Fourth Edition

Our Digital **World**

Introduction to Computing

Jon Gordon • Karen Lankisch
Nancy Muir • Denise Seguin • Anita Verno

PARADIGM
EDUCATION SOLUTIONS

St. Paul

Senior Vice President: Linda Hein
Editor in Chief: Christine Hurney
Developmental Editor, Digital and Print: Tamborah Moore
Director of Production: Timothy W. Larson
Production Editor: Shannon Kottke
Cover and Text Designer and
Senior Production Specialist: Jaana Bykonich
Vice President Sales and Marketing: Scott Burns
Director of Marketing: Lara Weber McLellan
Vice President Information Technology: Chuck Bratton
Digital Projects Manager: Tom Modl
Indexer: Ina Gravitz
Illustrators: Hespenheide Design,
Patrick Gnan/IllustrationOnline.com

Care has been taken to verify the accuracy of information presented in this book. However, the authors, editors, and publisher cannot accept responsibility for web, email, newsgroup, or chat room subject matter or content, or for consequences from application of the information in this book, and make no warranty, expressed or implied, with respect to its content.

Trademarks: Some of the product names and company names included in this book have been used for identification purposes only and may be trademarks or registered trade names of their respective manufacturers and sellers. The authors, editors, and publisher disclaim any affiliation, association, or connection with, or sponsorship or endorsement by, such owners.

Image credits: Image credits follow the Index on page 283.

We have made every effort to trace the ownership of all copyrighted material and to secure permission from copyright holders. In the event of any question arising as to the use of any material, we will be pleased to make the necessary corrections in future printings. Thanks are due to the aforementioned authors, publishers, and agents for permission to use the materials indicated.

ISBN 978-0-76386-831-4 (print)
ISBN 978-0-76386-832-1 (digital)

© 2017 by Paradigm Publishing, Inc.
875 Montreal Way
St. Paul, MN 55102
Email: educate@emcp.com
Website: ParadigmCollege.com

Printed in the United States of America

25 24 23 22 21 20 19 18 17 16   2 3 4 5 6 7 8 9 10

Brief Contents

Contents

Preface

Getting the Most Out of This Book

You've just paid good money for another textbook. It feels like every other textbook. You expect it to be something you have to get through, and something you'll be glad to leave behind when you finish the course.

The truth is, we actually hope you are somewhat surprised by this book.

As in the previous editions of *Our Digital World*, we've done a lot of work to make the writing in this book easy to read, to find ways to get you excited about how technology is evolving, and to make computing relevant to your work and personal life. We've included information about recent technologies such as cloud storage and mobile applications. We've also cut back on the amount you have to read by providing part of the content in multimedia formats that we think you'll find engaging. The result is more than a book—it's a combination of text and technology that together, provides a new learning experience.

The multimedia content of *Our Digital World*, Fourth Edition, is available as part of SNAP, a web-based training and assessment system.

Moving Your Learning Online

One of the fundamental ways that this book provides a different learning experience is by connecting this course with the way you experience computing in the twenty-first century. We have integrated the use of online technology into this textbook through a web-centric educational experience. The activities in this book involve accessing the book's SNAP course to view videos and animations, play with interactive hands-on tools, connect with other students and your instructor by learning how to use collaborative features such as blogs and wikis, and discover where technology is headed by reading stories from today's headlines. To see how this works, take a look at the Chapter Tour beginning on page xi.

Our hope is that you'll not only find our online features informative and interesting, but that you'll also become a more competent participant in our digital world by gaining practice with online technologies. After you finish the course, that practice will continue to help you enjoy computers on a personal and professional level.

Pay special attention to the Take the Next Step activities that are marked as "Core Content." These activities, available as part of the SNAP course, provide required learning in an alternative and visual way. Other activities are up to your instructor to assign to enhance your learning in the way that suits your class environment and interests.

Really Special Features

One way in which we tried to make this book different was by providing special content that answers common questions about planning for the future and using technology wisely. These features include:

- **Computers in Your Career**   We realize that just about every job today involves computers in some way, so rather than focus only on computing careers in IT, we tell you how computers are being used in a wide variety of work settings.
- **Playing It Safe**   Technology offers wonderful opportunities, but it also comes with some risk. In this feature we advise you about staying safe from threats such as ID theft, phishing scams, and virus attacks.
- **Spotlight on the Future**   These fascinating articles and companion podcasts are based on interviews by co-author Jon Gordon, a veteran technology reporter, with technology experts, including project leaders at the Pew Research Center. They give you a glimpse of the exciting directions technology is taking and what that could mean for you in the future. All Spotlight on the Future interviews from the previous editions will be available as additional podcasts.
- **Ethics and Technology Blog**   This ongoing classroom blog raises interesting ethical questions regarding technology and lets you share your ideas and opinions and engage in ongoing conversations with your classmates.

These features, along with the presentation of key computing concepts, are designed to help you become tech-savvy at home and at work, today and into the future.

Who Are You?

Finally, we know that you aren't one homogenous student so we've tried to address a variety of interests and backgrounds. You are 18 or 28 or 60 years old. You are comfortable with technology or you may be technophobic. You could be juggling a job and family with your education to take the next step in your career, or you could be just starting out on your initial career path. Maybe you recently retired and are looking for a new work experience.

This course could be a basic requirement for your degree that you hope to get through and get a grade. Or it could be a stepping stone to a career that is focused on computing in one of its many forms. Maybe it's simply going to help you keep up with the digital curve so you can explore ways that computers can connect you with friends and family.

Whatever your goals, we believe this book will help you, and we wish you success in exploring the amazing possibilities of our digital world.

Taking a Chapter Tour

Learning objectives establish clear goals and help you focus your study of the chapter. Numbers align with the major sections of the chapter.

Why Does It Matter? feature provides a context to help you picture the practical reasons for learning the chapter content.

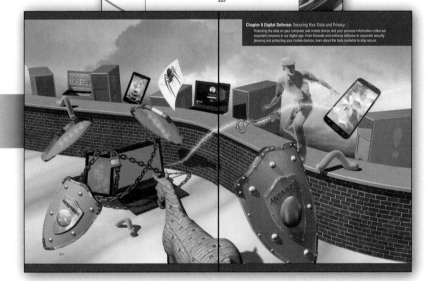

Chapter opening illustrations provide a sneak preview of the computing concepts discussed in the chapter.

Go to your SNAP course to take a Precheck for each chapter learning objective. Based on your results of that quiz, the SNAP Study Planner will provide a customized study plan to help you succeed in the course. After studying the content, take the Recheck quiz and see how much you have learned.

Thought-provoking quotes scattered throughout the text provide insights into what the famous and the not-so-famous think about our digital world.

Chapter 8

Digital Defense
Securing Your Data and Privacy

What You'll Accomplish
When you finish this chapter, you'll be able to:

8.1 Describe the risks associated with operating a computer connected to a network and the Internet and list the tools you can use to protect your computing devices and data from those risks.

8.2 Explain the steps to secure a home network, the various types of personal computer or mobile device malware, and methods used to obtain personal information from individuals.

8.3 Recognize security risks associated with mobile devices and with storing data in the cloud and give examples of tools and services to safeguard those devices and data.

8.4 Identify hardware and software tools and strategies used by organizations to secure corporate networks and prevent loss of data.

8.5 List security defenses that both organizations and individuals should adopt to prevent cyberattacks and data loss or theft.

Why Does It Matter ?

Would you leave your bank card and PIN sitting on an empty table in a food court at the mall? Would you leave your home for a vacation and not bother to lock the doors or windows? Many people who are used to protecting their wallets or houses may not take steps to guard their digital information against common threats. Even if you protect your computer with antivirus software, you might overlook routine tasks that can leave you vulnerable to losing important data. Everybody should learn the basic skills of computer security because replacing a computer is easy—replacing valuable data is not.

223

Chapter 8 Digital Defense: Securing Your Data and Privacy

Protecting the data on your computer and mobile device and your personal information online are important concerns in our digital age. From firewalls and antivirus software to corporate security planning and protecting your mobile devices, learn about the tools available to stay secure.

PRECHECK **7.1** The Social Web Phenomenon

You may belong to or have visited pages on websites such as Facebook, Twitter, YouTube, Pinterest, Google+, or Tumblr, or have read about these sites in the news. All of these are social sites, where people go to share their thoughts in text, video, or photos. Together with a wide variety of other social websites, these sites form the **social web**, a revolution in how people connect with each other, how news is delivered, and how our collective knowledge is formed. Social sites and the tools they offer create a vehicle for a two-way dialog between people and groups, rather than a one-way communication from the media to the public, stores to customers, or teachers to students.

> " Facebook was not originally created to be a company. It was built to accomplish a social mission—to make the world more open and connected. "
>
> —Mark Zuckerberg, founder of Facebook

The social web is still evolving and defining itself, and as such is likely to include more types of websites and services than you think. Any site that allows users to inter-

---

Operating system packages also offer security features such as password protection to keep others from using your computer and a firewall to prevent someone from remotely accessing your computer.

Operating system packages also include basic applications you can use to get your work done or be entertained, such as simple word processing programs like WordPad; games like Spider Solitaire; media players such as QuickTime Player to play music or videos; and tools such as a calculator, a calendar or address book, and an Internet browser.

Take a Survey *Online*

What experience do you have with operating systems?

A (Brief!) History of Operating Systems

There was a time when computers had no operating system. In this pre-OS time, every program had to have all the required **drivers** (software that allows an operating system to interface with hardware) and specifications needed to connect to

---

Take a Survey invites you to share your thoughts and experiences by answering a few questions on a topic related to the chapter. SNAP will compile your feedback with the feedback from the other students in your class to show you how people are really using technology.

Playing It Safe margin boxes provide practical tips for using the web safely and responsibly.

---

* Viruses can spread from a computer storage device such as a DVD or flash drive that you use on an infected computer and then insert into another computer drive.
* Worms can spread by simply connecting your computer to an infected network.
* Mobile devices can be infected by downloading an app, ringtone, game, or theme that carries malware.
* A mobile device with Bluetooth enabled in "discoverable mode" could be infected simply by coming within range of another Bluetooth device that has been infected and is running the same operating system.

Security threats are a reality in our digital world. What's also true is that several programs and technical tools are available to protect your computer against these potential hazards, as you'll learn later in the chapter. In addition, knowing how to recognize trustworthy websites and how to manage cookies are two proactive strategies everyone can use.

Playing It Safe

Be especially cautious when you receive a chain letter via email. These are often simply devices for delivering malware or collecting email addresses for the purpose of building spam lists.

Recognizing Secure Sites

Although even a reputable site occasionally may pass on a dangerous download to your computer, it's the sites that actively download malware that you have to be most cautious about.

---

pelting you with pop-up window advertisements to destroying your data to tracking your online activities with an eye toward stealing your identity or money.

In the early days of computers, individual hackers often planted viruses just to aggravate people or exploit a technological weakness. Today, most malware is created by less-than-ethical businesses, organized gangs, or criminals who aim to download dangerous code to your computer, co-opt your email contact list to send out **spam** (mass emails), or perform other illegal activities for profit-based motives. The following are descriptions of some common forms of malware.

Ethics and Technology Blog *Online*

Taking Advantage of an Unsecured Network

My apartment is next door to a café that offers Internet access. I hardly ever go to the café, but because I can pick up its Internet connection from my apartment, I do. It saves me lots of money. Does anybody think that's a problem?

The Ethics and Technology Blog feature prompts you to go to your SNAP course to blog about some of the thought-provoking, ethical questions related to living and working with technology.

Help features provide searchable support information and troubleshooting tools for the operating system, some of which are located on your computer and some of which you can access online. Windows even provides a remote assistance feature that allows another person to take control of your computer to pinpoint your problem and fix it for you.

Computers in Your Career

Computer support specialists may work in a small, local computer repair store, a larger national chain store, or an expansive technical support call center for a large software or hardware corporation. To become a computer support specialist, you must have a solid grounding in a computer-related field (at least an associate's degree or certification in a topic such as servers or databases) and be able to communicate well and deal with the public. Because many computer problems require troubleshooting within the OS, being comfortable with operating system settings, configurations, and utilities will help you succeed in your work.

Maintaining the Computer with Operating System Utilities

System maintenance is an important task for system software. This process is similar to taking your car into the shop on a regular basis for a tune-up to keep it running efficiently.

The Computers in Your Career feature gives ideas for how your computer studies could help you succeed in a career you may not have considered.

Spotlight on the Future *Online*

The Internet of Things

The Internet of Things will change how we connect to one another, and how we shop, travel, and learn, experts say.

The **Internet of Things (IoT)** means "connectivity between people and devices," according to Janna Anderson, associate professor at Elon University and a co-author of a recent report by the Pew Research Center. "Pretty much anything in the world can now be networked."

As an example, she notes that you might not want to take that hotel towel home with you—because the hotel could know that it has gone missing and track it to your home.

The Internet of Things will expand computing far beyond the devices we carry around now or have in our homes, she says.

"We could be computing through a contact lens."

Talk about It

1. What is meant by the term *Internet of Things*?

2. Discuss some examples of how items in the world are networked today, and how they may be more so in the future.

3. What are some types of wearable technology that already exist?

4. What are some predictions for how such wearable or implantable computing could develop in the future?

5. Discuss pros and cons of different ways that the Internet of Things might affect our lives in the next 25 years.

The Convergence of Computing Devices

Technological convergence is a term that describes the tendency of technical devices to take on each other's functions.

Do you enjoy audio content? Go to your SNAP course and listen to the full podcast for each of the Spotlight on the Future features. In addition to the Talk about It discussion questions in the book, each podcast is supported with a brief online quiz.

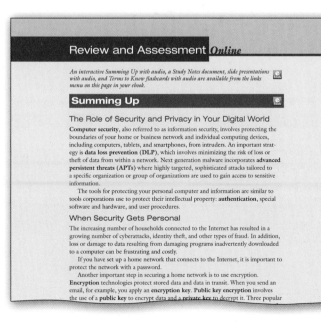

Illustrations help you visualize processes and concepts explained in the text. Even if you're not a visual learner, you may find that a picture can save you reading a thousand words.

Take the Next Step activities expand what you read in your textbook. Activities identified with the Core Content logo are accessed through your SNAP course, and include a brief online quiz. Activities marked with the ebook icon are accessed through the ebook.

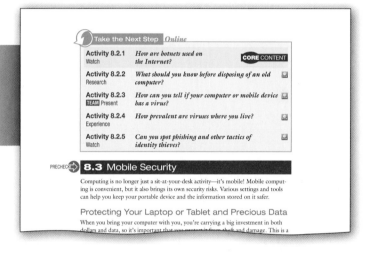

The chapter Review and Assessment section begins with Summing Up, a recap of the chapter concepts. Read it in the book or go to your ebook where you'll find an interactive version of the summary. The online summary provides pop-up definitions with audio of the bolded chapter key terms. A Study Notes document, slide presentations with audio, and Terms to Know flashcards with audio are also available from the links menu on this page in your ebook.

Terms to Know

Software's Role in the World of Computing
application software, 130

The Many Types of Application Software

productivity software, 131
word processor software, 132
spreadsheet software, 132
database software, 133
presentation software, 134
calendar software, 136
contact management software, 136
customer relationship management
   (CRM) software, 137
graphics software, 137
desktop publishing (DTP) software, 137
photo editing software, 137
screen capture software, 137
multimedia software, 138
animation software, 138
audio software, 138
podcast, 138

video editing software, 138
web authoring software, 138
WYSIWYG (what you see is what you
   get), 138
entertainment software, 139
query, Activity 5.2.1
table, Activity 5.2.1
record, Activity 5.2.1
field, Activity 5.2.1
entry, Activity 5.2.1
relational database, Activity 5.2.1
primary key, Activity 5.2.1
Structured Query Language (SQL),
   Activity 5.2.1
edutainment, Activity 5.2.2
web-based training, Activity 5.2.2
MOOC, Activity 5.2.2

Developing and Delivering Software

software development life cycle
   (SDLC), 144
alpha version, 144

cloud computing, 146
software as a service (SaaS), 146

Not sure what a key term means? Page numbers indicate where the term is bolded and defined within the chapter. For terms introduced within a Take the Next Step activity, the activity number is listed. To review the definitions of these terms, turn to the complete Glossary at the end of the book. Flash cards, one set for each learning objective, are available in your ebook.

Concepts Check activities are provided in your SNAP course. These interactive, scored exercises and word games offer a fun way to check how well you've learned the technology concepts presented in the chapter.

Concepts Check

Concepts Check 5.1 Multiple Choice
Take this quiz to test your understanding of key concepts in this chapter.

Concepts Check 5.2 Matching
Match the software application to the primary use of the software.

Concepts Check 5.3 Label It
Use the interactive tool to label the elements in a Microsoft Excel worksheet.

Concepts Check 5.4 Arrange It
Use the interactive tool to arrange the phases in the software development life cycle.

Projects

Check with your instructor for the preferred method to submit completed work.

---

se the interactive tool to idea_____re is designed to protect against.

Projects

Check with your instructor for the preferred method to submit completed work.

Project 8.1 Wireless Networks at Home

Project 8.1.1
Watch the video titled *Securing Your Wi-Fi* at http://ODW4.emcp.net /SecuringYourWi-Fi. After watching the Google video, research Wi-Fi Protected Access 2 (WPA2), Wi-Fi Protected Access (WPA), and Wired Equivalent Privacy (WEP) wireless security standards. Prepare a brief summary comparing the three security protocols. Include the URLs of the source material you used.

Project 8.1.2 TEAM
As employees of a new IT security company, your team has found that the typical homeowner is unaware of the risks of using an unsecured wireless network at home. To educate homeowners about these security issues, your company has decided to create a short video that presents a convincing demonstration of the need for securing wireless access in the home. As a team, create a video storyboard that shows a wireless network being breached by an outsider. Following this sequence of scenes, devote the remaining scenes of your storyboard to an explanation of security measures that homeowners can take to avoid being victimized by cybercriminals or having Internet connections accessed by people outside their homes. When you are finished with the storyboard, film and edit the video; then share the video with your class.

252   Our Digital World

Completing the Project activities allows you to put your new knowledge to work, either on your own or as a member of a team. These activities let you demonstrate the kind of thinking and problem-solving needed in today's workplace — plus you can use popular social media, such as wikis, in the process.

In the final chapter activity, you get a chance to talk about some key ideas and to share your thoughts on the effects of current and future technology applications. Take your discussion online (if your instructor sets this section up as a blog) or extend your conversations in class with the challenging questions presented in the Class Conversations section.

Class Conversations

Topic 8.1 Are two heads better than one?
Watch the video titled "Former Hacker: Information Systems Face Rising Threat" at http://ODW4.emcp.net/FormerHacker. In the interview, Kevin Mitnick, once the FBI's most wanted hacker who now is a security consultant, speaks about the difficulties faced by organizations to secure devices and information from all threats. Mitnick also discusses the two-person rule, a security strategy implemented when an individual has high-level access to computing system resources. Consider security threats that exist besides access to a server or other high-level computing resources and discuss whether the two-person rule should be used in more situations. Give at least one example of a situation in which you recommend the two-person rule should be used.

Topic 8.2 Do you care if advertisers are in your social network space?
Discuss the pros and cons of social networks selling targeted advertising to you based on your personal data, buying history, and web browsing practices outside the social network. Do you like that the advertising you see is customized to your life or does it bother you that businesses are exchanging data about your online presence without your knowledge? Why or why not?

Topic 8.3 Stop that data from walking out the door!

About the Components

As you can see from the Chapter Tour, *Our Digital World,* Fourth Edition, is more than just a textbook. The digital content, available as part of your SNAP 2016 course, is vital to your learning experience.

SNAP Web-Based Training and Assessment

You can access the activities in your SNAP 2016 course by using a Join Code provided by your instructor if you are accessing your course through the SNAP website, or through the course portal of your school's learning management system. In both cases, you will also need to provide a SNAP Activation Code, which you can purchase with your textbook or ebook. Through SNAP 2016, you'll be able to access the Take the Next Step activity sections with the *Core Content* label as you move through each chapter. Activities with the *Core Content* label and Spotlight on the Future podcasts include short quizzes. Scores for quizzes are reported automatically to a grade book.

You'll also be able to take the chapter survey, listen to the Spotlight on the Future podcasts, participate in the Ethics and Technology blogs, complete the end-of-chapter Review and Assessment activities, apply your knowledge playing interactive games, and take exams.

The SNAP Study Planner charts your performance on exams and assessments. Each exam question or assessment step is keyed to a topic. When you take an exam or assessment, a Study Planner report is generated showing how you did on each topic. The report can be filtered by topics mastered, topics still to be learned, and topics on which you haven't yet been assessed. The Study Planner can generate this report for a given exam, for a chapter, or for the whole course. For topics still to be learned, the Study Planner provides quick access to the specific ebook content covering the topic, for quick, focused review.

Ebook

Don't want to carry around a textbook? You can travel light by accessing the entire book's contents through the web-based ebook. The ebook features dynamic navigation tools including a linked table of contents and the ability to jump to specific pages, search for terms, bookmark, highlight, and take notes. You can also access valuable study tools through the ebook.

Instructor Resources

Instructor resources are available through an innovative, web-based ebook. These materials include:

- Answer keys and rubrics for evaluating chapter work
- Lesson plans and teaching tips
- Syllabus suggestions and course-planning resources
- PowerPoint® presentations with lecture notes

Because student assessment is important, the SNAP course includes a concept item bank for each chapter, which can be used to create custom exams. Exam items are based on key terminology and support chapter learning objectives.

Personalized approach.
Powerful technology.
Proven results.

Instructors can do more

As the classroom changes, you have the ability to do more through automation and powerful integrated tools.

Students are empowered

Learners demonstrate hands-on mastery, can identify their challenges and define their own individual paths to success.

Experience and support

Paradigm evolves its teaching tools in response to instructor and student needs, plus provides 24/7 on-site technical support.

Visit SNAP2016.com or contact your local Account Manager to schedule a demo of SNAP 2016.

About the Author Team

Jon Gordon

Journalist
Minnesota Public Radio News
St. Paul, Minnesota

Jon Gordon is director of digital news at Minnesota Public Radio (MPR) News, where he is responsible for the MPR News website, news apps, social media, and overall digital strategy. Gordon also served 14 years as creator, producer, and host of American Public Media's *Future Tense*, a daily technology report that aired on more than 125 stations across the United States and Canada, and by podcast. Gordon joined MPR in 1990 and has served as a producer and reporter covering general news, suburban issues, and politics. Gordon's work has been recognized by the Radio Television Digital News Association, the Society of Professional Journalists, the Associated Press, the Corporation for Public Broadcasting, and the Northwest Broadcast News Association. He's a recipient of the prestigious Edward R. Murrow Award and the Gerald Loeb Award for business journalism from UCLA's Anderson School of Business.

Karen Lankisch

Professor, Consultant
University of Cincinnati—Clermont College
Cincinnati, Ohio

Karen Lankisch is a professor at the University of Cincinnati—Clermont College. Lankisch is the program director of the Health Information Systems Technology program and teaches a variety of courses in the Health and Business Information Technology programs. In addition, she serves as a support faculty member for the Instructional Design and Technology graduate program, as well as an external mentor in the University of Cincinnati's New Faculty Institute Initiative. Lankisch is a Quality Matters Master Peer Reviewer and has completed reviews both nationally and internationally. She has a PhD in Education with a concentration in technology and adult learning and is certified through AHIMA as a Registered Health Information Administrator (RHIA). Along with co-authoring *Our Digital World*, Lankisch has co-authored *Exploring Electronic Health Records* for Paradigm Education Solutions. She has served as a national consultant for Paradigm Education Solutions, giving workshops and presentations to instructors on Paradigm's technology learning solutions. In 2013, she received the University of Cincinnati Faculty Award for Innovative Use of Technology in the Classroom. In 2016, she was selected for membership to the University of Cincinnati Academy of Fellows for Teaching and Learning.

Nancy Muir

Writer, Author, Instructor
Seattle, Washington

Nancy Muir is the owner of The Publishing Studio, a technology publishing company. Muir holds a Certificate in Distance Learning from the University of Washington. She was co-creator and instructor of a course called Internet Safety for Educators, offered through the distance learning programs at both Washington State University and The University of Alaska, Anchorage. Previously, she was an instructor of Technical Writing at Indiana University–Purdue University in Indianapolis. In addition to co-authoring *Our Digital World*, Muir has co-authored *Guidelines for Microsoft Office* for Paradigm Education Solutions and has written a number of technology and business books, including *Distance Learning for Dummies* and *Young Person's Guide to Character Education* (winner of the Benjamin Franklin Award for Excellence from the Independent Bookseller's Association). She also runs two websites focused on technology.

Denise Seguin

Author, Instructor
Fanshawe College
London, Ontario

Denise Seguin has served on the Faculty of Business at Fanshawe College of Applied Arts and Technology in London, Ontario, from 1986 until her retirement from full-time teaching in December 2012. She developed curriculum and taught a variety of office technology, software applications, and accounting courses to students in postsecondary Information Technology diploma programs and Continuing Education courses. Seguin served as Program Coordinator for Computer Systems Technician, Computer Systems Technology, Office Administration, and Law Clerk programs and was acting Chair of the School of Information Technology in 2001. Along with authoring *Seguin's COMPUTER Concepts*, First and Second Editions, and *Seguin's COMPUTER Applications with Microsoft® Office 2013*, First Edition, and *with Microsoft® Office 2016,* Second Edition, she has also authored Paradigm Education Solution's *Microsoft Outlook* 2000 to 2016 editions and co-authored *Our Digital World* First, Second, Third, and Fourth Editions, Benchmark Series *Microsoft® Excel®,* 2007, 2010, and 2013, Benchmark Series *Microsoft® Access®* 2007, 2010, and 2013, Marquee Series *Microsoft® Office*, 2000 to 2013, and *Using Computers in the Medical Office*, 2003 to 2010.

Anita Verno

Associate Professor
Bergen Community College
Paramus, New Jersey

Anita Verno is an associate professor of Information Technology at Bergen Community College and was IT coordinator/department chair from 2000 to 2010. A founding member of the Computer Science Teachers Association (CSTA) (http://csta.acm.org/), Verno was the elected "College Faculty Representative" to its Board of Directors and served as curriculum chair from inception until June 2009. She is currently serving on the CSTA Advisory Council. She also assisted in establishing CSTA's Northern New Jersey chapter to serve computing teachers in her home state. Verno served as an associate member of the ACM Committee for Computing Education in Community Colleges (CCECC), where she worked as part of a curriculum project team tasked with identifying the nature and breadth of IT-related programs of study in community colleges. Verno is the former college representative to the CSTA Northern New Jersey chapter, a former president of the Community College Computer Consortium, and a member of the Board of Advisors for the New Jersey Institute of Technology (NJIT) Bachelor of Science in Engineering Technology program. Her 40 years of professional experience cover software design and development, teaching in IT/CS, and development of curricula/degrees for high schools and colleges. Along with co-authoring *Our Digital World*, Verno has co-authored *Guidelines for Microsoft Office* for Paradigm Education Solutions.

Acknowledgments

We would like to thank the following reviewers who have offered valuable comments and suggestions on the content of this textbook.

Becky Anderson
Zane State College
Zanesville, Ohio

Martin S. Anderson, MBA
BGSU Firelands
Huron, Ohio

Roberta Baber
Fresno City College
Fresno, California

Roxanne Bengelink
Kalamazoo Valley Community College
Kalamazoo, Michigan

Dave Bequette
Butte College
Oroville, California

Shirley Brooks
Holmes Community College
Ridgeland, Mississippi

George Cheng
Hostos Community College
Bronx, New York

Scott Cline
Southwestern Community College
Sylva, North Carolina

James Cutietta
Cuyahoga Community College Metro
    Campus
Cleveland, Ohio

JD Davis
Southwestern College
Chula Vista, California

Alec Fehl
Asheville-Buncombe Technical
    Community College
Asheville, North Carolina

Lisa Giansante, BAS, CMA
Humber College
Toronto, Ontario

Debra Giblin
Mitchell Technical Institute
Mitchell, South Dakota

Glenda Greene
Rowan-Cabarrus Community College
Salisbury, North Carolina

Prosper Hevi
Kankakee Community College
Kankakee, Illinois

Marilyn Hibbert
Salt Lake Community College
Sandy, Utah

Terry Hoffer
City College at Montana State University
    Billings
Billings, Montana

Mardi Holliday
Community College of Philadelphia
Philadelphia, Pennsylvania

Stacy Hollins
Florissant Valley Community College
St. Louis, Missouri

Sherry Howard-Spreitzer
Northwestern Michigan College
Traverse City, Michigan

Ly Huong
UCSC Extension
Santa Clara, California

Vincent Kayes
Mount Saint Mary College
Newburgh, New York

David Kern
Whatcom Community College
Bellingham, Washington

Annette Kerwin
College of DuPage
Glen Ellyn, Illinois

Sylvia Knapp
Brunswick Community College
Leland, North Carolina

Paul Koester
Tarrant County College, Northwest
  Campus
Fort Worth, Texas

George Kontos, Ed.D
Bowling Green Community College
  of Western Kentucky University
Bowling Green, Kentucky

Kathy Lynch
University of Wisconsin–Oshkosh
Oshkosh, Wisconsin

Lana Mason
Wayne Community College
Goldsboro, NC

Lorraine Mastracchio
College of Westchester
White Plains, New York

Dr. Lisa McMillin
East Central Community College
Decatur, Mississippi

Jolene Meyers
Terra Community College
Fremont, Ohio

LeAnn Moreno
Minnesota State College
  Southeast Technical
Winona, Minnesota

Larry Morgan
Holmes Community College
Ridgeland, Mississippi

Tammie Munsen
Mitchell Technical Institute
Mitchell, South Dakota

Bonnie Murphy
County College of Morris
Randolph, New Hampshire

Gary Muskin
College of Westchester
White Plains, New York

Patricia Newman
Cuyamaca College
El Cajon, California

Phil Nielson
Salt Lake Community College
Salt Lake City, Utah

Greg Pauley
Moberly Area Community College
Moberly, Missouri

Stacy Peters-Walters
Kilian Community College
Sioux Falls, South Dakota

Pattie Roberts
Mesa Community College
Mesa, Arizona

Vicki Robertson
Southwest Tennessee Community College
Memphis, Tennessee

Wesley Scruggs
Brazosport College
Lake Jackson, Texas

Sue VanLanen
Gwinnett Technical College
Lawrenceville, Georgia

Wilma VanSegbrook
Forest Heights Collegiate Institute
Kitchener, Ontario

Scott Warman
ECPI Technical College
Roanoke, Virginia

Mary Ann Zlotow
College of DuPage
Glen Ellyn, Illinois

Digital Technologies
Exploring a Wealth of Possibilities

What You'll Accomplish

When you finish this chapter, you'll be able to:

1.1 Recognize the types of digital devices available today.

1.2 Differentiate the four categories of computers and how technological convergence has impacted the functions of computers.

1.3 Describe how digital devices are being used and how digital devices provide various career opportunities.

1.4 Explain the information processing cycle and identify and differentiate data and information.

Why Does It Matter ?

You encounter computers in their various forms, from desktop computers to smartphones to GPS navigation systems, almost every day. In whatever work you do now or are preparing for in the future, understanding the role of computing and the capabilities of computers can help you get ahead. Even a basic level of technical knowledge gives you an edge in the job market, although it is becoming increasingly important to expand your skills beyond the basics to compete for available positions.

Chapter 1 Digital Technologies: Exploring a Wealth of Possibilities

The world of computers includes several types of computing devices that people use for many different purposes. All digital devices process data and produce information that enriches our personal and work lives.

1.1 Just What Is a Computer?

On the simplest level, a **computer** is an electronic, programmable device that can assemble, process, and store data. An **analog computer** uses mechanical operations to perform calculations, as with an older car speedometer, slide rule, or adding machine. A **digital computer**, which is the category that includes your laptop, desktop, or tablet computer, uses symbols that represent data in the form of code. A digital computer has a much higher level of functionality than an analog computing device, including the ability to process words, numbers, images, and sounds.

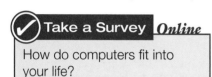

✓ **Take a Survey** *Online*

How do computers fit into your life?

The combination of digital computing capability with communications has brought us tools such as email and instant messaging, and resulted in new types of computing devices, including smartphones, gaming devices, and smart appliances.

Today, many devices beyond the traditional desktop or laptop computer have computing capabilities, including phones and gaming devices.

1.2 Computers in All Shapes and Sizes

Although there are many devices that have computing capability (which we'll talk about shortly), most of us think of a computer as the desktop, laptop, or tablet computer we use for work or entertainment. According to a 2014 Nielsen report, the average American has four digital devices and spends 60 hours a week looking at content across these devices.

Take a stroll down the computer aisle of a well-stocked office superstore (or click through its website) and you'll find that there are several kinds of computer models available. First, you'll notice two broad groups of computers: Windows- or Linux-based personal computers (PCs) manufactured by a wide variety of companies such as Hewlett-Packard, Dell, Acer, and Lenovo; and Mac computers, available at Apple stores or other authorized retailers. A third category of computers, Chromebooks, run Google's Chrome operating system for web-based computing and are made by manufacturers such as Samsung and Acer. Manufacturers are also beginning to produce **wearable computers** in the form of glasses, clothing, and watches.

TABLE 1.1	Examples of Computers by Size	
Category	**Examples**	
Larger	Supercomputer, mainframe, server	
Mid-sized	Personal computer, desktop, laptop, convertible laptop, ultrabook	
Mobile	Tablet, smartphone, digital audio player, e-reader, handheld game console, wearable computer	

Table 1.1 lists some common computers categorized by size, which usually correlates with **computing power**, or the amount of data that can be processed and the speed at which it can be processed. For example, the computers common in homes and offices range from portable devices to larger units that sit on a desk or table. But the computing world also includes very powerful larger computers used in science and medicine.

Supercomputer

The computing power in your laptop today would astound personal computer users of ten years ago. But the fact remains that there are some tasks your personal computer doesn't have the power to handle.

That's where supercomputers and their cousins, mainframe computers (now typically used as servers, which will be discussed in Chapter 6), come in. A **supercomputer** is a computer with the ability to perform trillions of calculations per second. A supercomputer is usually custom-made for a particular use. For example, when a scientist wants to run a computer model of what happens when a star explodes, or a medical researcher has to process the millions of data points from an MRI scan, he or she turns to a supercomputer, because processing the amount of data required could take years on a personal computer. Supercomputer processing power is measured in petaflops of processing power. While a **flop** is one floating-point operation per second, a **petaflop** represents a thousand trillion floating-point operations.

Supercomputers often function as very large servers in a network. Another model for supercomputers involves **computer clusters**. The moviemaking and computer gaming industries, for example, use clusters of computers joined together with custom-designed connections (known as a **render farm**) to make full-length animated movies and feature-rich games that require high-quality images. These same images would take up to a hundred years to build on a personal computer.

Desktop

A **desktop computer** is a computer whose central processing unit (CPU) might be housed in a tower configuration or, in some cases, within the monitor, as with the Apple iMac. Though models vary, typically a desktop computer setup includes a CPU, monitor, keyboard, and mouse. Most desktop models would not be considered portable, though you may be able to move some mini-towers or other compact designs around the house with relative ease.

The distinctive design of Macs comes from only one source: Apple.

Laptop

Laptops, also known as notebook computers, contain a monitor, keyboard, mouse, CPU, and battery, all in one device. Laptops are essentially portable, although today many are intended as replacements for desktop computers and may come with a large monitor that can cause them to weigh as much as seven pounds. Other smaller models weigh only three or four pounds and are designed to be taken on the road. While a category of small, easily portable laptops known as **netbooks** became popular in the early 2000s, these lightweight computers contained limited computing power and today have largely been replaced by tablets and **ultrabooks** (very lightweight laptops).

> "Computers get better faster than anything else ever. A child's PlayStation today is more powerful than a military supercomputer from 1996."
>
> —Erik Brynjolfsson, director, MIT Center for Digital Business

Laptops weigh less today than they ever have before because most no longer include an optical (CD or DVD) drive. This change is due to the fact that most content can now be accessed and downloaded online from the Internet. Another development in the design of laptop computers is the inclusion of touchscreen monitors. Some of these monitors can even be detached from the keyboard and used independently as a tablet, further blurring the lines between the different categories of computers.

Tablet

Tablet PCs, which appeared around 2002, were designed to be held like a legal pad, and weighed about three pounds. Perhaps inspired by the Star Trek PADD that appeared in the 1966 show, they were great for taking to meetings or conferences to make notes either by writing on the screen or using an onscreen keyboard. Some models also included a traditional keyboard; you could swivel the unit to go from the pad configuration to a more traditional laptop look. (These were called *clamshells*.)

In early 2010, a new form of tablet appeared on the scene and essentially replaced Tablet PCs. The Apple iPad hit the market with high demand and created the benchmark for the new tablet niche in computing devices. **Tablets** are portable computing devices with a touchscreen interface. A tablet can be used as an e-reader, web browser, and media player, among other functions. Tablets can access a wide variety of apps ranging from games to word processors and spreadsheet software. Several tablets are now available, including the Samsung Galaxy, Google Nexus 10, Amazon Fire, and Apple iPad. The tablet market is expected to continue to grow in the future.

Tablets enable you to use onscreen controls to navigate by touch.

The Internet of Things

The Internet of Things will change how we connect to one another, and how we shop, travel, and learn, experts say.

The **Internet of Things (IoT)** means "connectivity between people and devices," according to Janna Anderson, associate professor at Elon University and a co-author of a recent report by the Pew Research Center. "Pretty much anything in the world can now be networked."

As an example, she notes that you might not want to take that hotel towel home with you—because the hotel could know that it has gone missing and track it to your home.

The Internet of Things will expand computing far beyond the devices we carry around now or have in our homes, she says.

"We could be computing through a contact lens."

Talk about It

1. What is meant by the term *Internet of Things*?

2. Discuss some examples of how items in the world are networked today, and how they may be more so in the future.

3. What are some types of wearable technology that already exist?

4. What are some predictions for how such wearable or implantable computing could develop in the future?

5. Discuss pros and cons of different ways that the Internet of Things might affect our lives in the next 25 years.

The Convergence of Computing Devices

Technological convergence is a term that describes the tendency of technical devices to take on each other's functions. Today computers take many forms beyond the traditional desktop or laptop computer. Some are specialized in their functionality; others tackle some big computer tasks despite their compact design. Many combine communications, media, and information processing features in one package. The ability to access many services online rather than loading applications into a device is helping to make this combination of more features in one small package a reality.

One of the most prevalent examples of a **converged device** is the smartphone, which now contains the functionalities of a phone, digital camera, GPS navigation system, and web browsing device, among others, in one package. People use these devices for many tasks. It is estimated that there are over 2 billion smartphone users across the globe—an average of more than two smartphones for every nine people. So what are users doing with their smartphones and other converged devices, such as tablets? Which functions are the most popular? Table 1.2 shows the results of a survey asking people how they are using their smartphones and tablets for non-voice data applications. (Note that survey respondents could respond yes to multiple activities.)

TABLE 1.2 Top Ten Activities by Mobile Device Users

Users of Smartphones Do This		Users of Tablets Do This	
Sent text message to another phone	90.5%	Accessed search	73.9%
Took photos	83.4%	Used email	73.6%
Used email	77.8%	Accessed social networking	67.5%
Accessed weather reports	67.1%	Played games	66.3%
Accessed social networking	65.3%	Accessed weather reports	64.6%
Accessed search	58.7%	Accessed news	58.8%
Played games	52.9%	Accessed photo/video sharing site	51.5%
Accessed maps	51.2%	Read books	51.2%
Accessed news	49.2%	Watched videos	50.9%
Listened to music	48.0%	Accessed retail	49.8%

Source: comScore.com.

Take the Next Step *Online*

Activity 1.2.1 Watch	*What makes up a computer system?*	CORE CONTENT
Activity 1.2.2 Research	*What is the most powerful supercomputer on the planet?*	ebook
Activity 1.2.3 TEAM Present	*How many devices do you need to carry around?*	ebook
Activity 1.2.4 Research	*When and how did the tablet begin?*	ebook

PRECHECK

1.3 Who Is Using Computers and How?

Computers are used in most businesses to create memos and letters, analyze expenses and sales figures, research and organize data, and communicate with customers. At home, you may have played a computer game, sent email, or watched a movie on your computer. But you may not be aware of how computers are used by people who work in different industries or by people with specialized interests.

Computers Are Everywhere

Although it would probably be easier to give you a list of settings where computers *aren't* being used than to tell you where they are used, the following are some examples of industries in which computers play a major role: government, medicine, publishing, finance, education, arts, law enforcement, the entertainment industry, gaming, and more.

Here are a few interesting uses of computers to ponder:

- While you may already be aware that retail websites track your shopping and spending habits online, you may not know that computers are also being used to track your behavior in bricks-and-mortar stores. Some stores are now equipped with hidden cameras that contain high-tech facial recognition software. These cameras can be stashed inside mannequins or store displays, and their software can be used for a variety of purposes, from determining a person's age and gender to identifying whether that person is a VIP customer or a known shoplifter. Although this technology can provide retailers with valuable information about their customers, it also raises privacy issues that many shoppers may not be comfortable with.

> "I want the entire smartphone, the entire Internet, on my wrist."
> —Steve Wozniak, co-founder of Apple Inc.

- Automobile manufacturers are enabling various handsfree functionality in the latest cars, and are even experimenting with automated cars. In the future, cars may drive themselves by use of computer technology.
- The ability to archive electronic images such as CAT scans from medical imaging devices and retrieve them from any location, as well as the use of web conferencing to connect specialists at large urban hospitals with healthcare providers in remote locations, is helping doctors diagnose and treat patients more efficiently.
- Nike, Sony, and LG are using technology to help people live healthier lifestyles through the creation of wearable devices that can track physical activity, heart rate, calories burned, and hours of sleep. These devices interact with apps on smartphones to make it easy for busy users to maintain an active lifestyle.

Automobile manufacturers are experimenting with automated cars, replacing certain driver functions with hands-free computer technology.

- Korean retailer Tesco used QR codes to enable customers to order groceries for home delivery from subway stations. Users simply scan a product code with their smartphone from a wall display to add the item to their shopping cart. After they check out, the items will be delivered to the customer's home on the same day. Chapter 2 explains what QR codes are and how to use them.
- Retailers are installing technology to read RFID chips embedded in credit cards to process transactions. These chips are essentially like computer chips, storing data and initiating actions. This new technology replaces the easier to steal magnetic strip and signature method used in older credit cards.
- Location technologies use GPS or Wi-Fi to track people, fleet vehicles such as delivery vehicles, and products and components in transit from one location to

another. Location technologies help ensure that employees and customers have assets where they are needed, find items quickly, avoid excess inventory situations, increase security, and more.

Ethics and Technology Blog *Online*

Computing All around You

Ubiquitous computing (also called *embedded technology*) places computing power in your environment. That means the walls of your house might have the ability to sense your body's temperature and turn up the heat, or sense that you have fallen asleep on the couch and turn down the lighting. Do you think it would be right to monitor your family with such technology?

Finding a Career in Computing

Though you are likely to use computers in your work no matter what your profession, there are several computer-specific fields that exist today. These fields are fast-paced and constantly evolving, so new career options come up on a regular basis. Even in bad economic times, employers look to information technology workers to save money with more efficient systems and procedures.

Today, there are several computer careers you can prepare for, including:

- **Computer engineering (CE).** This field involves the study of computer hardware and software systems and programming how devices interface with each other.

- **Computer science (CS).** People working in this field may design software, solve problems such as computer security threats, or come up with better ways of handling data storage.

> *Someday a computer will give a wrong answer to spare someone's feelings and [humans] will have invented artificial intelligence.*
>
> —Robert Brault, freelance journalist

- **Information systems (IS).** Those who work with information systems design technology solutions to help companies solve business problems. An IS professional considers who needs what data to get work done and how it can be delivered most efficiently.

- **Information technology (IT).** IT workers make sure the technology infrastructure is in place to support users. They may set up or maintain a network, or recommend the right hardware and software for their companies. IT workers are also responsible for ensuring that devices within a network are able to communicate with one another and share data.

- **Software engineering (SE).** This field involves writing software programs, which might be developed for a software manufacturer to sell to the public or involve a custom program written for a large organization to use in-house.

- **Web development.** The World Wide Web provides another group of technology career paths. Programming websites, developing the text and visual content, explaining how clients can use tools such as Search Engine Optimization (SEO) to maximize site traffic, and using social media to promote goods and services are just a few examples of careers in this area.

- **Database administrator (DBA).** Workers in this field help to create and organize databases of information. DBAs make sure that information stored in a database is available and usable. These folks also make sure that data is secure from hackers and unauthorized access. According to the *2014 Occupational Outlook Handbook*, computer professionals are in demand and it's expected that many new jobs will be created in this field between now and 2022. To prepare for a degree in a computer field, you should focus on analytical subjects such as math and science. Usually employers look

A wide variety of careers exists in computer fields, with more being created every day.

for a minimum of an associate's degree with a computer science or information technology focus, although many positions require a bachelor's degree or higher. Because computer technology is constantly changing, employers may be more impressed with your résumé if you stay current with changes by obtaining professional certifications. Some employers will pay for or subsidize your professional development; others won't.

Take the Next Step *Online*

Activity 1.3.1 Watch	*What computer jobs has the web produced?*	CORE CONTENT
Activity 1.3.2 Research	*Who provides professional certifications for IT workers?*	e book
Activity 1.3.3 Research	*How have computers redefined some industries?*	e book
Activity 1.3.4 Research	*How will you use computers in your career?*	e book
Activity 1.3.5 Research	*How are computers being used in various industries?*	e book

PRECHECK

1.4 What Is Information Technology?

The Information Technology (IT) department in an organization is in charge of its most valuable asset: information. IT is a department you are likely to come into contact with, whether as an IT employee or as a user of a company computer system, so it's important for you to understand just what information technology is.

According to the former Information Technology Association of America (ITAA), now merged with other organizations to form TechAmerica, information technology is "the study, design, development, implementation, support, or management of computer-based information systems, particularly software applications and computer hardware."

There are a few basic concepts that will help you understand IT. One is the difference between data and information; the other is what's involved in information processing.

Computers in Your Career

Fashion designers are embracing 3-D printing technology to produce customized printable clothing in an emerging field known as computational fashion. Fashion designs can be customized to a specific person by using body scanning technology, and 3-D printing allows for intricate details to be included that couldn't be designed on fabric. The use of this technology is still in its infancy, and it will require fashion designers to learn a variety of new software applications, but as the technology continues to evolve, the creative opportunities for designers are limitless.

Differentiating between Data and Information

Data such as these numbers may be the basis of information organized in the form of a graph or table.

Say that your job is to predict which new toys will prove most popular next holiday season. You might gather data about popular toys, their prices, and their sales to date. When you take that raw data and organize it into a chart or table that compares sales and prices, it becomes information that you can use to make a business decision.

Computers can take data and turn it into useful information by processing and organizing it. **Data** is what you put into a computer. **Information** is what you can get out of it.

The Information Processing Cycle

What happens between obtaining raw data and getting information based on that data from your computer? That's what the **information processing cycle** is all about. This cycle, shown in Figure 1.1, has four parts: input of data, processing of data, output of information, and storage of data and information.

Input In a typical day, you use a decimal system as you go about your tasks. For example, if you have your car repaired and the bill is $321, you've spent three hundreds, two tens, and one dollar. All this is based on a system of ten possible digits, 0 through 9. Computers, on the other hand, use a **binary system** with two possible values, 0 and 1, called *binary digits*. The term **bit** is a shortening of **binary digits**. Bits are found together in 8-bit collections. Each collection is called a **byte**. Each byte can store one thing like a digit, a special character, or a letter of the alphabet. You'll hear

FIGURE 1.1 **The Information Processing Cycle**
There are four parts to the information processing cycle.

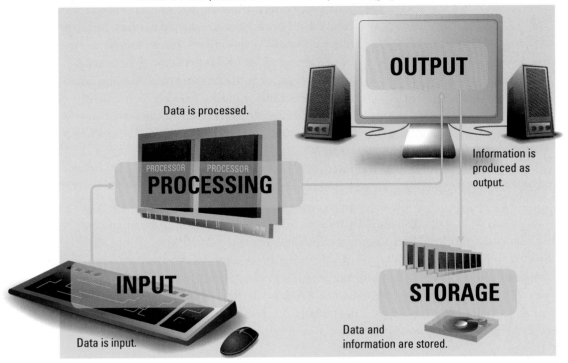

the terms bits and bytes used in the descriptions of processors (for example, 64-bit Pentium) and data storage capacity (500 gigabytes memory).

When you **input** data into a computer, it is converted to bits and bytes. Though typing on a keyboard may leap to mind when you think of getting data into your computer, there are actually several methods of inputting data. For example, you might provide your computer with input using a mouse, keyboard, scanner, gaming joystick, bar code scanner, microphone, camera, or the touchscreen on your smartphone. (You'll learn more about input and output devices in Chapter 3.)

Devices such as scanners turn existing printed materials into digital data.

Processing The **central processing unit (CPU)** in your computer is what interprets instructions and performs the **processing** of data. CPUs are integrated electronic circuits called **microprocessors** that are contained on chips, which are small squares of silicon. These microprocessors accept programming instructions that tell them what to do with the data they receive. Processors are often rated by the speed with which they can process the data, measured in hertz (Hz), or cycles of current per second. One hertz is one cycle per second. One megahertz (MHz) is one million cycles per second. A notebook computer might have a processing speed of two gigahertz (GHz), or two billion cycles per second.

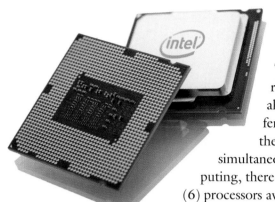

Processor speed has increased dramatically in recent years.

In addition, processors can be 32-bit or 64-bit, which is an indicator of how much data the processors can handle at a given point in time. The 64-bit processors are more powerful, but they require that the operating system and applications also be designed for 64-bit processing. Another differentiating factor is the number of processing cores the microprocessor contains, because each core can simultaneously read execute instructions. In personal computing, there are dual-core (2), quad-core (4), and hexa-core (6) processors available today. Some processors, such as Intel's Atom, which draws less power, have specialized features that make them a good match for mobile computing.

While a computer is processing data, it temporarily stores both the data and instructions from the CPU in **computer memory** in the form of **random access memory (RAM)**. There is a constant exchange of information between the CPU and RAM during processing. When you turn your computer off, the data temporarily stored in RAM disappears; therefore RAM is also referred to as **volatile memory**. Think of RAM as similar to a shopping cart—while you're shopping, you can temporarily place items in the cart. If you walk out of the store without buying the items, somebody will empty the cart, causing the items to "disappear."

Cache memory is an area of computer memory between RAM and the processor that serves as a holding area for the most frequently used data. As illustrated in Figure 1.2, your processor checks the cache memory first, because it is located on or near the microprocessor chip and therefore quicker to access. This procedure saves the processor from having to troll through the entire RAM holding area to find what it needs.

FIGURE 1.2 **Cache Memory**

Cache memory quickens computer processing time.

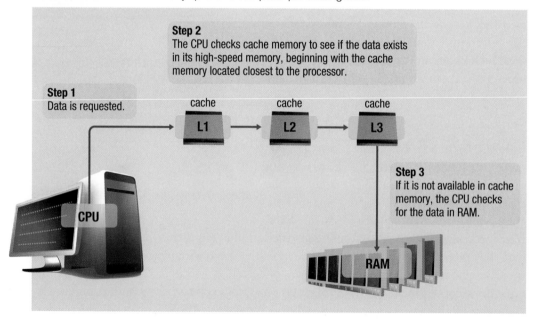

Step 1
Data is requested.

Step 2
The CPU checks cache memory to see if the data exists in its high-speed memory, beginning with the cache memory located closest to the processor.

Step 3
If it is not available in cache memory, the CPU checks for the data in RAM.

cache L1 → cache L2 → cache L3

CPU

RAM

Output Once you've put a lot of data into your computer, you'll typically want to see that data in some form. **Output** is the information that results from computer processing. Output might include the information you view on your monitor, a printed hard copy of a document, or an X-ray produced by a medical imaging computer. Your mobile device's screen can also provide output.

A monitor can display your computer's output at various resolutions. **Resolution** refers to the number of **pixels** (short for picture elements, which relates to the number of dots of color) used to generate an image on your screen. The higher the number of pixels, the more clearly defined the image.

Speakers are another form of output device. You might receive output of audio files through your computer or smartphone speakers, for example.

Printers are another method of output. They create a hard-copy record of your computing results. Though there have been predictions of a paperless office for years, people still seem to like paper copies of documents to keep records or make notes on. Many printer types are available, such as laser and inkjet, which you will learn more about in Chapter 3.

Monitors come in a variety of sizes and types. This 27-inch widescreen monitor provides a large-screen view of computer programs and data, and is especially beneficial for users who work with detailed drawings.

Storage **Storage** is a key part of the information processing cycle. If you have ever spent hours creating a document only to discover that your work was somehow lost, you know how important storage is. Your computer temporarily stores data while it runs processes, but that data is lost when you turn off your computer. You use a permanent storage device, such as a flash drive or your computer's hard drive, to save a version of your work that will be available long after you have shut off your computer. Early permanent storage media included paper punch cards, followed by floppy plastic disks and then floppy disks in hard cases. The most common long-term storage medium is your computer's internal hard drive, which is a metallic disk that uses magnetic or flash technology to store data. You can also store data on removable media (a flash drive or DVD, for example) so you can retrieve it using any computer. Today, an increasingly popular storage medium is **cloud storage**, which involves storing information on the web. Users can access the stored information from any computer with an Internet connection by entering a username and password. A popular cloud storage service is Microsoft's OneDrive. OneDrive is free and users get 7 GB of free space but can get additional space up to 25 GB for a fee. Any type of file may be uploaded and may be set to private, shared, or public. Other popular cloud storage services are Google Drive, Dropbox, iCloud, Box.net, and ADrive.

> ### 🔒 Playing It Safe
>
> It's a good idea to get in the habit of saving your files as you work and backing up your files on a regular basis. The cost in time and money of losing your work could be tremendous. In addition, in your working life you may be required to keep backup copies of files for a period of time to meet government regulations or prove your ownership of the work. Always keep a backup separate from your computer hard drive (for example on a DVD, flash drive, or in the cloud) in case your hard drive fails.

Flash drives (also called *USB sticks*) provide lots of storage in a small package.

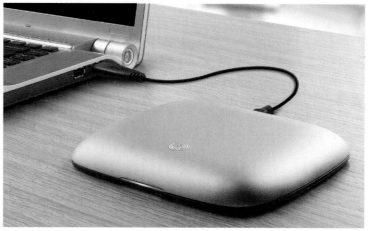

External hard drives provide an easy way to get extra storage capacity.

The basic unit of storage for data is the **file**, which might contain a report, spreadsheet, or picture, for example. Storage capacity is measured in kilobytes (approximately 1,000 bytes), megabytes (approximately 1 million bytes), gigabytes (approximately 1 billion bytes) and terabytes (approximately 1 trillion bytes).

Storage devices include your computer's hard disk, CDs or DVDs (also called *optical discs*), USB or flash drives (thumb-sized cartridges that slot into a USB port on your computer), and external hard drives (small boxes that connect to your computer via a cable in a USB port). Future forms of computer memory and storage may be made of conductive gels, making them suitable to use in conditions that would destroy current types of memory and storage, such as wet environments.

Take the Next Step *Online*

Activity 1.4.1 Watch	*What are the various types of RAM?*	**CORE** CONTENT
Activity 1.4.2 Watch	*What is the machine cycle?*	**CORE** CONTENT
Activity 1.4.3 Watch	*How does your computer translate text into numbers?*	**CORE** CONTENT
Activity 1.4.4 **TEAM** Present	*Is it data or information?*	e book
Activity 1.4.5 Research	*What is the best way to back up files?*	e book
Activity 1.4.6 Present	*What does the term* computer *mean to you?*	e book

Review and Assessment *Online*

An interactive Summing Up with audio, a Study Notes document, slide presentations with audio, and Terms to Know flashcards with audio are available from the links menu on this page in your ebook.

Summing Up

Just What Is a Computer?

On the simplest level, a **computer** is a programmable device that can assemble, process, and store data.

An **analog computer** uses mechanical operations to perform calculations, as with an older car speedometer or slide rule. A **digital computer** uses symbols that represent data in the form of code.

The combination of digital computing capability with communications has brought us tools such as email and instant messaging and new types of computing devices, including mobile phones, gaming devices, and GPS navigation systems.

Computers in All Shapes and Sizes

Computers fall into three broad groups based on operating system and manufacturer: Windows- or Linux-based personal computers (PCs) manufactured by a wide variety of companies such as Hewlett-Packard, Dell, Acer, and Lenovo; Mac computers available only through Apple; and Chromebooks using Google's Chrome OS. Manufacturers are also beginning to produce **wearable computers** in the form of glasses, clothing, and watches, but this category of computers is still emerging.

Computing power is the amount of data that can be processed and the speed with which it can be processed. A **supercomputer** is a computer with the ability to perform trillions of calculations per second and is usually custom-made for a particular use.

A **desktop computer** includes a central processing unit (CPU), which might be housed in a tower configuration or, in some cases, within the monitor, as with the Apple iMac.

Also known as notebook computers, **laptops** are usually portable, though today many are intended as desktop replacements and therefore may come with a large monitor and weigh as much as seven pounds. **Netbooks**, which became popular in the early 2000s, were lightweight and portable but contained limited computing power. Today they have largely been replaced by tablets and **ultrabooks** (very lightweight laptops).

Tablets are manufactured by several companies and enable you to navigate by touching easy-to-use onscreen tools. Tablets run several newer operating systems, such as Apple's iOS and Android.

Technological convergence is a term that describes the tendency of technical devices to take on each other's functions, resulting in communications, media, and information computing features in one package. So-called **converged devices** include your smartphone, which now contains functionalities of a phone, digital camera, GPS navigation system, and web browser.

Who Is Using Computers and How?

Computers are used in government, medicine, publishing, finance, education, arts, law enforcement, social settings, the entertainment industry, gaming, and more.

Though you are likely to use computers in your work no matter what your profession, there are several computer-specific fields that exist today. **Computer engineering (CE)** involves the study of computer hardware and software systems and programming devices to interface with each other. **Computer science (CS)** workers may design software, solve problems such as computer security threats, or come up with better ways of handling data storage. **Information systems (IS)** workers identify the kinds of data company employees need and design the technology systems to solve business problems. **Information technology (IT)** workers make sure the technology infrastructure is in place to support users. They may set up or maintain a network, or recommend the right hardware and software for their companies. **Software engineering (SE)** involves writing software programs that a software manufacturer sells to the public, or custom programs that a large organization uses in-house. There are also a number of **web development**-focused career tracks, as well.

What Is Information Technology?

According to the former Information Technology Association of America (ITAA), now part of TechAmerica, information technology is "the study, design, development, implementation, support or management of computer-based information systems, particularly software applications and computer hardware."

Computers take **data** and turn it into useful **information** by processing and organizing it. For example, if you take raw data about sales and prices and put it into a chart, it becomes information that you can use to make a business decision.

The **information processing cycle** has four parts: input of data, processing of data, output of information, and storage of data and information. Computers use a **binary system** of data based on two possible values, 0 and 1, called **binary digits** or **bits**.

You provide your computer with **input**-using devices such as a mouse, keyboard, scanner, gaming joystick, bar code scanner, or the number pad on your smartphone.

The **central processing unit (CPU)** in your computer interprets instructions and performs the **processing** of data. CPUs are made up of integrated circuits called **microprocessors** contained on chips. Processors are often rated by the speed with which they can process data, measured in hertz (Hz), megahertz (MHz), or gigahertz (GHz). While 64-bit processors generally can handle more data at once than 32-bit processors, they also require matching 64-bit software. The number of cores indicates how many simultaneous program instructions the processor can execute, with dual-core (2), quad-core (4), hexa-core (6), and octo-core (8) processors available today. Some processors, such as Intel's Atom, which draws less power, have specialized features that make them a good match for mobile computing.

While a computer is processing data, it temporarily stores both the data and instructions from the CPU in **computer memory** in the form of **random access memory (RAM)**, also called **volatile memory**. When you turn off your computer, the data temporarily stored in RAM disappears. There is also an area of computer memory between RAM and the processor called *cache memory*. **Cache memory** is a holding area for the most frequently used data.

Output is the information that results from computer processing. Output can include the information you view on your monitor or a printed hard copy of a document.

Our Digital World

Storage is a key part of the information processing cycle. Your computer temporarily stores data while it runs processes, but that temporarily stored data is lost when you turn your computer off. You use a permanent storage device to save a copy of your data or information that's available long after you have shut off your computer. The basic unit of storage for data is the **file**. Storage devices include your computer's hard disk, CDs or DVDs (also called *optical discs*), USB or flash drives, and external hard drives. **Cloud storage** involves storing information on the web. Future memory and storage technologies might use conductive gels that can stand up in wet environments.

Terms to Know

Just What Is a Computer?

Computers in All Shapes and Sizes

Who Is Using Computers and How?

What Is Information Technology?

Concepts Check

Concepts Check 1.1 Multiple Choice

Take this quiz to test your understanding of key concepts in this chapter.

Concepts Check 1.2 Matching

Test your understanding of terms and concepts presented in this chapter.

Concepts Check 1.3 Label It

Use the interactive tool to identify the categories of computers.

Concepts Check 1.4 Label It

Use the interactive tool to identify the parts of a computer system.

Projects

Check with your instructor for the preferred method to submit completed work.

Project 1.1 Computers Then and Now

Project 1.1.1

As a computer user, you may be curious about the people behind the development of computers and peripheral devices. To gain a better understanding of these people, research on the Internet and prepare a pictorial timeline of the work of these innovators along with their contributions. Your pictorial timeline should include 10 to 15 innovators who contributed to the development of computer hardware. The following questions, along with the names of the innovators you choose, will provide a head start for your timeline.

1. A slide rule is often associated with the early days of information tools; who is associated with the invention of the slide rule?
2. Who is known as the "Father of Computers"?
3. Who invented Z series computers?
4. The first fully electronic digital computer, known as the Atanasoff-Berry Computer (ABC), was invented by a professor and his student. What were their names?
5. Who invented the input device known as the mouse?

Be prepared to present your completed timeline according to your instructor's directions.

Project 1.1.2

Because of the prevalence of computers in today's society, it's essentially guaranteed that you and your classmates will work in jobs that require the use of some type of computing device. Select two different careers that are of interest to you. Research the ways in which computers and technology are used in performing these jobs by addressing the following questions:

1. What aspects of the job require the use of a computing device?
2. In what ways does using a computer support efficiency, effectiveness, and productivity in this position?
3. How have computers changed the way the job is performed over the last 20 years?
4. What types of advances in computer technology do you think might affect this job in the future?

Prepare a presentation summarizing the information you discovered. Be prepared to share the presentation with the class.

Project 1.2   Making Computer-Related Recommendations

Project 1.2.1

As the IT manager for a large physician's practice, the practice manager has asked you to determine what type of computing devices to provide to the physicians in the practice. The physicians will use these devices both for their own work and to provide healthcare information and services to patients. Research the capabilities of smartphones, tablets, and laptops in a healthcare setting. Using the information you have found, prepare a table that addresses the following questions:
1. What is the approximate cost of each category of device?
2. What features does each type of device offer?
3. What components could be added to each device to improve functionality?
4. How can each device uniquely improve how the physicians deliver healthcare services?

Use the information from your table to determine which type of computing device would be the best option for the physicians in the practice. Prepare a report making a recommendation of the type and model of device the practice should provide and include the details to support your recommendation. Submit the report to your instructor.

Project 1.2.2   TEAM

The owners of a toy manufacturing company believe that new computer input and output devices will result in improved worker efficiency. Your IT team has been asked to study the issue and make a recommendation. To accomplish this project, you and your teammates should complete the following tasks:
1. Prepare a list of all possible input/output devices in general use.
2. Describe what type of training each input/output device requires.
3. Identify which company departments (such as marketing, sales, finance, manufacturing, customer service) might use a specific input/output device.
4. List the cost of each device, assuming that mice and keyboards do not need to be purchased. Include your reference sources.
5. Recommend three input/output devices that should be purchased.

Prepare a table that displays your research findings, and attach a summary of your written recommendation.

Project 1.3   How Are Computing Devices Being Used?

Project 1.3.1

Substantial evidence indicates that individuals who frequently use computers at work are at risk for computer-related injuries. As you start your new data entry job, you want to ensure that you don't become another statistic. Research the topic of work-related injuries for computer users. Prepare a blog post that lists common injuries, the causes of these injuries, and suggestions for creating a safe working environment.

Project 1.3.2   TEAM

As members of the human resources department, your team has been assigned to investigate an increase in employee work-related injuries. Specifically, employees who work at computer workstations have reported chronic musculoskeletal problems. To help these employees, your team will prepare a slide presentation on how to create an ergonomic workstation. Your presentation should address chair requirements, including height adjustments and lumbar support, monitor and keyboard locations and settings, ergonomic accessories, and training. Be prepared to share your presentation with the class.

Project 1.4   Storage and Processing

Project 1.4.1

You recently left your flash drive in the college computer lab and lost all of your assignments. You now have to redo all your work. You have heard of cloud storage services such as OneDrive, Google Drive, and Dropbox from your friends. You decide to research the different types of cloud storage to back up your assignments. Using the Internet, research four different cloud storage services and prepare a table that includes the following information:

- Web address of the service
- Image of the cloud service website
- Storage fee, either by month or year or indicate if free
- Storage capacity
- Speed of uploads and downloads
- Available support services

Include with your table a written summary of your research, and state which cloud storage service will best meet your needs. Be sure to document your resources.

Project 1.4.2   TEAM

Read or listen to the "History of the Computer Processors" article at http://ODW4 .emcp.net/ProcessorHistory. Prepare a presentation about how the processor has evolved and improved the performance of computing devices.

Project 1.5   Wiki Project—Backing Up Data

Project 1.5.1

Interview one person who works at your college or a local business to find out how and why they back up data. If possible, pursue interesting industries that might have unique data needs such as nuclear power facilities, hospitals, or the stock exchange. Post your interview in podcast or transcript form on the class wiki. Be sure to include references for verification of content.

Project 1.5.2   TEAM

Natural disasters often occur without notice. For example, a few years ago a tornado damaged St. John's Hospital in Joplin, MO. Fortunately, the hospital had begun to use electronic health records. Even though the hospital was extensively damaged, the patient records were still accessible because the hospital had a disaster recovery plan that enabled employees to access the data and information. As a class, design a disaster recovery plan to be used in a particular industry such as health care or telecommunications. The disaster recovery plan might include backup methods, and comments about why these methods are important in that industry. Break into small teams. Every team should post the information it gathered about disaster recovery plans on the class wiki. If two teams post information about the same industry, they should combine the entries. In addition to posting an entry, add a comment or more information to other teams' posts. When you post or edit content, make sure you include a notation with the page that includes your team name and the date you posted or edited the content.

Project 1.6   Choosing a Computing Device

Project 1.6.1

You are the Director of IT for a two-year community college. The dean of the Business School has informed you that all incoming business students will be required to purchase a computing device to be used in the BYOD (bring your own device) pilot project. The dean wants to provide a list of recommended devices to the students. Research computing device options, focusing on current tablets. Prepare a table or spreadsheet listing the tablet specifications and costs. Include any upgrades or additional components (along with their costs) that would enhance the BYOD system. In a memo addressed to the dean, state your computing device recommendations and include your table or spreadsheet showing your cost analysis. In addition, provide a list of sources used in your research.

Project 1.6.2

You're ready to purchase a new smartphone to take advantage of newer technologies. There are many choices. Using the Internet, research three different smartphones from manufacturers such as Samsung, Apple, or Nokia. Prepare a presentation that includes an image of each smartphone and discuss the operating system, weight, screen size, dimensions, camera specs, screen resolution, battery life, features, and carriers. Explain what you use a smartphone for and make a recommendation based on the features you use most. Submit your presentation to your instructor. Be prepared to share your research with the class.

Class Conversations

Topic 1.1   Do computers cause us to work less efficiently?

Computers have changed the way we work. Most employees would say that computers have helped them become more effective and efficient in the workplace. Some think that computers just create more work and cause problems when they crash or slow down. Discuss a career or place of employment where you think computers have actually decreased effectiveness and efficiency. Why do you think this is the case? Be prepared to support your position.

Topic 1.2   What will computing in the future look like?

Technology changes rapidly. Since the first personal computer appeared on the cover of *Popular Electronics* in 1975, the computer has changed in performance, cost, size, and capabilities. The personal computer has morphed from a desktop to a handheld device. Consider what you think the computer of the future will be like. Discuss what the computer might look like, its functionality, capacity, and performance.

Topic 1.3   What is the impact of going overseas for technology services?

Computers and technology have enabled outsourcing by large organizations for many years. Now, small businesses often need workers for a one-time project such as website design or software development, so they are using online job marketplaces that contract with skilled foreign workers to lower costs. Discuss the advantages and disadvantages of small business outsourcing technology work to other countries. Discuss how this will have an impact on the US and Canadian economies and small business job markets in the future.

The Internet
Gateway to a World of Resources

What You'll Accomplish

When you finish this chapter, you'll be able to:

2.1 Describe how the Internet and the web have changed the ways in which people interact with each other.

2.2 Describe the Internet and the web in terms of the Internet's infrastructure and the web's phases of evolution.

2.3 Select the services, equipment, and software you need to connect to and browse the Internet.

2.4 Describe the organization of web pages and how they are accessed.

2.5 Distinguish between appropriate and inappropriate use of intellectual property and copyright as they apply to the web.

2.6 Differentiate between the three types of e-commerce.

2.7 Compare various Internet services and applications such as email, instant messaging, and audio and video conferencing.

Why Does It Matter ?

Online caring site CaringBridge is visited by over 500,000 people a day to get updates about and support loved ones who are dealing with healthcare challenges. A study by IBM indicated that 80 percent of the students surveyed "anticipate running into new technology that they will have to adapt to and learn upon entering the workforce." The Internet can be used for this purpose. By the time President Obama was starting his second term in office in 2013, he had already supported changes to better control digital data, appointed the first chief technology and chief information officers in the country, and made the position of the White House cybersecurity coordinator more prominent. In December 2015, Obama became the first US President to write a line of computer code. From protecting our health to electing our officials, the Internet has become an indispensable part of our lives. Understanding what the Internet is, how it works, and the dynamics of its growth will help you succeed personally and professionally in our digital age.

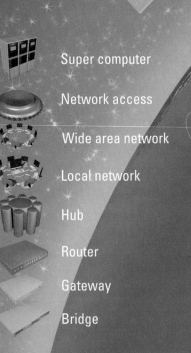

Super computer

Network access

Wide area network

Local network

Hub

Router

Gateway

Bridge

The Internet has changed the way we live, work, and play. From communicating to searching for information to socializing to conducting business, a vast web of resources and activities is at our fingertips 24/7.

——— Internet backbone

——— Commerce

——— Information

——— Communication

2.1 The World Goes Online

Many people, for much of the day, use the Internet for a wide variety of activities. People learn, work, play, and connect with others using several types of devices, such as computers, tablets, smartphones, gaming devices, and information kiosks. We can even **sync** our own electronic devices with one another to keep our data up to date. This enables us to do things like view our calendar and contacts and post to social media and other sites from any Internet-connected device.

According to the Pew Internet Project, as of January 2015, 92 percent of American adults owned a cell phone, 68 percent owned a smartphone, 45 percent owned a tablet, and 19 percent owned an e-reader. As of October 2015, 76 percent of those online used social networking sites. Of all adult Internet users, 54 percent posted original photos or videos that they themselves had taken, and 47 percent took photos or videos they found online and reposted them on sites designed for sharing with many other users. All these activities performed using various devices take advantage of the Internet to do things that would have seemed miraculous only a dozen years ago.

Your smartphone is a tiny computer with enormous potential.

Cutting-Edge Internet

Activities such as shopping, communicating, and researching online are probably familiar to you, but some other uses of the Internet may be new to you. For example:

- Today, scientists share the use of extremely expensive, specialized microscopes over the Internet.
- Doctors learn surgery techniques through online cyberscalpel simulations.
- Entertainers release albums strictly online—no disc required. In 2014, digital album sales totaled 27.8 million.
- Airline pilots practice landing a plane on water with web-based flight simulators.
- NASA, through a program called *NASA Quest*, offers web-based, interactive explorations of space to students.
- A **quick response (QR) code** provides a shortcut you can use to go to a website using your smartphone. Rather than entering the web address, you use your phone (with a reader application installed) to scan this 2-D code and let it connect

Pilots practice air disaster recovery maneuvers by training online.

your phone to the site. Figure 2.1 shows how this process works. QR codes are a marketing tool used to bring potential clients or customers to a target website. A school library can use a QR code to direct a student to a website to search for a particular book.

- More people make purchasing decisions based on information gleaned from social media, forcing today's corporations to include social media as a regular and vital part of every marketing plan.
- Cloud computing lets you access your files and programs from anywhere in the world via the Internet. Because the files and programs reside on the web, they are always available.
- Your car has become a computer. Automobile manufacturers are building in smart systems that allow drivers to make phone calls with their cars; play music on your smartphone over the car speakers; receive, listen to, and respond to incoming text messages, all handsfree.

- Microblogging sites such as Twitter are pushing the boundaries of citizen journalism as participants often send out updates on current news stories before news agencies do, as was the case during the hunt for a downed Malaysia Airlines plane in 2014.

What remarkable uses of the Internet are you aware of?

Many colleges are phasing out computer labs and requiring that freshmen have a laptop computer to complete coursework and communicate with instructors.

FIGURE 2.1 **A QR Code in Action**
Scanner software enables your smartphone to read the QR code and go to the destination website.

smartphone

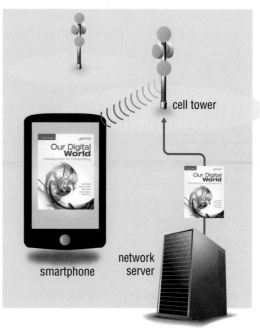

smartphone   network server

cell tower

The Future of the Internet

Some current uses of the Internet are amazing, and in the future, this technology will only become more ingrained in your daily life. Consider how quickly technology advances:

- Astronauts sent the first tweets (Twitter messages) just years ago from the space shuttle Atlantis and the International Space Station. The Mars Phoenix lander tweeted its progress as it explored that planet. With no Internet connection they had to send their tweets to Earth where others posted them, but at some point, our global Internet could reach directly out to other planets.
- Collaboration and social media keep converging in the cloud. Whether it's recommending a Hulu video to your Facebook friends with the click of a button or developing the specs for a new product via a company wiki, online collaboration is quickly becoming a real-time tool for teams and colleagues.
- Nanotechnology-enabled robots can be injected into your body, move around to deliver drugs and monitor vital signs, and then send information to your doctor over a wireless Internet connection.

In fact, what was once science fiction is becoming reality through technologies that are being thought of or developed today. Nobody imagined texting or video streaming over YouTube twenty years ago, yet these types of significant additions to our culture explode on the scene rapidly. Tomorrow is anybody's guess—will you be there to adopt or even introduce the next great online innovation?

> "You can't just ask customers what they want and then try to give that to them. By the time you get it built, they'll want something new."
>
> —Steve Jobs,
> former CEO of Apple

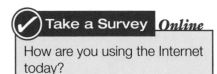

Take a Survey *Online*

How are you using the Internet today?

PRECHECK ## 2.2 What Are the Internet and World Wide Web?

Together the Internet and World Wide Web (better known as simply the web) have made it possible for the world to connect and communicate in remarkable ways. But what role does each of these play?

What Is the Internet?

The **Internet** is the world's largest computer network—a physical infrastructure that provides us with the ability to share resources and communicate with others around the world. It is possible to "see, touch, and feel" elements of the Internet because it's made up of hardware such as servers, routers, switches, transmission lines, and towers that store and transmit vast amounts of data (Figure 2.2).

The Internet is the pathway on which data, sounds, and images flow from person to person around the globe.

> "I must confess that I've never trusted the web. Where does it live? How do I hold it personally responsible? And is it male or female? In other words, can I challenge it to a fight?"
>
> —Stephen Colbert,
> Comedian

FIGURE 2.2 **The Infrastructure of the Internet**

Data moves across the Internet by traveling through a collective of physical objects.

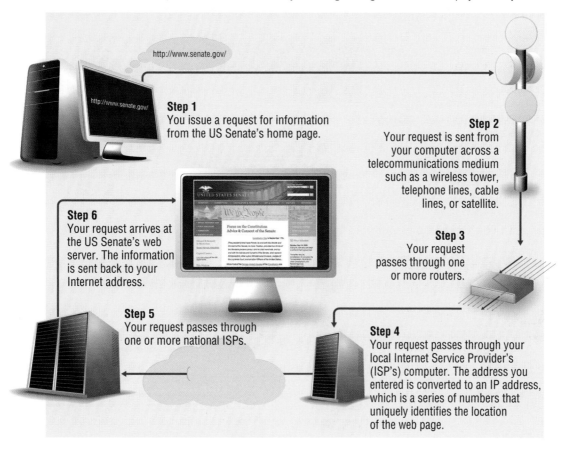

Step 1
You issue a request for information from the US Senate's home page.

Step 2
Your request is sent from your computer across a telecommunications medium such as a wireless tower, telephone lines, cable lines, or satellite.

Step 3
Your request passes through one or more routers.

Step 4
Your request passes through your local Internet Service Provider's (ISP's) computer. The address you entered is converted to an IP address, which is a series of numbers that uniquely identifies the location of the web page.

Step 5
Your request passes through one or more national ISPs.

Step 6
Your request arrives at the US Senate's web server. The information is sent back to your Internet address.

What Is the Web?

If the Internet is a pathway for information, the web is one type of content that travels along that path. The **web** is a body of content that is available as web pages. The pages are stored on Internet servers around the world. A **web page** may contain text, images, interactive animations, games, music, and more. Several web pages may make up a single **website** (Figure 2.3).

The documents, images, and other information that you choose to put on the web are the ones you want other people to see. You can also choose whether you want everyone in the world to view your content or limit access to a few close friends.

Because anyone can publish just about anything to the web, it has become very popular very fast, and has grown with little oversight or regulation. Many people feel that what makes the web appealing is that it is a largely unregulated environment. However, that very lack of regulation and supervision means that some people feel free to abuse others or commit crimes using online tools and sites. The web is therefore sometimes referred to as the wild, wild West.

Although certain countries have regulations and laws in place regarding the web, it is hard to enforce them across borders and cultures. For example, many forms of online gambling are illegal in the United States, but it's easy for US citizens to gamble online using off-shore hosted online casinos. Still, many people feel that the benefits of freedom of expression and sharing of ideas and information on the web far outweigh the problems that result from the lack of regulation and control.

FIGURE 2.3 A Website

A single website is made up of one or more web pages. You use a web browser, a type of software, to find and view a website.

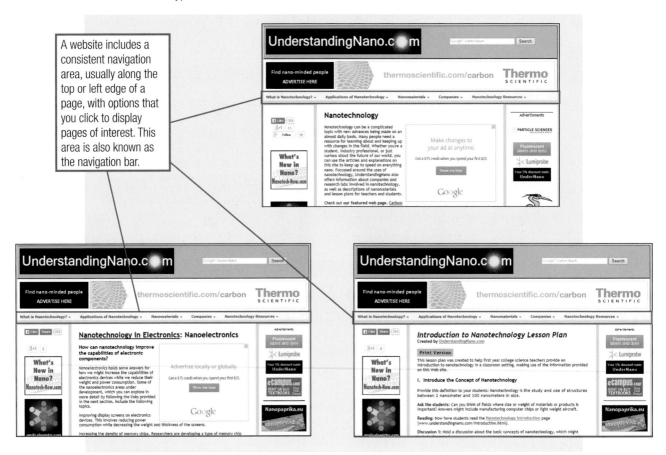

A website includes a consistent navigation area, usually along the top or left edge of a page, with options that you click to display pages of interest. This area is also known as the navigation bar.

Web 2.0 The different phases of the web are not like software releases. Rather, they represent new trends in online usage and technologies brought about both by the way people use the Internet and technologies that enable new activities in the online world. We have already experienced the first shift in online usage. This shift is considered to be the start of the second phase of the web, referred to as Web 2.0. **Web 2.0** marks a change from people simply reading information online to people interacting with information by both reading and writing online content.

The concept of Web 2.0 came out of the "dot-com collapse" of 2001, when many online businesses failed. Internet users appeared to be unwilling to pay fees to use online services such as email and news and sought a more collaborative experience. New applications and websites began popping up with surprising regularity, marking a turning point for the web, according to an article by Tim O'Reilly, founder of O'Reilly Publishing.

Playing It Safe

Connecting with billions of people from different cultures and with different agendas can be a wonderful learning opportunity, but use care when sharing personal information online. If you wouldn't shout your home address and social security number from a street corner, why would you post it online for the world to read?

Ethics and Technology Blog *Online*

Regulating Web Behavior

Some people think the web should be regulated by a central body. Other people think the freedom to say and do what you want on the web should be protected. What do you think? Should the web be under anybody's control?

 Computers in Your Career

The Internet and web have made available a wide variety of careers that didn't exist 10 years ago, and not all are high-tech in nature. For example, consider jobs such as web content writer, Internet law expert, and online trainer. If you are more technically inclined, a variety of developer jobs allow you to work with tasks from programming an e-commerce shopping cart to creating environments in virtual reality worlds.

Over time, Web 2.0 has become associated with interactive web services such as Wikipedia and Facebook that provide users with a way to collaborate by sharing and exchanging ideas and adding or editing content. The premise of this generation of web usage is that people are not passively viewing information but are also interacting with and helping to create content.

Web 3.0 **Web 3.0**, which has already begun and will evolve over time, is seen as the next phase in online usage. Web 3.0 will host collaborative content that is connected in meaningful ways. For example, while in the past you could post a photo from your vacation online and also keep an online calendar with your trip itinerary, in the world of Web 3.0 your photos appear within the calendar on the date and at the time you took them. Web 3.0 is also called the **Semantic Web**, appropriately named because semantics is the study of meaning in language.

In Web 3.0, machines can talk to machines. For example, TiVo searches the Internet and gathers information from various websites about programs that you might like to watch. In Web 3.0, machines go beyond just gathering information; they can also draw conclusions about the data they share. The Semantic Web makes it possible for websites to "understand" the relationships between elements of web content. An intelligent agent, or search program, may even be able to update and modify your documents on the fly based on information you read on the Internet. For this to come about, we have to find common formats so that data can be integrated, rather than just exchanged.

Web 3.0 also has an impact on how we search. Beginning with the Windows 8.1 operating system, Microsoft introduced a new way of searching that is built on Web 3.0 technology. With this new feature, conducting a search on your computer can return results that include a list of related files, applications, or features stored on your hard drive, plus websites, music, or images from the web. Microsoft's Bing search service finds information and provides recommendations to help you make choices and decisions for shopping, travel, and more. Stephen Wolfram's WolframAlpha search engine lets you ask questions in natural human language rather than entering keywords. Instead of simply searching for matches, this engine computes answers to your questions.

Computers in Your Career

Huge volumes of patient data create a record-keeping challenge in the medical field. Medical informatics professionals work to tame the mountains of data by designing medical information systems that make it easier to enter, update, and retrieve medical data. This drive toward online medical records was given a boost when the US government mandated digital record keeping from the healthcare industry as of January 2014. Today, in addition to making data retrieval easier, expert systems have been created to present and summarize information in a way that assists medical professionals in diagnosing and treating illnesses.

 Spotlight on the Future *Online*

Utopian or Dystopian Future?

Will the growth of connected sensors and monitoring devices lead to a more utopian (perfect) or dystopian (imperfect) experience? Experts argue for both outcomes, according to a recent report from the Pew Research Center.

"There will be a whole host of ways that life gets more convenient, more productive, potentially safer, potentially healthier," says Lee Rainie, project director. For example, if you are wearing a device that monitors your health, you can head off health problems.

Other experts answering the survey had a drastically different view.

"People are saying that the biggest effect of the Internet of Things will be government-sanctioned spyware in every aspect of our lives," Rainie says. "As we extend ourselves and open ourselves up and share our personal information . . . we also extend ourselves out to the threat of . . . people with other goals in mind."

Talk about It

1. In what ways could the Internet of Things lead to a more utopian future?

2. How would you react to technology that is so common and ubiquitous it is like electricity? Do you think you would notice it?

3. In what ways could the Internet of Things lead to a more dystopian future?

4. What are some "middle ground" arguments that don't predict either extreme coming to pass?

5. How will the complexity of these systems and technologies affect the speed and success of the most forward-looking visions of what might occur?

Activity 2.2.1 Research	*If anyone can post content to the web, who manages the web and in what ways?*	**CORE** CONTENT
Activity 2.2.2 Watch	*How is Web 2.0 changing our world?*	**CORE** CONTENT
Activity 2.2.3 Research	*Who founded the web?*	e book
Activity 2.2.4 Research	*What might the web of the future look like?*	e book

PRECHECK

2.3 Joining the Digital World

You may have been going online for many years and it may seem as natural as turning on a television set, or you may have only skimmed the surface of the Internet, which came into the public mainstream less than twenty years ago.

Whichever the case, you are probably aware that today, the Internet is truly a global phenomenon. According to Internet World Stats, in 2015 more than 3.3 billion people are now online, up from almost 361 million people in 2000. This represents more than 800 percent growth over approximately 15 years.

Figure 2.4 shows how many people use the Internet worldwide.

- Asia has the highest number of Internet users, at more than 1.6 billion users (almost half of the world's total users).
- North America, including the United States and Canada, comes in fifth with 313,867,363 users.

However, these statistics can be misleading. In fact, relative to the size of our population, North America has the greatest penetration of Internet usage: 87.9 percent of us are online, compared to only 40.2 percent of the population of Asia.

To appreciate how the online world works, it's useful to understand how we all connect to this vast community with a combination of hardware and software technology.

Ethics and Technology Blog *Online*

Good Business vs. an Invasion of Privacy

The advertising and marketing world are eager to find new opportunities for collecting information about how people use the Internet. Search engines return results based on your searching and buying habits and sometimes sell information about your search habits to other companies. Do you think the ability of search engines to track your actions and to sell that information to others is "business as usual" or an invasion of your privacy?

FIGURE 2.4 Worldwide Internet Use

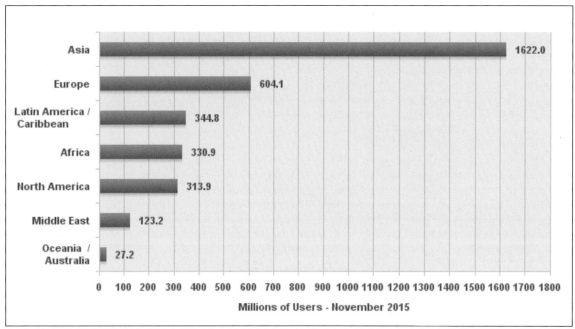

Source: http://InternetWorldStats.com, November 2015.

Hardware to Make the Connection

Most of today's computers come ready to connect to the Internet through the use of wireless technology. After you establish an account with an **Internet service provider (ISP)**, which is a company that lets you use its servers and software to connect to the Internet for a fee, you will need hardware such as a DSL, cable, or satellite modem to connect (see Figure 2.5). If you want to connect wirelessly, you will need additional hardware such as a router.

You might connect in a number of ways:

- You can get access via a cable modem that connects your computer via a coaxial cable (the same type of cable that carries a cable TV signal), by using a high speed digital subscriber line (DSL) modem that connects your computer via regular phone lines or by using fiber optic cable, which transmits your data via light waves. You can share any of these connections over a wireless router.
- You can connect your wireless computer to a WiMAX tower. The WiMAX tower connects directly to the Internet or transmits to one or more additional towers that then connect to the Internet. This technology provides high-speed long distance connectivity when cable and DSL are not available.
- Use a wireless modem (most newer computers offer this option) to go online by way of a cellular network.
- Tap into a wireless fidelity (Wi-Fi) network, which uses radio signals for a wireless connection from hotspots located in places such as hotels, airports, and Internet cafes. These may be free or may require that you pay a fee to connect. Some ISPs now offer a wireless cloud over their service areas, making wireless access available in open places like your hometown's parks and recreation areas.

FIGURE 2.5 **Connecting to the Internet**
Depending on the type of Internet connection available, you will need different types of equipment to connect to the Internet.

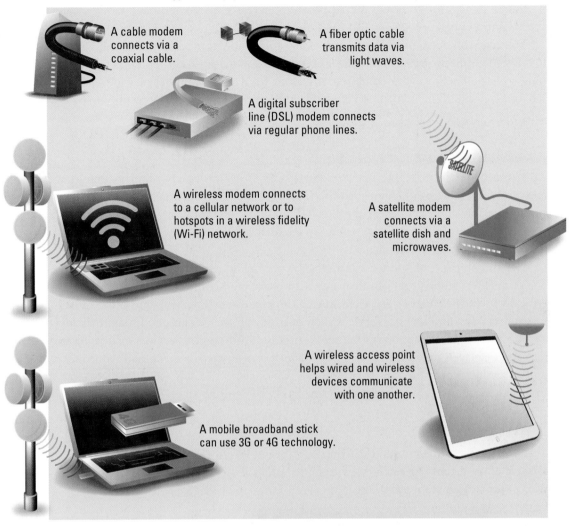

A cable modem connects via a coaxial cable.

A fiber optic cable transmits data via light waves.

A digital subscriber line (DSL) modem connects via regular phone lines.

A wireless modem connects to a cellular network or to hotspots in a wireless fidelity (Wi-Fi) network.

A satellite modem connects via a satellite dish and microwaves.

A wireless access point helps wired and wireless devices communicate with one another.

A mobile broadband stick can use 3G or 4G technology.

- **Multihomed devices** allow you to connect to the Internet in multiple ways. For example, your smartphone can connect using your cell plan or a Wi-Fi connection. The best method for connection is determined based on those currently available, and if the existing connection becomes unavailable (such as if you leave the area of a Wi-Fi network), the device will automatically switch to another connection, if possible.

A smartphone is a multihomed device, which allows you to access the Internet using a cell plan or a Wi-Fi connection.

- Mobile broadband sticks are essentially portable modems about the size of a USB stick. They use 3G or 4G technology to connect via a provider such as T-Mobile or Verizon for a monthly fee. 3G is the third generation of cellular technology. 4G is fourth generation technology that provides increased speed and bandwidth. Both 3G and 4G technology are also used on smartphones.

You may still occasionally come across an old-fashioned modem that is used for a low-speed connection method called *dial-up*. With a dial-up Internet connection, you plug a phone line into your computer and dial a local access number provided by your ISP to go online. The connection is usually slow and you can't use your phone for calls while you're connected.

Paying for the Privilege: Internet Service Providers

As mentioned earlier, an Internet service provider (ISP) lets you use their technology (servers and software) to connect to the Internet for a fee. Your ISP might be your phone or cable company. There are also national ISPs such as EarthLink and local and regional ISP companies that use technologies such as DSL and fiber optic access provided by local utility companies.

Depending on your connection method, your ISP may provide you with a modem and/or router and instructions for using it to make your connection. ISP accounts typically include a variety of services, such as an email account, news and other information services, and security services such as a firewall, virus scans, and spam management for your monthly subscription fee. Email and information services may be identified and displayed on your ISP start page, which is often personalized with your name and a weather report for your area. You can personalize your start page further—for example, by choosing which news services send news to the page.

How Browsers View What's Online

You use browser software such as **Microsoft Edge**, Firefox (Figure 2.6), Safari, Google Chrome, and Opera to view online content. Essentially, a **browser** renders web pages (which are typically created using a language such as HTML) into text, graphics, and multimedia.

FIGURE 2.6 Mozilla Firefox
Mozilla Firefox is a popular browser.

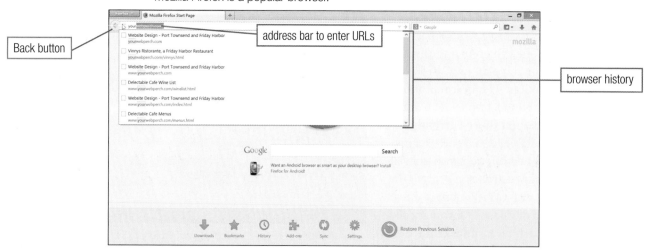

Back button

address bar to enter URLs

browser history

Browsers allow you to move from page to page on the World Wide Web while retaining a list of your favorite sites and a record of your browsing history. Browsers have become an ally in protecting your privacy online with built-in filters and security features.

Mobile devices use web browsers designed to display web pages on smaller screens. For example, Opera Mobile allows a smartphone running the Windows, iOS, or Android operating systems to browse the web on the go. (Chapter 4 provides more information about mobile phone operating systems.) Web 2.0 sites such as ChaCha allow you to text questions from your cell phones and get nearly immediate answers. As many people now surf the web from their mobile devices, more companies are providing mobile apps or responsive websites. Responsive websites contain all or most of the same content, but they are specially formatted to be viewed and interacted with more easily on small screens.

Smartphones allow you to browse the web with mobile versions of your favorite browsers, such as Safari, Chrome, and Opera Mobile.

 Take the Next Step *Online*

Activity 2.3.1 Watch	*Why choose one Internet connection method over another?*	**CORE** CONTENT
Activity 2.3.2 Watch	*What is your Internet connection and how does your browser display web pages?*	

PRECHECK **2.4** Navigating and Searching the Web

With so many web pages out there created by lots of different people, the web ought to be pretty chaotic. However, there are underlying systems as to how pages are organized on the web and how they are delivered to your computer. This involves unique addresses used to access each web page, a unique address for each computer, and browser features for locating and retrieving online content.

IPs and URLs: What's in an Address?

An **Internet Protocol (IP) address** is a series of numbers that uniquely identifies a location on the Internet. An IP address consists of four groups of numbers separated by periods; for example: 225.73.110.102. A nonprofit organization called *ICANN* keeps track of IP addresses around the world.

Due to the explosion of Internet users and websites, the number of available unique four-group addresses (under IPv4) has been nearly consumed. A new standard known as IPv6 uses addresses with eight groups of hexadecimal characters separated by colons and should provide enough addresses for the foreseeable future.

> " The goal has always been the same. The progression is from data to useful information to knowledge that answers questions people have or helps them do things. Knowledge is the quest. "
>
> —Amit Singhal, senior vice president at Google

Because numbers would be difficult to remember for retrieving pages, we use a text-based address referred to as a **uniform resource locator (URL)** to go to a website (Figure 2.7). A URL, also called a **web address**, has several parts separated by a colon (:), slashes (/), and dots (.). The first part of a URL is called a *protocol* and identifies a certain way for interpreting computer information in the transmission process. *Http*, which stands for hypertext transfer protocol, and *ftp*, which stands for file transfer protocol, are examples of protocols. Some sites use a secondary identifier for the type of site being contacted, such as *www* for a World Wide Web site, but this is often optional.

The next part of the URL is the **domain name**, which identifies the group of servers (the domain) to which the site belongs and the particular company or organization name (such as *emcp* in the Figure 2.7 example).

A suffix, such as *.com* or *.edu*, further identifies the domain. For example, the *.com* in the example shown in Figure 2.7 is a **top-level domain (TLD)**. These TLDs with three or more characters are also called **generic top-level domains (gTLDs)**, in contrast to two-character country code TLDs such as .jp and .de. To accommodate growth, ICANN is delegating new gTLDs on a rolling basis and expects to eventually move the domain name system to over 1,300 new names. Table 2.1 on the next page provides a rundown of some common gTLDs.

FIGURE 2.7 Parts of a URL

A domain name is an easy-to-remember way to get to a specific IP address.

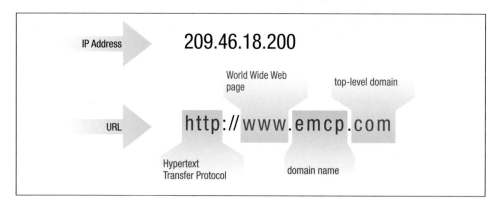

TABLE 2.1 Common Generic Top-Level Domain Suffixes Used in URLs

Suffix	Type of Organization	Example
.biz	business site	Billboard: http://www.billboard.biz
.com	company or commercial institution	Intel: http://www.intel.com
.edu	educational institution	Harvard University: http://www.harvard.edu
.gov	government site	Internal Revenue Service: http://www.irs.gov
.int	international organizations endorsed by treaty	World Health Organization: http://www.who.int
.mil	military site	US Army: http://www.army.mil
.net	administrative site for ISPs	Earthlink: http://www.earthlink.net
.org	nonprofit or private organization	Red Cross: http://www.redcross.org

Browsing Web Pages

You may already be quite comfortable with browsing the Internet, but you may not have pondered how browsers move around the web and retrieve data.

Any element of a web page (text, graphic, audio, or video) can be linked to another page using a hyperlink. A **hyperlink** describes a destination within a web document and can be inserted in text or a graphical object such as a company logo. Text that is linked is called **hypertext**.

A website is a series of related web pages that are linked together. You get to a website by entering the URL, such as http://amazon.com, into your browser. Every website has a starting page, called the **home page**, which is the first page displayed when you visit the site's TLD. For example, the home page of the US Copyright Office is shown in

FIGURE 2.8 Parts of a Web Page

Web pages are designed with tools to help you access their content.

Figure 2.8. You can also enter a URL to jump to a specific page within a site, such as the page showing copyright fees at http://copyright.gov/docs/fees.html, or search within the site to find specific content.

Searching for Content Online

A **search engine**, such as Google, Ask, and Yahoo, catalogs and indexes web pages for you. A type of search engine called a **search directory** can also catalog pages by topic, such as finance, health, news, shopping, and so on.

Search engines may seem to be free services, but they are typically financed by selling advertising. Some also make money by selling information about your online activities and interests to advertisers.

Some current search engines, including Microsoft Bing and Google, not only search for content but make choices among content to deliver more targeted results. Such search engines allow you, for example, to ask for a list of female tennis stars from 1900 on and they then assemble a table of them for you.

Table 2.2 shows some common search tools with their URLs.

TABLE 2.2	Common Search Tools
Search Tool	**URL**
Ask	ask.com
Bing	bing.com
Dogpile	dogpile.com
DuckDuckGo	duckduckgo.com
Google	google.com
Yahoo!	yahoo.com

 Ethics and Technology Blog *Online*

Sharing Information from Search Directories

Do search engine companies such as Google have the right to make your personal information (a picture of your home, your phone number, or whatever) available to others? Should you have the right to opt out of being included in these directories?

Searches That Succeed So how do search engines work? You search for information by going to the search engine's website and typing in your search text, which is comprised of one or more **keywords** or keyword phrases. You can search within a specific website by entering your search text into a search text box, which you'll find on most websites.

For example, to find information about the international space station you might type *international space station* in the search engine's search text box and press Enter. You can then narrow your search by specifying that you want to view links to certain types of results such as images, maps, or videos, as on Google's site, shown in Figure 2.9.

You can get more targeted search results by honing your searching technique. Effective searching is a skill that you gain through practice. For example, typing *space station* into a search engine could easily return more than 80 million results. If what you really need to find out is the cost to build the station, consider a more targeted keyword phrase like *space station cost*. Search engines provide advanced search options that you can use to include or exclude certain results. For example, you can exclude pages with certain domain suffixes (such as .com and .net) to limit your search results to educational and government sites. Table 2.3 explains how to narrow your search by entering keywords in various ways. Figure 2.10 shows Yahoo!'s search parameters, which include specifying the category of content to search, when the content was last updated, and the quality of the image (if applicable).

A **metasearch engine**, such as dogpile.com, uses several search engines to search keywords across several websites at the same time. This helps optimize the search by providing the top results from the best search engines. For example, imagine you need

FIGURE 2.9   **The Google Search Page**

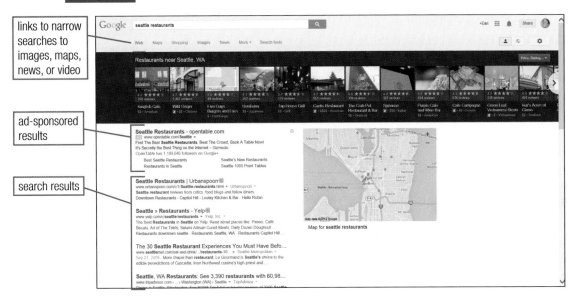

links to narrow searches to images, maps, news, or video

ad-sponsored results

search results

TABLE 2.3   **Advanced Search Parameters**

Item	What It Does	Example
Quotes ("")	Instruction to use exact word or words in the exact order given	"Pearl Harbor"
Minus symbol (-)	Excludes words preceded by the minus symbol from the search	jaguar -car
Wildcard (*)	Treat the asterisk as a placeholder for any possible word	*bird for bluebird, redbird, etc.
Or	Allow either one word or the other	Economy 2006 or 2007

FIGURE 2.10   **Examples of Yahoo!'s Advanced Search Options**

terms to include in search

categories

Safe Search

when content was last updated

image quality

search results

to write a report on cocoa production. Instead of typing *cocoa production process* into several search engines individually, you can type the search text into one metasearch engine that initiates searches on several engines at the same time.

Specialized Search Sites Many websites are essentially specialized search services. Some simply provide you with information while others use your search results to sell you merchandise or services. Here are some examples:

- Mapquest and Google Maps let you look for locational information including maps and driving directions.
- Expedia is a travel site that searches a multitude of resources for rates on airfares, hotels, and rental cars to help you plan a trip. Similarly, KAYAK searches hundreds of travel websites so you can compare results and find the best deal.
- BizRate is a site you can use to compare and shop by gathering results for prices at dozens of retailers.
- Sites such as Google Video index videos that have been posted online from around the world.

Some of these sites charge a fee. For example, if you book a trip on Expedia, you pay for the trip plus a small fee to Expedia for providing your itinerary. Other sites such as Mapquest are free.

The Role of Plug-ins and Players Some multimedia components on a web page may require that you install a **plug-in** or **player** on your computer to view or hear content. Many players are installed with your browser; however, you've probably come across a web page that uses a plug-in or player that you need to download and install. These programs are free and simply require that you go to the publisher's site to download and install them.

For example, to play **streaming video**, which is video that is delivered to your computer as a constant stream of content, you may need a media player. To read a file saved in PDF format, you must install Adobe Acrobat Reader. Table 2.4 contains a list of some of the most common plug-ins and players.

> **🔒 Playing It Safe**
>
> Most people don't realize how much information about them exists online. Maybe you posted a résumé or made some blog entries on a publicly viewable page. Perhaps schools, employers, friends, or the government placed your information online. Do a web search of your name. If you find information about you that you'd rather not have online, ask the host site to remove it.

BizRate is a metasearch engine that allows you to compare information from several retailers to find the best price available for a product.

Our Digital World

TABLE 2.4 Common Plug-Ins and Players

Name	Home Page	Purpose
Adobe Reader	http://adobe.com	Read and print PDF files
QuickTime	http://apple.com	Play MP3 music, animations, and video files
RealPlayer	http://real.com	Play streaming audio and video files
Shockwave	http://adobe.com	Play interactive games and various multimedia files online
Windows Media Player	http://microsoft.com	Play streaming audio, video, animations, and multimedia presentations on the web

Windows Media Player allows you to play a variety of multimedia files.

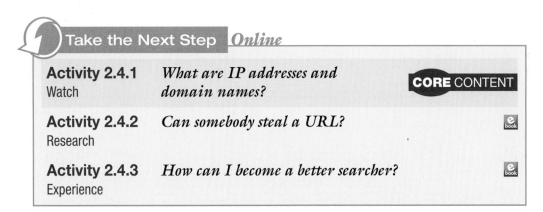

Activity 2.4.1 Watch — *What are IP addresses and domain names?* — CORE CONTENT

Activity 2.4.2 Research — *Can somebody steal a URL?*

Activity 2.4.3 Experience — *How can I become a better searcher?*

PRECHECK

2.5 The Vast Sea of Online Content

Though it's difficult to calculate exactly how many websites and web pages exist today, information from the Netcraft Secure Server Survey in 2013 indicated an increase of over three times the number of websites it reported in 2010. With that kind of constant activity, it's logical to conclude that not all of the content that is online is of the same quality or accuracy. In addition, some of that content is free for the taking, while other content is protected by **copyright**, or legal ownership of that content. It's important that you learn how to evaluate the quality of content, learn to respect laws that govern your use of that content, and understand when free exchange of content is allowed and encouraged.

Some information posted online occurs in social transactions such as on blogs and social networking sites. Chapter 7 takes a look at the social web and the kinds of content and activity you'll find there.

Evaluating Web Content

The web contains a wealth of accurate and useful information. However, not all information found online is true, just as newspaper stories can contain inaccuracies. As in the offline world, you have to consider the source of online content. If you trust technology information from *Wired* magazine in print, you can have a similar level of trust in its online site. If you don't know a source at all, you may have to do some digging to discover if it is reputable by looking at the source's credentials (what individuals or organizations are involved in the venture?), methods (for example, is the information based on surveys and experiment, or personal opinion?), and reputation (what do other online users say in reviews of the site or the company's products?).

Because anyone can publish to the web, to gauge the accuracy of what you read, you have to verify the three Ws (or WWW) of online content (Figure 2.11):

- *Who* is the author or publisher? Is the source credible?
- *What* is the message? Is the information verifiable? Is there a possibility of bias? Always try to crosscheck the information with other sources. Look for sponsors of a site to determine if the content could have a bias.
- *When* was it published? Is the information current? If no date is published, is it possible to figure out how current the information is from the text? Online information may remain available even after it becomes outdated. Always look for the most current information on any topic.

Some academics prefer more authoritative sources than the collaborative Wikipedia. Still, many people find the shared knowledge it provides innovative and valuable.

The Wikipedia unified mark is a trademark of the Wikimedia Foundation and is used with the permission of the Wikimedia Foundation. We are not endorsed by or affiliated with the Wikimedia Foundation.

FIGURE 2.11 The Three Ws of Online Content

Use *Who*, *What*, and *When* information to gauge the accuracy of content found on the web.

Computers in Your Career

A wide variety of careers rely heavily on using the Internet for research. Librarians, government policy analysts, economists, insurance risk analysts, and others make use of online encyclopedias, survey results, and online professional journals on a regular basis. Human resource workers search online for the latest compensation models for jobs in different areas of the country. Purchasing agents search for vendors and the best prices online. What career are you considering and how could online research help you succeed in that field?

Intellectual Property

Some works found online are placed there to be shared and passed on. Other content falls into the category of intellectual property, much of which is copyrighted. According to the World Intellectual Property Organization (WIPO), **intellectual property (IP)** refers to "the creations of the mind; inventions, literary and artistic works; and symbols, names, images, and designs used in commerce." It is illegal to copy or distribute intellectual property without appropriate permission.

> "You can't say that you work in research and not worry about IP because as soon as you do any research you are doing intellectual property – it goes with the research and you have a responsibility to look after it."
>
> —Dr. Philip Graham, director of the Association for University and Industry Links

The Internet has brought the issue of illegal treatment of intellectual property front and center. Because it's so simple to copy and paste content online, many people who would never dream of stealing a CD from a music store or a book from a bookstore download music illegally or plagiarize by using text or images from a website and representing that content as their own work.

Peer-to-peer (P2P) file sharing programs such as BearShare are used by millions of people to share music, video, and other types of files by downloading them from each others' hard drives, rather than from the Internet. This type of sharing is ripe for copyright abuse because materials that might be downloaded from a legitimate source by paying a fee are instead exchanged freely with no payment going to the copyright owner.

However, some people feel that copyright law in the digital age has gone too far. There's a strong sense among many Internet activists that laws such as the Digital Millennium Copyright Act distort the balance between fair use (the right to reuse content that is available to all) and intellectual property rights and therefore are a threat to creativity and technological innovation.

The Invisible Web (aka the Deep Web)

The content you typically find online is only the tip of the web-content iceberg. There are huge "hidden" collections of information that are collectively known as the **invisible web** or **deep web**. A typical search engine won't return links to these databases or documents when you enter a search keyword or phrase. To get to some databases on the invisible web, libraries and companies have to pay for access to them.

In the future, as search engines get more sophisticated, you will probably be able to more easily find this content. You can try now by entering the word *database* after your keyword(s) in services such as Google. Doing this may help you locate some hidden content. You can also try to locate hidden content in directories such as the Librarians' Internet Index, free and paid-for databases such as LexisNexis for legal research, and some specialized search engines such as Scirus, a science search engine. If you're willing to pay for help accessing the invisible web, companies such as BrightPlanet specialize in harvesting information.

Take the Next Step *Online*

Activity 2.5.1 Research	*What is copyright?*	**CORE** CONTENT
Activity 2.5.2 Watch	*How and why is the deep web hidden from us?*	**CORE** CONTENT
Activity 2.5.3 Research	*Which source do you trust?*	ebook
Activity 2.5.4 Research	*Is it legal for me to use these images, songs, and videos?*	ebook
Activity 2.5.5 TEAM Research	*What happens when intellectual property protection crosses borders?*	ebook

PRECHECK ⇒ ## 2.6 E-Commerce

Electronic commerce, or **e-commerce**, involves using the Internet to transact business. When you're buying downloadable music or software, shopping for shoes, or paying to access your credit report, for example, you're involved in e-commerce.

There are three main kinds of e-commerce that describe how money flows in an online business. Money can flow from business-to-consumer (B2C), business-to-business (B2B), or consumer-to-consumer (C2C). Sometimes more than one of these models occurs on a single site (for example, when a consumer on eBay buys a product from another consumer (C2C), but eBay makes money from advertisers (B2B).

B2C E-Commerce

Business-to-consumer (B2C) e-commerce is probably the kind of online commerce with which you are most familiar. It involves companies, such as Amazon and Zappos, that sell products and services to individual consumers. This is the model that most resembles shopping for books or shoes at brick-and-mortar stores in the mall.

The steps in the B2C online shopping process are shown in Figure 2.12.

B2B E-Commerce

Business-to-business (B2B) e-commerce involves businesses selling to businesses. In some cases, a business provides supplies or services to another business, such as a plumbing supply site that caters to building contractors.

In another B2B model, businesses provide a service to consumers but do not charge those consumers directly. Instead, their business model involves making money from selling ad space or information about their customers to advertisers. Given that e-commerce models are defined by how money flows, Facebook is an example of this second kind of B2B site because it gets no money from its members, only from advertisers (other businesses).

C2C E-Commerce

Consumer-to-consumer (C2C) e-commerce activity occurs on sites such as craigslist and eBay, where consumers buy and sell items from each other over the Internet. Though the host site provides the infrastructure, the money flows from one consumer to another. What e-commerce model do you think supports the companies that host C2C sites? If you guessed B2B (they get their money from advertisers), you'd be right!

FIGURE 2.12 **The B2C Online Shopping Process**

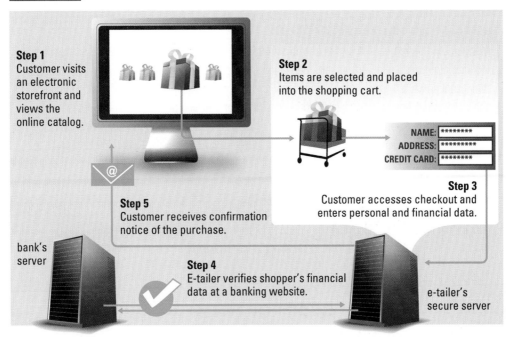

Step 1
Customer visits an electronic storefront and views the online catalog.

Step 2
Items are selected and placed into the shopping cart.

NAME: ********
ADDRESS: ********
CREDIT CARD: ********

Step 3
Customer accesses checkout and enters personal and financial data.

Step 5
Customer receives confirmation notice of the purchase.

bank's server

Step 4
E-tailer verifies shopper's financial data at a banking website.

e-tailer's secure server

eBay is a popular auction site with B2B, B2C, and C2C characteristics because transactions can occur between two consumers, two businesses, or a business and a consumer.

E-Commerce and Consumer Safety

In many cases, buying and selling items online is safer than doing so offline. That's because, rather than handing your credit card to a clerk in a store, you are performing a transaction over a secure connection, providing payment information to a system rather than an individual. Of course, every system has its problems, and online stores, banks, and investment sites are hacked into now and then. Still, if you use care in choosing trusted shopping sites, pay by a third-party payment service such as PayPal or by credit card (these purchases are protected from theft, while a check or debit card purchase is not), and make sure that while performing a transaction the URL prefix reads *https* (indicating a secure connection), you can be fairly confident that you'll have a safe shopping experience.

🔒 Playing It Safe

When using online auctions or classified sites:
- Use payment services—never pay by check or debit card.
- Never let the buyer come to your home—meet in a public place to show or hand over the product. Some towns have set up safe locations for such exchanges.
- Never let the buyer talk you into completing the transaction outside of the auction service.

Computers in Your Career

Many people have become online entrepreneurs by starting their own eBay store or creating a website about a special interest such as baking bread. Others become affiliates or associates; they get a small fee for sending online browsers to a partner site. Some post videos on YouTube earning money from embedded ads. Whether you use e-commerce to supplement your regular job or as your main source of income, it can offer challenges and rewards.

Take the Next Step *Online*

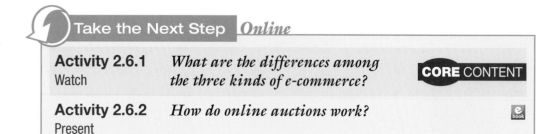

Activity 2.6.1 Watch	*What are the differences among the three kinds of e-commerce?*	**CORE** CONTENT
Activity 2.6.2 Present	*How do online auctions work?*	📘 book

2.7 Connecting in Cyberspace

The Internet offers a variety of ways to communicate that people are using to get work done or stay in touch with family and friends. The results of a July 2012 McKinsey Global Institute report showed that the average worker now spends 28 percent of his or her day reading, responding to, and organizing emails. Voice over Internet Protocol (VoIP) allows subscribers to make phone calls via the Internet; VoIP provider Skype had a record 74 million users as of January 2015. Skype is also adding call minutes at twice the rate of all other phone companies combined worldwide. Individuals and companies are also taking advantage of combinations of technologies to work collaboratively using web conferencing and collaborative learning and working spaces. Social networking tools provide a variety of ways to network and collaborate, both professionally and personally. Chapter 7 will cover social networking communications in more detail.

> ❝The Internet is just a world passing around notes in a classroom. ❞
>
> —Jon Stewart, comedian

The computer used to send the first email in 1971 was huge by today's standards.

Email

Electronic mail (**email**) was one of the first services available on the Internet, even before consumers started coming online and the web appeared on the scene. In fact, the first email was sent between two computers in 1971. Following the advent of the commercially available Internet, email soon became the standard method of communication for businesses and individuals. Today, email allows people to communicate with one another almost instantaneously from anywhere on the planet that offers an Internet connection.

Many ISPs provide a web-based method that you can use to access your email (a service typically included free with your account), or you can use an email client application such as Outlook on your computer. You use **web-based email** to create and send messages, add attachments, receive and reply to messages, store contact information, and manage messages in folders. Hotmail and Gmail are examples of popular web-based email services. Many email programs include calendaring options.

An **email client** such as Microsoft's Outlook or Apple's Mail can perform the same functions as a web-based email service and can also manage messages that come to any number of email accounts you might have created on the Internet. For example, if you have a Gmail account for work, an AOL account for personal messages, and a

 **Playing It Safe**

Email is a wonderful communications tool, but it is also used to deliver threats such as viruses, terrorist messages, and financial scams. Use caution when downloading file attachments and read unsolicited emails carefully to understand the sender's intent.

Hotmail account you use to make online purchases, you can access and manage them all using an email client.

Services such as iCloud from Apple go a step further. They help you to access multiple email accounts and sync your email and contacts among multiple devices such as a PC, iPhone, and iPod (Figure 2.13).

You may have already observed that email services use a specific address format for sending messages, but you may not know what each piece of that address means. An **email address** includes a user name, the domain name for the email service, and the domain suffix, as in YourName@gmail.com. The user name and domain name are separated by the @ symbol. Email addresses are all unique, and a user name can be made up of a combination of letters and numbers and some special characters such as the underscore and period.

Instant Messaging

Messaging between mobile phones and other portable devices is another growing form of communication. When you send a **text message**, you are exchanging a written message of 160 characters or less with another person using **short message service (SMS)** through a cell phone provider. Sending a text message is called **texting**. The text message celebrated its 20th birthday in 2012. Approximately 2.2 trillion text messages were sent that year in the United States, and 8.6 trillion messages were sent worldwide.

The growth of texting has slowed in recent years in favor of mobile instant messaging. An **instant message (IM)** is a message transferred between devices over a network. A **mobile instant message** is a message transferred between mobile devices using Wi-Fi. Both instant messaging and mobile instant messaging require that the sender and receiver have compatible messaging app software. Messaging apps like iMessage and messaging services within social media like Facebook are taking over this form of communication. The use of mobile instant messaging is expected to increase from over 1.4 billion accounts in 2014 to over 3.8 billion accounts by the end of 2018.

FIGURE 2.13 **iCloud from Apple**
This service allows you to gather data such as email, contacts, and calendar items from several accounts and sync it among multiple devices.

Our Digital World

Audio and Video Conferencing

Voice over Internet Protocol (VoIP) is a transmission technology that allows you to make voice calls over the Internet using a service such as Skype. When you speak into a microphone, software and hardware convert the analog signals of your voice into digital signals that are then transferred over the Internet, a process called **audio conferencing**. VoIP is also used for collaborative services such as **web conferencing**, a technology that allows companies to conduct interactive live meetings and deliver presentations over the Internet with employee groups or clients across the country.

Other audio conferencing services such as ViaTalk provide free calls to other ViaTalk users and may charge a monthly fee if you want to call landline numbers that run through a phone network. Even traditional phone providers such as AT&T are now offering VoIP service.

Video conferencing is very much like audio conferencing. It simply transfers video signals over the Internet along with the audio signals. Since video conferencing permits all parties to see one another as well as hear one another, all participants must have a web cam on their devices.

Email, IM, and audio and video conferencing are only a few of the ways people are connecting using their computers and other devices. Today people are using text, video, audio, and images to share with others in creative and exciting ways. You'll hear about many of these as you explore other chapters in this book.

Skype was one of the early leaders in VoIP. The company offers various tiers of Internet calling services; some are free, and some are fee based.

Take the Next Step *Online*

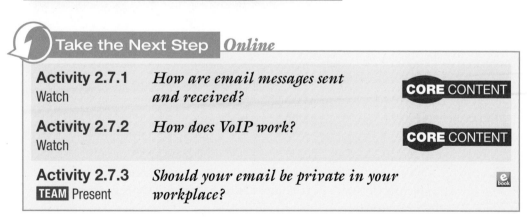

Activity 2.7.1 Watch	*How are email messages sent and received?*	**CORE** CONTENT
Activity 2.7.2 Watch	*How does VoIP work?*	**CORE** CONTENT
Activity 2.7.3 **TEAM** Present	*Should your email be private in your workplace?*	e book

Review and Assessment *Online*

An interactive Summing Up with audio, a Study Notes document, slide presentations with audio, and Terms to Know flashcards with audio are available from the links menu on this page in your ebook.

Summing Up

The World Goes Online

Today more people are using the Internet for a variety of activities over several kinds of devices, such as smartphones and tablets. Devices can be **synced** to share data for calendars, contacts, and more.

There are many examples of cutting-edge uses of the Internet in fields such as science, medicine, and even space travel. People are influenced in their purchasing decisions by the Internet. **QR codes** are turning up everywhere for you to scan from your smartphone to get information about businesses and historical locations.

In the future, we will see even more uses of technology, more social collaboration, and advances in everything from healthcare to communication from space, all because of the Internet.

What Are the Internet and World Wide Web?

The **Internet** is the physical infrastructure that allows us to share resources and communicate with others around the world. It is made up of hardware such as servers, routers, switches, transmission lines, and towers that store and transmit vast amounts of data.

The **web** is a body of content that is available as web pages. The pages are stored on servers around the world. A **web page** may contain text, images, interactive animations, games, music, and more. Several web pages make up a single **website**.

The web continues to evolve, and the different phases of the web represent shifts in online usage and technologies. **Web 2.0** has become associated with interactive web services such as Wikipedia and Facebook. These services allow users to collaborate— share, exchange ideas, and add or edit content. Where Web 2.0 focused on *exchange* of data by individuals, **Web 3.0** (also called the **Semantic Web**) is evolving and will involve *integration* of data from a variety of sources in a meaningful way.

Joining the Digital World

You can connect to the Internet through various methods, such as through a broadband cable, satellite, or DSL phone connection. An **Internet service provider (ISP)** lets you use their hardware to connect to the Internet for a monthly fee. To go online, you need an Internet account, which generally involves connecting a piece of hardware such as a cable, DSL, or satellite modem, and often a wireless access point and/or router to share the connection. With newer computers, hardware and software for connecting to the Internet may be built in, as with wireless technology.

A **browser** such as Microsoft Edge is what you use to view online content. Essentially a browser renders web page content, which is typically created using a language such as hypertext markup language (HTML) into text, graphics, and multimedia. Browsers also allow you to navigate the web.

Navigating and Searching the Web

An **Internet Protocol (IP) address** is a series of numbers that uniquely identifies a location on the Internet. Current IP addresses consist of four groups of numbers, IPv4, separated by periods. New addresses with eight groups of hexadecimal characters, IPv6, separated by colons will ensure a pool of future addresses. Because numbers would be difficult to remember for retrieving pages, we can use a text address referred to as a **uniform resource locator (URL)** to go to a website. The text-based addresses are cross-referenced to IP addresses.

To get to a website, enter a URL, such as http://amazon.com, in the address bar of the browser. Every website has a starting page called the **home page**. Any element of a page (text, graphic, audio, or video) can be linked to another web page using a hyperlink. A **hyperlink** describes a destination within a web document and can be added to text or to an image such as a company logo. Text that is linked is called **hypertext**. Navigating among pages using a browser is called *browsing the web*.

A **search engine** allows you to search for information by going to the search engine's website and typing one or more **keywords** or keyword phrases.

Some components on a web page may require that you install a **plug-in** or **player** on your computer to view or hear content. These programs are free and simply require that you go to the publisher's site to download and install them.

The Vast Sea of Online Content

As in the offline world, you have to consider the source of content online. Look at the credibility of who has written and published the information, the quality of the information, and how current it is to evaluate its quality and accuracy.

Some online content is free to exchange, share, and remix. **Intellectual property**, which includes inventions and literary and artistic works, cannot be copied or distributed without permission. Much of this material has the additional legal protection of a **copyright**. The Internet can make it easy to copy and use other people's property, so intellectual property abuse is rife.

Databases and other collections of information on the web that are hidden or are not catalogued by most search engines are collectively known as the **invisible web** or **deep web**. To get to some databases on the invisible web, libraries and companies have to buy access to them.

E-Commerce

Electronic commerce, or **e-commerce**, involves using the Internet to transact business such as shopping and banking. E-commerce sites are classified based on the flow of money. There are three main kinds of e-commerce: **business-to-consumer (B2C)**, **business-to-business (B2B)**, and **consumer-to-consumer (C2C)**.

Connecting in Cyberspace

You use an **email** program to create and send messages, add attachments, receive and reply to messages, store contact information, and manage messages in folders.

Voice over Internet Protocol (VoIP) is a transmission technology that allows you to make voice calls over the Internet using a service such as Skype.

Using the Internet for phone meetings is called **audio conferencing**. **Video conferencing** allows you to see, as well as hear, the conference participants.

Web conferencing is a service that combines several technologies such as VoIP and webcams that allow users to view presentations and participate interactively while conducting live meetings over the Internet.

A **text message** is a brief message of up to 160 characters sent using **short message service (SMS)** through a cell phone provider. An **instant message (IM)** is sent over a network and does not require an SMS, while a **mobile instant message (MIM)** can be sent by a mobile device over Wi-Fi. Both instant messaging and mobile instant messaging require that the sender and receiver have compatible message app software.

Terms to Know

The World Goes Online
sync, 28
quick response (QR) code, 28

What Are the Internet and World Wide Web?
Internet, 30
web, 31
web page, 31
website, 31

Web 2.0, 32
Web 3.0, 33
Semantic Web, 33

Joining the Digital World
Internet service provider (ISP), 36
multihomed device, 37
browser, 38

download, Activity 2.3.1
upload, Activity 2.3.1

Navigating and Searching the Web
Internet Protocol (IP) address, 39
uniform resource locator (URL), 40
web address, 40
domain name, 40
top-level domain (TLD), 40
generic top-level domain (gTLD), 40
hyperlink, 41
hypertext, 41
Microsoft Edge, 41

home page, 41
search engine, 42
search directory, 42
keyword, 42
metasearch engine, 43
plug-in, 44
player, 44
streaming video, 44

The Vast Sea of Online Content
copyright, 45
intellectual property (IP), 47
peer-to-peer (P2P) file sharing
    program, 47

invisible web, 48
deep web, 48
crawler, Activity 2.5.2
data integration, Activity 2.5.2

E-Commerce
e-commerce, 48
business-to-consumer (B2C)
    e-commerce, 49

business-to-business (B2B) e-commerce, 49
consumer-to-consumer (C2C)
    e-commerce, 49

Connecting in Cyberspace

Concepts Check

Concepts Check 2.1   Multiple Choice
Take this quiz to test your understanding of key concepts in this chapter.

Concepts Check 2.2   Matching
Test your understanding of terms and concepts presented in this chapter.

Concepts Check 2.3   Label It
Use the interactive tool to identify the components of a URL.

Concepts Check 2.4   Arrange It
Use the interactive tool to order the steps followed by data moving over the Internet.

Projects

Check with your instructor for the preferred method to submit completed work.

Project 2.1   Smartphones—Staying Well While Staying Connected

Project 2.1.1 TEAM
Play the interview with Dr. Eric Topol at http://ODW4.emcp.net/iDoctor. Consider the ways he suggests that smartphones can be used to replace more expensive medical treatments, and then respond to the following:
1. List three uses for smartphones that are demonstrated by Dr. Topol in the video.
2. What does Dr. Topol say about the future possibility of using a smartphone app to replace a visit to the doctor?
3. Do you believe your smartphone can be used to replace your physician? Defend your answer.

Individually or in teams, prepare for a debate. Can smartphones replace physicians? Your instructor will assign you to the pro or con position.

Project 2.1.2

Texting while driving is a safety hazard. Countries around the world have acted to help keep roads safe by enacting laws that prohibit texting while driving. According to the FCC (United States) article at http://ODW4.emcp.net/TextDriving, the Virginia Tech Transportation Institute found that "text messaging creates a crash risk 23 times worse than driving while not distracted. Eleven percent of drivers aged 18 to 20 who were involved in an automobile accident and survived admitted they were sending or receiving texts when they crashed." Texting and making or receiving calls using a handheld cell phone while driving is illegal in many locations. Search online to learn about texting and driving laws in your location. If you live in the United States, visit http://ODW4.emcp.net/Map and find your state on the map. Is it illegal to use a handheld cell phone while driving in your state? Follow the link to the penalties map at http://ODW4.emcp.net/Penalties. What is the penalty for texting while driving in your state? Do you think this is an appropriate penalty? Prepare a three-paragraph letter to be sent to your state's governor that explains your position on smartphone use while driving and the related penalties in your state.

Project 2.2   Net Neutrality—Should Everyone on the Internet Be Considered Equal?

Project 2.2.1

You have been assigned to research the principle of net neutrality. To start your investigation of this controversial topic, go to http://ODW4.emcp.net/NetNeutrality and watch a video discussion of net neutrality by Tim Berners-Lee. Also visit http://ODW4.emcp.net/Court to read about a January 2014 Federal Court of Appeals ruling on net neutrality. Conduct an Internet search to learn more about this principle. When you have finished, prepare a summary that defines net neutrality, covers its main concepts, and explains the controversy surrounding this topic. Include any necessary text citations and a list of Internet sources.

Project 2.2.2 `TEAM`

Discuss with your team the results of your individual research from Project 2.2.1. Next, address the following questions with team members: Do you agree with the Court of Appeals decision? Should corporations be able to treat Internet users differently depending on the services to which the users have subscribed? Why or why not? Based on your discussion, arrive at a joint conclusion that either supports or opposes net neutrality. Prepare a summary explaining your team's position and the information that led your group to reach this conclusion. Have one person submit the document to your instructor with all team members' names included.

Project 2.2.3 `TEAM`

Using your summary from Project 2.2.2, prepare an oral presentation and a brief slideshow to present your team's position and rationale on net neutrality. First, write a script for an oral presentation and assign each team member a speaking part. Then create a series of slides to accompany your presentation. The slides should highlight the main points of your position and provide effective visuals. Give your oral presentation to your classmates and provide an opportunity for student discussion.

Project 2.3   Investigating Climate Change

Project 2.3.1

According to NASA, climate change is "a long-term change in the Earth's climate, or of a region on Earth." Use your favorite search engine to find two articles about climate change: one article should clearly support the science of climate change, and the other article should present opposing views. Apply advanced search techniques so that the articles you choose to read have been published since January 1, 2013. When you have finished locating and reading the articles, write a one-paragraph summary of each article and include the URL below each summary.

Project 2.3.2

Evaluating the credibility and accuracy of articles on the Internet is an important part of the research process. Using the three Ws (or WWW) technique you learned in this chapter, evaluate the credibility and accuracy of the two articles that you read for Project 2.3.1. To your existing document, add a table after each article that includes your three Ws analysis of the article's content.

Project 2.3.3 `TEAM`

Each team member should search the Internet to find a web page that has inflammatory or provocative content regarding climate change. Team members should share their web pages with their group and choose one of the pages to analyze for this project. As a team, write a one-page document that summarizes the content of the web page and offers the reasons for your team's decision that the content is unreliable or not credible. Include a second page that lists the URLs and brief summaries of the other articles that were found by team members.

Project 2.3.4 `TEAM`

Prepare a short slide presentation for the class that displays the web page and then presents your reasons for finding the content unreliable or not credible.

Project 2.4   Wiki—Internet Telephones

Project 2.4.1 `TEAM`

You or your team will be assigned to research the answers to one or more of the following questions related to Internet consumer telephone service:

- What is Voice over Internet Protocol (VoIP)?
- How does VoIP work?
- What are the advantages and disadvantages to converting to VoIP?
- Who offers Internet telephone service in your area?
- What are the costs of Internet telephone service for each provider in your area?
- How do you subscribe to an Internet telephone service? What if you want to cancel at some point?
- What equipment will you need for Internet telephone service?
- Does the government regulate Internet telephone service? If yes, in what ways?

- What emergency and security issues, if any, might be concerns in Internet telephone service?
- How does a subscriber place an overseas call using an Internet telephone service? What costs are incurred?

Prepare a post to the course wiki site that summarizes what you learned in clear, concise language. Make sure you include the research question, citations, and references to the articles from which you obtained your information.

Project 2.4.2 `TEAM`

You or your team will be assigned to edit and verify content posted on the wiki site about Internet phone services. If you add or edit any content, make sure you include a notation within the page that includes your name or the team members' names and the date you edited the content—for example, "Edited by [student name or team members' names] on [date]." Keep a list of references that you used to verify your content changes. When you are finished with your verification, include a notation at the end of the entry—for example, "Verified by [student name or team members' names] on [date]."

Class Conversations

Topic 2.1   Is web research enough?

You are taking a sociology course and have been asked to write an essay on various kinds of bullying in high schools. Assume you conduct all of your research online making sure that you use credible sources for your information. Another classmate conducts all of her research at the library using traditional reference materials such as sociology journals and books.

Discuss the advantages of your Internet-research-based approach and the advantages of your classmate's library-research-based work. Should the two papers be considered equal when graded? Do you think others will view the journal- and book-researched paper as being of stronger academic quality? Why or why not? Is your web-researched paper likely to have a different perspective? Why or why not?

Optional: Create a blog entry that states your response to the previous questions and provides your rationale.

Topic 2.2   How is YouTube changing society?

The popularity of YouTube has made it possible for anyone to become a media publisher and can make an average person suddenly famous for a day. It seems that every week another video is posted that becomes a popular topic among friends and family members. Some of these videos are taken of other people with or without their knowledge.

Consider the following scenario. You are enjoying an afternoon with friends at a football game. You jump up to cheer and accidentally trip, causing the person next to you to dump a carton of popcorn all over you. You are not injured, but are somewhat embarrassed by the popcorn on your clothes and in your hair. Your friend, who thought you looked funny covered in popcorn, filmed the accident using a cell phone. While you head to the bathroom to clean up, your friend posts the video on YouTube.

a. What is the likelihood you would know this video existed on YouTube?
b. Should the friend who filmed the accident be required to get your release before posting the video? Why or why not?
c. Does this scenario violate any guidelines provided by YouTube?
d. If you became aware of the video, what would you do?
e. Should someone be allowed to capture video of you without your knowledge? If you answer no, how could society police this action?

Topic 2.3 What's after Web 3.0?

If the evolution of the web makes it possible for intelligent agents to locate information for you on the Internet based on your preferences and even update and modify your documents when you read a related article, what will that mean for the role of the Internet in learning? If student work is updated automatically, what will be the role of individual contribution and how much inaccuracy could be introduced? What role will humans play in the development of information on the web in future?

Computer Hardware and Peripherals
Your Digital Toolbox

What You'll Accomplish

When you finish this chapter, you'll be able to:

3.1 Identify the major types of digital devices.

3.2 Recognize the components that make up a digital device and give an example of each part of a digital device.

3.3 Identify and differentiate input and output devices that are used with today's digital devices.

3.4 List the components to assess and factors to consider when purchasing a digital device.

Why Does It Matter ?

We live in a time when digital devices rule. Whether you always have to have the latest gadget or are hesitant to adopt new technology, you still must realize that these devices, from the tablet you use to browse the web and email to the Xbox One you use to play games and stream videos, are an important part of your life. Understanding the parts of the hardware that make up these devices, how you get information in and out of them, and how to make wise choices when purchasing new technology can help you cope and prosper in our digital age.

Output
Display the drawing on the monitor screen

Optical drive

Power supply

Processor

Battery backup

RAM

Motherboard

Hard drive

Video card

Input
Draw and label the parts of the CPU

Chapter 3 Computer Hardware and Peripherals: Your Digital Toolbox

The tangible part of computing starts with hardware. Components for input, processing, output, and storage allow you to put data in and get useful information out.

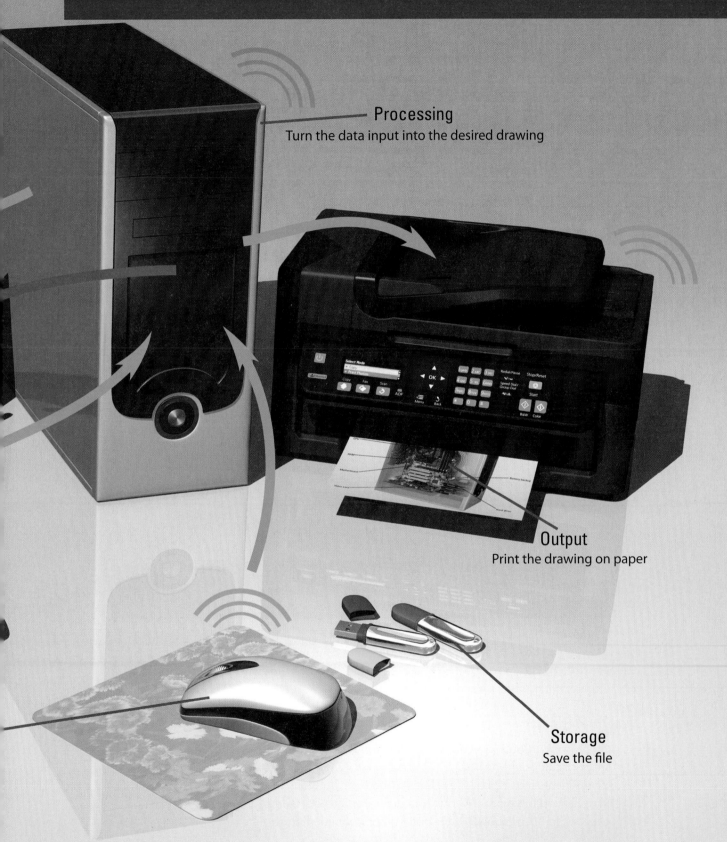

Processing
Turn the data input into the desired drawing

Output
Print the drawing on paper

Storage
Save the file

3.1 A World of Digital Devices

As you read in Chapter 1, digital devices differ from analog devices in that they use symbolic representations of data in the form of code and can process words, numbers, images, and sounds. Today the number of devices that fit that definition has expanded far beyond your desktop computer, but these devices still have certain things in common. They all have some form of memory and, however basic, an operating system; they provide a way to input and store data and output information; and they have a source of power.

Some digital devices have input and/or output features built in, such as with a laptop computer or smartphone. Others use **peripheral devices** that physically or wirelessly connect with them. For example, your desktop computer keyboard is a peripheral device used to input data, and your printer is a peripheral device used to produce output.

Take a Survey *Online*

What's in your digital toolkit?

Digital devices come in many forms and sizes.

3.2 The Parts That Make Up Your Computer

Compare a typical desktop and laptop computer and you'll find that, although they may be packaged differently, they each contain similar hardware that processes data, provides battery power, offers ports for making connections with peripheral devices and networks, and stores data.

The Motherboard

If you were to open up your computer, you'd see that the **motherboard** is the primary circuit board. It holds the central processing unit, BIOS, memory, and other components (see Figure 3.1). The motherboard is really just a container where the various working pieces of your computer slot into one compact package. Circuits on the motherboard connect the components contained on it.

Our Digital World

FIGURE 3.1 The Operations of the Motherboard

The motherboard is a container for various processors and expansion slots for cards that add functionality such as sound, graphics, or memory.

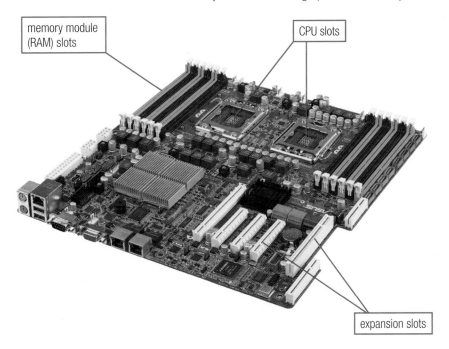

memory module (RAM) slots

CPU slots

expansion slots

The central processing unit (CPU), which is a microprocessor (also called by the shorter terms *processor* or *core*), sits on the motherboard. The CPU processes a user's requests, such as opening documents or formatting text. A CPU is a thin wafer or **chip** made up of a semiconducting material, such as silicon. It contains an integrated circuit made up of a combination of miniaturized components and drives the system's computing capabilities. (Note that the term *central processing unit* is sometimes, albeit incorrectly, used to refer to the case that contains the processor and everything else within this case.)

The motherboard also holds different types of memory. **Read-only memory (ROM)** is the permanent memory, or **nonvolatile memory**. ROM is hardwired into a chip. In a PC, the read-only memory stores the **BIOS**, which stands for basic input/output system. During the boot-up sequence, the BIOS checks devices such as your memory, monitor, keyboard, and disc drives to ensure they are working properly and to start them up. It also directs the hard drive to boot up and load the operating system (OS) to memory.

Random access memory (RAM) chips are slotted into the motherboard and are used to store programs and data while the computer is in use. This memory is temporary, or volatile. Each memory location in RAM can be accessed in any order, which speeds up processing. (This differs from storage devices, such as USB sticks or DVDs, that store and retrieve data one file at a time.)

" Researchers at IBM have created computer chips that behave more like actual brains when processing information. Systems built with these chips will be called "cognitive computers."… Cognitive computers are expected to learn through experiences, find correlations, create hypotheses and remember. "

—Rob Spiegel, TechNewsWorld

While some computers have built-in sound or graphics cards, others include them as **expansion cards**. These cards enable input and output of sound or images. Your laptop computer can also accommodate **PC Cards** that slot into a built-in card reader to provide other kinds of functionality such as additional USB ports or wireless networking capabilities.

Power Supply

All computing devices require power to work, whether that power is accessed by plugging a cord into a wall outlet, operating off a charged battery, or using power from solar cells.

A **power supply** in a desktop or laptop computer is located where the power cord is inserted into the system unit. This metal box housed in the CPU contains the connection for the power cord and a cooling fan to keep the connection from overheating. The power supply switches alternating current (AC) provided from your wall outlet to lower voltages in the form of direct current (DC). A laptop computer also contains a battery that is charged when you plug the power cord into your wall outlet.

Your operating system is capable of sending a signal to the power supply to instruct it to sleep or hibernate. This action puts the computer into a lower power mode or no power mode without losing your unsaved work. To take some computers out of sleep or hibernation mode, you can simply move the mouse or press any key. For most systems, however, you have to briefly press the power button.

Charging mats are a way to charge more than one device.

Tablets and smartphones use USB chargers that can be connected to the device and then plugged into a wall outlet or a computer using an adapter. You can also purchase USB charger hubs, which are devices you plug into an outlet and then use to insert multiple USB connectors so that you can charge multiple devices at once. Charging from an outlet is much faster than charging from a computer.

A newer technology trend that is emerging is the charging mat. A **charging mat** or **pad** allows you to charge multiple devices simultaneously without connecting them to the mat with a cable. Charging mats typically use the same level of power that it takes to charge a device from an outlet.

Ports

A computer uses a **port** to connect with a peripheral device such as a monitor or printer or to connect to a network. A **physical port** connects a computer to another device, sending a signal via a cable (as for a USB port), infrared light (as with an infrared port), or a wireless transmitter (as with a wireless mouse or keyboard).

Some types of physical ports (commonly called just *ports*) in use today, shown in Figure 3.2, are serial, USB, FireWire, Thunderbolt, and infrared.

A **serial port** is a port, built into the computer, that is used to connect a peripheral device to the serial bus, typically by means of a plug with 9 pins. (A bus is essentially a subsystem of your computer that transfers data between the various components inside your computer.) Network routers in a business setting use serial ports for administration, although they are being replaced by web-based administration interfaces.

FIGURE 3.2 **Ports in Your Computer**

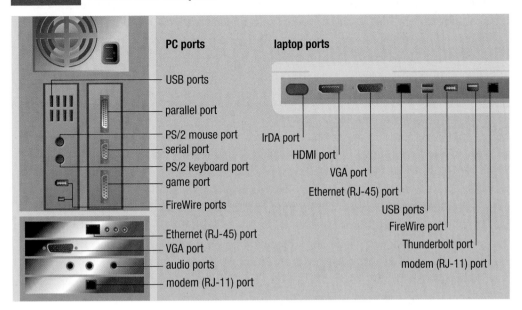

A **universal serial bus (USB) port** is a small rectangular slot that has become the most popular way to attach everything from wireless mouse and keyboard transmitters (the small devices that send wireless signals to wireless devices) to USB flash drives for storing data. USB first came out in version 1.0, which supported a 12 megabits per second (Mbps) data rate (the measurement of the speed at which data can be transmitted). USB 3.0 became available in 2010, providing a transfer rate of up to 5 Gbps, and USB 3.1 introduced an even faster transfer, called *SuperSpeed*, with a data rate of 10 Gbps. USB-C, introduced in 2014, provides a small, reversible plug connector.

Usually a computer has two to four USB ports that you can use to attach peripheral devices. Should you need to plug in more peripherals than your computer has USB ports, you can add a hub that increases the number of available USB ports. Plug the USB hub into one of your computer's USB sockets, and then plug USB devices into the ports on the hub. Most USB hubs offer four ports, but some offer more.

A **FireWire port** is based on the same serial bus architecture as a USB port. FireWire provides a high-speed serial interface for peripheral devices such as digital cameras, camcorders, or external hard disk drives. Generally used for devices that require high performance, the newest version of FireWire, called FireWire 800, is capable of transferring data up to 800 Mbps.

The **Thunderbolt port**, introduced on Apple's MacBook Pro in 2011, was developed by Intel and Apple to provide a peripheral connection standard that combines data, audio, video, and power within a single high-speed connection. The newest version of Thunderbolt, Thunderbolt 3 doubled bandwidth and cut power consumption in half. Thunderbolt's high-speed connection supports high-resolution displays and other devices that require a lot of bandwidth, such as high-end video cameras or data storage devices, and is generally expected to replace FireWire. Originally added to Apple devices, Thunderbolt is now being added to some PCs, making the port no longer strictly an Apple favorite.

An **Infrared Data Association (IrDA) port** allows you to transfer data from one device to another using infrared light waves. Today the ability to transmit wirelessly between devices using Bluetooth (a wireless communications standard) is making IrDA ports obsolete. You can add Bluetooth connectivity via a device that connects to the USB port.

MIDI is a communications protocol that allows computers and devices, such as musical synthesizers and sound cards, to control each other. Game ports on older computers allowed the connections of the MIDI device to a computer. A new version of MIDI that uses a high-definition protocol is being created. This HD MIDI protocol will accommodate more channels to carry data, as well as create improved resolution of data values that will allow for clearer rendering of audio.

Storage

Because saving the work you've done on your computer is so important, computer manufacturers have devised several ways to store all kinds of data, from numbers and images to words and music. All storage media have methods for reading and writing data.

The various storage media used on a computer are accessed using **drives**, which are identified on a Windows-based computer by a unique letter. For example, your computer's hard disk is typically identified as the C drive, while a DVD or USB drive might be labeled E, F, or G. Mac computers give each drive a name, such as Mac HD for the hard drive and DVD_VIDEO for a DVD drive in which you have inserted a video. If you are connected to a network, you may also be able to access shared network drives.

Hard Disks The first place most of us save a copy of our work is on our **hard disk**, which is the disk drive that is built in to the computer. When you save a file to your Documents folder in Windows 10, for example, it is saved to your hard disk. The platters or disks in the drive rotate and one or more so-called "heads" read and write data to them. Because all hard disks eventually fail, the wise person uses other media storage or cloud storage to make backup copies.

Optical Drives Your desktop computer is likely to have a built-in drive where you can place a **CD** or **DVD** to read content stored there or store data of your own. This type of drive is called an **optical drive**. To save on weight and size, many laptops today have no CD/DVD drive. Manufacturers assume you will download most of your software or content, or use an external CD/DVD drive when necessary. Another type of optical drive that is built into some computers is a **Blu-ray disc** drive, mostly used for high-definition movies and games. Discs placed in optical drives are covered with tiny variations, or bumps, that can be read as data by a laser beam in the drive. Optical drives use these **optoelectronic sensors** to detect changes in light caused by the irregularities on the disc's surface. If you buy a movie or game on a disc rather than accessing the content online, it is likely to be in the Blu-ray format.

You can connect to some external hard drives with USB or Thunderbolt cables.

External Hard Drives If you'd like additional storage, you might consider buying an **external hard drive**. External hard drives typically connect to your computer via a USB, FireWire, Thunderbolt, or Serial ATA cable, but select high-capacity models can connect to a network via a wireless connection. Some call these devices networked external hard drives while others refer to them as **network attached storage (NAS)**.

External hard drives are useful for backing up your entire computer system. Some portable external hard drives don't even need a separate power source. Networked models can provide centralized storage for multiple teammates or family members, or can serve as a "juke-box" for storing various forms of media such as music or videos.

Flash Drives

Call them **flash drives**, USB sticks, or thumb drives, these small devices are a convenient way to store your data and take it with you. As of this writing, they come with capacities as big as 512 gigabytes (bigger than most hard drives just a few years ago), and some manufacturers have begun to release sticks whose capacity is measured in terabytes.

Flash drives use **flash memory** to record and erase stored data and to transfer data to and from your computer. Flash memory is also used in tablets, mobile phones, and digital cameras because it is much less expensive than other types of memory. Flash memory is also nonvolatile, meaning that it retains information even in a powered-off state.

Flash drives are very portable storage devices that are gaining larger capacities all the time.

Wireless Mobile Storage Devices

Similar to a flash drive, a wireless mobile storage device allows you to store as much as 2 terabytes, wirelessly stream movies and music, and share content with your computer or other devices. This technology allows multiple devices to connect at the same time and can work over its own Wi-Fi network so no Internet connection is required.

Solid-State Drives (SSDs)

A **solid-state drive (SSD)** is essentially a flash-based replacement for an internal hard disk. These drives are lighter and more durable than traditional hard disks and have paved the way for smaller, more portable computers with longer battery. In 2007, SSDs began to show up in commercially available computers. One of the first was the XO Laptop (part of the One Laptop Per Child initiative in developing countries), and internal SSDs were also included in the new Apple MacBook Air and MacBook Pro released that year. Dell also began shipping an ultra-portable laptop with an SSD in 2007, and many other PC manufacturers have since followed suit, though the cost of SSDs have to come down before they appear in most PC models.

Cloud Storage

In addition to using physical storage, many users increasingly rely on cloud storage. Cloud storage refers to the storage of data on a web-connected server operated by a third party. You can access your files stored in the cloud from any location using any computer with an Internet connection. Cloud storage may be used for backing up information as well as sharing files with others. If you've ever lost or damaged your flash drive, you can appreciate how valuable it would be to have backup copies of your information that you could access via the web from your school, on a trip, or in your office. Depending on your needs, you can choose either a fee-based cloud storage service or free services such as Microsoft OneDrive. Some of the most popular cloud storage services today are Dropbox, Google Drive, Amazon S3, Box, Carbonite, iCloud, and iStorage.

Activity 3.2.1 Watch	*How does a multicore processor system work?*	**CORE** CONTENT
Activity 3.2.2 Watch	*What devices can be built into your computer to enable communications?*	**CORE** CONTENT
Activity 3.2.3 Research	*What are my portable power options?*	e book
Activity 3.2.4 Research	*What's inside my computer?*	e book
Activity 3.2.5 Research	*What's the difference between static and dynamic RAM?*	e book
Activity 3.2.6 Research	*How do I keep my storage media safe?*	e book

PRECHECK

3.3 Input and Output Devices

Your computer is capable of processing and storing data, but if you can't get data into your computer and information out of it, this capability isn't of much use. That's where input and output devices come in. Examples of **input devices** are your keyboard to enter text or a microphone to record sound.

Output devices produce information in one of several forms: printed text on a page, sound from a speaker, or an image on your monitor, for example.

What goes into your computer in the form of digital files may come out as printed text, a movie, an image, or sound.

A Wide Assortment of Input Devices

A computer **keyboard** contains keys that you press to activate electronic switches. These switches in turn tell the active software on your computer or in the cloud to insert numbers, letters, or characters in a document or form. Today's computer keyboards also allow you to combine some keystrokes to accommodate additional commands (the familiar Ctrl, Shift, or Alt combinations and function keys, for example). Some keyboards also include shortcut keys that allow you to manage media functions such as video or audio playback. Many users today also use onscreen keyboards, which require the user to switch among two or more keyboards to input letters, numbers, and symbols.

Key presses are interpreted by the software program that controls the keyboard, called a *device driver*. The operating system then provides the key press information to the currently active program, such as a word processor or email client. Keyboards can

The option to use wireless input devices permits greater flexibility in positioning your keyboard and mouse.

plug into your computer, be built into a laptop, or use a wireless connection.

Your **mouse**, also referred to as a *pointing device*, detects motion in relation to the surface you rest it on and provides an onscreen pointer representing that motion. You might think of a mouse as being like the lever that a crane operator moves to control the crane, which moves up or down in the air according to the movements of the lever. A mouse prototype was invented in 1964 at Stanford University. The first mouse was sold with a computer when the first Apple Macintosh appeared in 1984.

A mouse can plug into your computer, be built into a laptop, or use a wireless connection. However it is connected to your computer, a mouse can function in several different ways. It can use:

- a mechanical device, such as a ball that rolls on a surface, to track motion.
- a light-emitting diode or **infrared (IR) technology** to sense motion (used by optical mice).
- an optoelectronic sensor that actually takes pictures of the surface.
- ultrasound technology to detect movement, as with 3-D mice.

There are two other input devices that are commonly used with today's digital devices: the touchscreen and the touchpad. A **touchscreen** is a visual display that permits the user to interact with a digital device by touching various areas on the screen, either with a finger or a **stylus**. A **digital pen**, such as the one that comes with Microsoft's Surface 4, is used to write or draw on a touchscreen. The touchscreen has evolved with the development of portable devices and smartphones. Touchscreens are used in many different areas from ATMs to airline kiosks. A **touchpad**, which senses finger movement, may be built into many computing devices. Both the touchscreen and touchpad use the motion and position of a person's finger to locate a position on the computer screen, either directly (touchscreen) or indirectly (touchpad).

The **scanner** has a very descriptive name, as its function is to optically scan hard copy of text or images to convert them into electronic files. Scanners may sit on your desktop (called *flatbed models*), be built into an all-in-one printer, or be handheld. In the world of industrial design, 3-D scanners can scan all sides of objects and produce three-dimensional models of them.

A **webcam** is a video camera that can be built into your computer monitor or purchased separately and mounted onto your computer. Both webcams and digital cameras can become input devices

Webcams are often used with online calling or meeting services so both callers can see each other as they chat.

when they interface with your computer to upload photos or videos in digital file formats.

Gaming devices such as Xbox One and Wii U provide controllers you can use to input moves in a game. The controllers often combine multiple buttons, a joystick, and even motion sensors. Virtual reality systems that are used to simulate situations for learning, such as for astronauts, offer **wired data gloves** that allow users to communicate with the system.

Gaming consoles use controllers as input devices.

Speech recognition software can be used as an input device that turns the user's voice into text. Leading voice recognition programs include Dragon Naturally Speaking and Dragon Dictate for Mac. The user typically completes a setup process to train the voice recognition software to understand his or her voice. The software then adjusts to the user's speech patterns, enabling that person to give commands and create documents such as spreadsheets and emails.

A **microphone** is an input device for getting sounds, from narrations to music, into your computer in the form of audio files. Microphones might be built into your computer, be plugged in via a cable, or be part of a headphone set.

Mobile Internet devices (MIDs) also use a variety of input devices. MIDs offer virtual keyboards, foldable keyboards, touchscreens, voice recognition, or a stylus for providing input. There has been a great deal of debate regarding mobile devices being used in automobiles. Today, automobile and mobile device manufacturers are working to improve devices and software for hands-free use while driving. There are currently voice devices that enable a user to find local businesses and open, create, and respond to email and SMS messages totally hands-free.

Today, wearable devices are becoming more popular. Computers incorporated into watches, glasses, and clothing are always on. A user's skin, hands, speech, or even eye movement can be used to provide input. WPAN (wireless personal area network) and WBAN (wireless body area network) protocols are being developed so you can make your body's environment a moveable Wi-Fi network.

Assistive technologies include a variety of devices and methods that enable physically challenged computer users to control their computer and provide input. For example, sip-and-puff or wand and stick devices enable users to give computer input using their mouths. Other assistive devices include Braille embossers, screen readers, and speech synthesizers.

The Tongue Drive System is an example of adaptive technology.

If you are interested in a career in healthcare, you need to know about how computers are being used to enhance the delivery of care. By using the Internet, healthcare providers and patients can connect through two-way video calls, email, smartphones, and other forms of technology and computer devices. Telemedicine is extending care to patients in remote areas, emergency situations, and workplaces. Technology is also enabling the use of live interactive video and the ability to remotely collect and send diagnostic data. Healthcare professionals can participate in online discussion groups regarding health issues and even observe remote surgical procedures. Sites such as meMD and TakeCareHealth can even provide online medical consultations and prescriptions for a fee.

Retail store or manufacturing employees often use bar code readers and RFID readers. **Bar code readers** optically scan a set of lines to identify a product. **RFID readers** scan an embedded tag that emits a radio frequency. Both are used to provide input to a computer system so software can track inventory and sales activity.

> 66 Garbage in, garbage out. 99
>
> —George Fuechsel, IBM technician, advising that bad input results in bad output

Getting Things Out of Your Computer with Output Devices

Any device that displays, prints, or plays content stored in your computer is an output device, including your monitor, speakers, headphones, printer, or a projector.

Monitors and Speakers You may not think of your **monitor** as an output device, but because it delivers information stored inside your computer in the form of images, it is. In the case of a mobile phone or gaming device, the screens are output devices. Monitor output is temporary; once you turn the computer off, there is no record of what was displayed.

Monitors may also include a **speaker** to add audio output. Laptop computers usually have an internal speaker while desktop computers use external speakers. Another way to get audio from your computing device is by plugging in a headset or by using a wireless **Bluetooth headset**.

Monitors come in a variety of sizes, from a few inches on your smartphone to ultra-portable laptops with 10 inch screens to huge screens that may be over 30 inches across. Display size is the measurement between two diagonally opposite corners. The latest USB 3.1 cables are enabling lightning-fast transfer of data such as high-definition 3-D video to your computer monitor or TV screen.

Playing It Safe

Keystroke logging software is a kind of malware that can be delivered to your computer in several ways, but most commonly is downloaded when you go to an untrustworthy site or click on an attachment in an email. The software records your keystrokes as you type and sends the information to a remote location. In this way someone might obtain your bank account password and account number, for example. Antivirus and antispyware software can help you locate such a program on your system and get rid of it.

Bluetooth headsets let you talk on a mobile phone handsfree.

Modern computer monitors use one of three technologies:

- **TFT active matrix liquid crystal displays (LCD)** are the most prevalent type of monitor today. They use a thin film transistor (TFT) to display output from your computer.
- **LED displays** use light-emitting diodes. They conserve power and provide a truer picture than LCD models.
- **Plasma displays** are flat panel displays mainly used for televisions, but they can also be used as multifunctional monitor/TV devices. They use a great deal of power but have a truer level of color reproduction when compared with LCDs.

Some new display technologies beginning to appear on computer monitors and television sets include the following:

- **Surface-conduction electron-emitter displays (SED)** use nanoscopic electron emitters (extremely tiny wires smaller than human hairs) to send electrons that illuminate a thin screen.
- **Organic light emitting diodes (OLED)** project light through an electroluminescent (a blue/red/ green-emitting) thin film layer made of organic materials.
- 3-D or 3-D-ready technology uses a polarized lens to display images. Usually, the viewer must purchase special glasses and may have to install separate IR equipment for use with the computer in order to view the 3-D effect. This 3-D technology is being used for both computer monitors and televisions.

Plasma displays are often used in television sets. Most computers can connect to a TV display to generate output.

Printers and Faxes A **printer** is the main way in which you can get a hard copy (print on paper) output from your computer. The foundation for today's printers was a dry printing process called *electrophotography*, also known as *Xerox* (hence the company of the same name). When the use of a laser beam was added, the business world saw the introduction of the laser printer in 1971 and inkjets (printers that spray jets of ink onto paper) in 1976. Hewlett-Packard threw their hat into the printer ring in 1984 with the first laser printer for sale to the general public.

A **photo printer** that prints high-quality photos directly from a camera storage card and a **thermal printer** that heats coated paper to produce an image, like the kind you've seen printing receipts in retail stores, can also be used to created printed output. You may also encounter high-end commercial printers like the ones you see at your local copy store, and **plotters**, which are used to print large blueprints and other technical drawings.

You can use fax programs to send content from your computer that comes out as printed copy at the receiving end. If you use a **fax machine** to scan content and then send it, the machine converts the scanned content into an electronic file and then sends it to the recipient's fax machine, which prints it as a hard copy on the other end. In this case, the sending fax machine is an input device and the receiving machine an output device.

3-D printing is a method of using printers to create 3-D objects from digital models. A 3-D printer prints layers on top of one another to build a precise, physical object, as opposed to traditional manufacturing in which material is often removed to carve out an object. 3-D printing is being used to manufacture customized equipment, such as automotive parts, and patient-specific devices, such as orthopedic implants. The 3-D printing industry reached over $5 billion in sales in 2015 and is projected to top $20 billion by 2020.

Devices That Project Computer Content There are several different devices that can be used to project computer content as part of a presentation, either in person or across the web.

Liquid crystal display (LCD) projectors project light through silicone panels colored red, green, and blue. The light passing through these panels displays an image on a surface such as a screen or wall. By blocking or allowing light to pass through pixels on the panels, these projectors can output a huge range of colors.

Used with a projector, a **document camera** can be used to display on a screen text from a book, slides, a 3-D object, or any other printed material.

If you give presentations, you will encounter LCD projectors. These output devices are popular for displaying PowerPoint slides and other types of content.

An **interactive whiteboard (IWB)** is a display device that receives input from a computer keyboard, special pen, finger, tablet, or other device. The IWB may connect directly to a computer to show the computer desktop, or you might need a projector to show the desktop on the IWB. IWBs help improve communication in settings such as the classroom, the corporate world, sports coaching, and broadcasting. Information displayed on an IWB may be saved as a document and shared or printed later. Popular IWB brands include SMART Board, Promethean, mimio, eBeam, and PolyVision.

Virtual Reality Displays A

virtual reality system connects you to a computer-simulated world. Most provide visuals to the user and some provide sound as well. The user wears a head-mounted display and headphones if sound is being provided. In the more sophisticated systems, gloves with wiring allow you to control actions with your hands. Virtual reality is a connection between user and computer that allows both input and output. This technology is used to train pilots, astronauts, doctors, and others by having them deal with simulated situations.

An interactive whiteboard display device.

Virtual reality equipment like the Sony Morpheus headset for PlayStation is helping people in various industries to simulate and prepare for situations they might encounter in their work.

Ethics and Technology Blog *Online*

Free for the Taking

I bought a computer from this guy and was surprised to see that he left a bunch of software and files on it, including his assignments from a course I'm taking next year. I'm definitely going to use the software, but I'm also thinking of changing his assignments slightly and submitting them. Is that wrong?

Take the Next Step *Online*

Activity 3.3.1 Watch	*How do touchscreens work?*	**CORE** CONTENT
Activity 3.3.2 Research	*How has technology helped people with physical challenges?*	
Activity 3.3.3 **TEAM** Present	*What new monitor technologies are on the horizon?*	

PRECHECK

3.4 Purchasing a Computer

When faced with buying a new computer, many people get overwhelmed trying to figure out all the features and tech terms. The challenge is compounded because the specifications for what makes up the latest and greatest computing device change frequently as manufacturers try to outdo each other. However, there are certain questions you can answer to make an informed and intelligent computer purchase.

What Are Your Computing Needs?

Not everybody needs the newest, fastest, most high-powered computer, so don't let sales hype sway you into buying more computer than you need.

Activities that require higher levels of speed and performance include:

- Working with sophisticated graphics when performing tasks such as photo manipulation or web design.
- Working with audio and video.
- Uploading and downloading larger files over a network using a more recent Wi-Fi specification.
- Rich multimedia experiences such as gaming.

Also consider how much time you will spend on the computer. If you work at home and will use the computer eight hours a day, five days a week, you need a better quality (which often means more expensive) model. But if you only log on to read email a few days a week and manage your checkbook with a financial program once a month, a lower-end model will probably do. Efficient power consumption is one last consideration. Many systems do comply with Energy Star requirements, but double-check the labeling and specifications to make sure.

Also consider how your choices create a larger impact on the world around you. Think about how the rapid change and constant upgrading of electronic devices has an impact on the environment. Technology doesn't seem green when you think about all the computer monitors, cases, keyboards, hard drives, and printers that get disposed of each day. The green computing movement focuses on several important goals:

- Reduce hazardous materials.
- Make computing devices energy efficient.
- Recycle outdated computing devices.
- Limit factory waste.

Technology companies have been developing products that are more energy efficient with batteries that last longer and promoting recycling efforts to make computing more green. Solid state drives with fewer moving parts are also a growing trend.

What Processor Speed Do You Need?

As you learned earlier in this chapter, computers contain a processor that is located on a computer chip. Your computer **processor speed** influences how fast your computer runs programs and completes various tasks.

Processor speed is measured in **gigahertz (GHz)**. The more gigahertz, the faster the processor speed. Processor speed gets faster all the time. As of the writing of this textbook, 2.6 to 5.0 gigahertz was the higher end for the average computer, though some have reached 5.5 gigahertz.

Gordon Moore, one of the founders of Intel, is the creator of **Moore's Law**, which states that over time the number of transistors that can be placed on a chip will increase exponentially, with a corresponding increase in processing speed and memory capacity. Since proposing this idea in 1970, Moore has largely been proved correct.

Those who want to play games and work with graphics require a more powerful computer system.

How Much Memory and Storage Is Enough?

Your computer has a certain amount of **memory capacity** that it uses to run programs and store data. When you buy a computer, you'll notice specifications for the amount of RAM and hard drive storage each model offers.

- As you read previously, RAM is the memory your computer uses to access and run programs. RAM chips come in different types, including DRAM, SRAM, and SDRAM. Most modern computer memory is some variation of SDRAM including DDR-SDRAM, DDR2-SDRAM, DDR3-SDRAM, and DDR4-SDRAM. Performance has steadily improved with each successive generation. The more sophisticated programs you run and the more you want to run several programs at one time, the higher RAM you should look for.

- RAM chips are rated by **access speed**. This rating measures how quickly a request for data from your system is completed. Your computer will also use some RAM to run the operating system and application programs. RAM access speed is measured in **megahertz (MHz)**. For example, 800 MHz is a typical access speed that would be sufficient to run most computers. Chip manufacturers continue to work to develop new, faster processors. Adding RAM to your computer is simple to do and one of the least expensive ways to improve the speed of your computer.
- The average computer's hard drive capacity for data storage is measured in **gigabytes (GB)**. A typical consumer PC might have anywhere from 250 GB to 750 GB of storage capacity though terabyte systems measured in thousands of gigabytes are becoming common. Large systems used by business and research institutes may have storage measured in petabytes (PB, measured as one quadrillion bytes). Likewise, data storage size is an issue for smartphones and tablets. Many smartphones and tablets feature up to 128 GB of storage.

Which Operating System Is Right for You?

Chapter 4 of this book goes into operating systems in detail, but when you go out shopping for a computer, there are a few reasons you should consider which operating system to use.

All new computers come with an operating system installed, so the cost of the operating system (OS) isn't usually a factor. However, if you are buying OS software on its own (for example, to upgrade to a newer version), there are variations in cost to consider.

Windows is a popular operating system, but if you are buying the software (as opposed to buying a computer with it already installed), it is costly. Also, because of its popularity, Windows computers are more often the target of viruses (though Macs are gaining in both popularity and virus problems).

Linux is a Windows-like operating system that comes in different "flavors" such as Mint and Ubuntu. You can use the free, open source version of Linux or you can

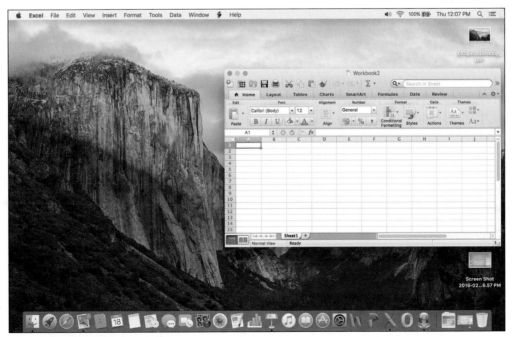

Operating systems are getting better at allowing users to interact with files created on other systems.

purchase a packaged edition. For a packaged edition, the company may charge a fee and add something extra, such as support and documentation. The Linux community offers lots of applications and add-ins to choose from.

Mac computers are manufactured by Apple and use the Mac OS X operating system. While Apple offers its own software written by Apple or third-party Apple developers, many software applications originally written for Windows are also available in Mac versions, such as Microsoft Office. You can also set up your Mac to run the Windows operating system alongside the Mac OS X, so you can take advantage of a wide variety of software.

How Do You Want to Connect with the Online World?

Computers come with various features that allow them to connect to the Internet, such as a port for connecting a cable to your computer and a built-in **wireless adapter**.

What Are You Willing to Spend?

Computers range in price from a few hundred dollars to several thousand. Often, buying a base model and customizing it with additional memory and an upgraded monitor will get you the system you need. Laptops are still slightly more expensive than desktop models, but lightweight laptops such as ultrabooks have leveled the playing field. It's a good idea to use online sites to check out the best prices and read consumer reviews before buying.

Where you shop can have an impact on price. You can shop for a computer in an online store, in a traditional retail store, or use online auctions or classifieds to find deals on new or refurbished models. Retail stores provide the ability to try before you buy. You can spend time with the computer, getting the feel of the keyboard and viewing the display to see if it meets your needs. You can also direct any questions you have about the computer to a real, live salesperson. Manufacturer sites allow you to customize computers to your requirements. To help you answer your specific questions, many online sites provide shopping support using real-time chat, which can make buying online easy.

Check to see whether memberships in organizations such as your university or member-discount retail stores such as Costco give you access to good deals. Also, think about shipping costs if you buy online, and note that retail stores often charge a restocking fee if you return a computer.

Should You Opt for Higher-End Graphics and Sound?

Those who work with a lot of visual elements (for example, photographers, gamers, or movie buffs), should opt for a better quality graphics card when purchasing a computer. Movies and games also use sound, so a high-end sound card is a plus.

Computers that have higher-end sound and image capabilities are referred to as *gaming* or *multimedia models*. In addition to more sophisticated sound and video cards, they usually have higher memory specifications.

Companies such as Dell and Lenovo offer buyers the opportunity to build a custom computer online.

Spotlight on the Future *Online*

Augmented Reality

The basic concept of **augmented reality** is to add overlays of technology to improve our experiences.

Janna Anderson, associate professor at Elon University and a co-author of a recent report by the Pew Research Center, says our smart devices will get even smarter.

"For instance you may be on a tour of New York and walking down the street and it will give you information about the buildings you're passing."

We are already seeing the start of this trend with devices like Google Glass, which puts a tiny computer screen within your field of vision where you can use the Internet, and record video of your interactions with other people, raising privacy implications.

"The voices in this survey expressed optimism well tempered by fairly urgent warnings that negatives come with the positives," she said.

Talk about It

1. What is meant by the term *augmented reality*?

2. What are some of the applications that augmented reality may have in our society, both now and in the future?

3. Is it possible that our smart devices will become too "smart" and distance us from actual reality?

4. What breakthroughs will be needed in areas such as storage and energy to fully realize the potential of augmented reality?

5. Discuss the positives and negatives of the ability to augment or change the reality of our experiences.

Activity 3.4.1 Watch	*What affects your computer's speed?*	**CORE** CONTENT
Activity 3.4.2 Watch	*How does 3-D printing work?*	**CORE** CONTENT
Activity 3.4.3 Research	*How do different styles of computers compare in weight, size, and portability?*	e book
Activity 3.4.4 **TEAM** Research	*How much battery life is enough for a computing device?*	e book
Activity 3.4.5 Research	*Which operating system is right for me?*	e book
Activity 3.4.6 Research	*What can I customize in a computer?*	e book

Review and Assessment *Online*

An interactive Summing Up with audio, a Study Notes document, slide presentations with audio, and Terms to Know flashcards with audio are available from the links menu on this page in your ebook.

Summing Up

A World of Digital Devices

Some digital devices have certain features built into one unit, such as a laptop computer or cell phone. Others use other **peripheral devices** that physically or wirelessly connect with them.

The Parts That Make Up Your Computer

The **motherboard** is the primary circuit board on your computer, and holds the central processing unit (CPU), BIOS, memory, and so on. The motherboard is a container where the various working pieces of your computer slot into one compact package. Circuits on the motherboard connect the various components contained on it.

The central processing unit (CPU), which is a microprocessor, sits on the motherboard. The CPU processes a user's requests. A **multicore processor** contains more than one CPU, which in this situation is referred to as a *core*.

The motherboard also holds different types of memory. **Read-only memory (ROM)** is the permanent, or nonvolatile, memory of a computer hardwired into a chip. In a **PC**, the **BIOS** is stored in ROM. BIOS stands for basic input/output system. This is code embedded in a memory chip also residing on the motherboard. During the boot-up sequence, the BIOS checks devices to insure they are working properly and to start them up. It also directs the hard drive to boot up and load the operating system (OS) to memory. Random access memory (RAM) chips store data and programs and allow access in any order, which speeds up processing.

While some computers have built-in sound or graphics cards, others include them as **expansion cards**.

A **power supply** in a desktop or laptop computer is located where the power cord is inserted at the back of the CPU. The power supply switches alternating current (AC) provided from your wall outlet to lower voltages in the form of direct current (DC).

A computer uses a **port** to connect with a peripheral device such as a monitor or printer or to connect to a network. A **serial port** is used to connect a peripheral device to the serial bus via a cable with a plug that typically contains nine pins. A **universal serial bus (USB) port** is a small rectangular slot that provides a popular way to attach peripherals and storage devices. You can add a hub to expand the number of available USB ports. A **FireWire port** is based on the same serial bus architecture as a USB port. FireWire provides a high-speed serial interface for peripheral devices that require high performance such as digital cameras, camcorders, or external hard disk drives. A **Thunderbolt port** is a peripheral connection standard that supports high-resolution displays and other devices that require a lot of bandwidth, such as high-end video cameras or data storage devices. An **Infrared Data Association (IrDA) port** allows you to transfer data from one device to another using infrared light waves.

All storage media have methods for reading the data from the media (input) and for writing the data to the media (output). The various storage media used on a computer are accessed using **drives**.

Storage media include the **hard disk** built into your computer; an **optical drive** to read a **CD**, **DVD**, or **Blu-ray disc**; an **external hard drive** or a **network attached storage (NAS)** shared external hard disk; a **flash drive**; and a **solid-state drive (SSD)**. Third-party cloud storage systems store and manage data on a web-connected server.

Input and Output Devices

You use **input devices** to get data into your computer and **output devices** to get information out.

In addition to a **keyboard** and a **mouse**, computer input devices include **touchscreens**, **touchpads**, **scanners**, digital cameras and **webcams**, **gaming devices**, and **microphones**. Specialty input devices include foldable keyboards for **mobile Internet devices (MIDs)**, **assistive technology** devices, and devices often used in retail or manufacturing settings such as **bar code readers** and **RFID readers**.

Output devices include any device that displays, prints, or plays content stored in your computer, including your **monitor**, **speakers**, headphones, **printer**, or an **LCD projector**.

Some devices provide both input and output functionality, such as a **fax machine**.

3-D printing is a method of using printers to create 3-D objects from digital models. A 3-D printer prints layers on top of one another to build a physical object, and 3-D printing is increasing in popularity as the technology develops.

Purchasing a Computer

When buying a computer, you should consider the following questions:

- What are your computing needs?
- What **processor speed** do you need?
- How much memory and storage is enough?
- What operating system is right for you?
- How do you want to connect to the Internet?
- What are you willing to spend?
- Should you opt for higher-end graphics and sound?

Your computer has a certain amount of **memory capacity** that it uses to run programs and store data. When you buy a computer you'll notice specifications for the amount of RAM and hard drive storage each model offers. RAM **access speed** is measured in **megahertz (MHz)**. The average computer's hard drive capacity for data storage and the storage capacity for smartphones and tablets is measured in **gigabytes (GB)**.

All new computers come with an operating system installed, so consider whether you want Windows, Linux, or a Mac OS X system. Computers also come with various features that allow them to connect to the Internet.

Computers range in price from a few hundred dollars to several thousand. Often, buying a base model and customizing it with additional memory and an upgraded monitor will get you the system you need. Laptops are still slightly more expensive than desktop models. Where you shop can have an impact on price.

Those who work with a lot of visual elements (for example, photographers, gamers, or movie buffs) should opt for a better quality graphics card. Movies and games also use sound, so a high-end sound card is a plus.

Terms to Know

e book

A World of Digital Devices

peripheral device, 66

The Parts That Make Up Your Computer

motherboard, 66

chip, 67

read-only memory (ROM), 67

nonvolatile memory, 67

BIOS, 67

expansion card, 68

PC Card, 68

power supply, 68

charging mat, 68

port, 68

physical port, 68

serial port, 68

universal serial bus (USB) port, 69

FireWire port, 69

Thunderbolt port, 69

Infrared Data Association (IrDA) port, 69

MIDI, 70

drive, 70

hard disk, 70

CD, 70

DVD, 70

optical drive, 70

Blu-ray disc, 70

optoelectronic sensor, 70

external hard drive, 70

network attached storage (NAS), 70

flash drive, 71

flash memory, 71

solid-state drive (SSD), 71

multicore processor, Activity 3.2.1

parallelized, Activity 3.2.1

Input and Output Devices

input device, 72

output device, 72

keyboard, 72

mouse, 73

infrared (IR) technology, 73

touchscreen, 73

stylus, 73

digital pen, 73

touchpad, 73

scanner, 73

webcam, 73

gaming device, 74

wired data gloves, 74

microphone, 74

mobile Internet device (MID), 74

assistive technology, 74

bar code reader, 75

RFID reader, 75

keystroke logging software, 75

monitor, 75

speaker, 75

Bluetooth headset, 75

TFT active matrix LCD, 76

LED display, 76

plasma display, 76

surface-conduction electron-emitter display (SED), 76

organic light emitting diode (OLED), 76

printer, 77

photo printer, 77

thermal printer, 77

plotter, 77

fax machine, 77

3-D printing, 77

liquid crystal display (LCD) projector, 77

document camera, 77

interactive whiteboard (IWB), 78

virtual reality system, 78

Purchasing a Computer

processor speed, 80

gigahertz (GHz), 80

Moore's Law, 80

memory capacity, 80

access speed, 81

megahertz (MHz), 81

gigabytes (GB), 81

wireless adapter, 82

augmented reality, 83

clock speed, Activity 3.4.1

Concepts Check

Concepts Check 3.1   Multiple Choice
Take this quiz to test your understanding of key concepts in this chapter.

Concepts Check 3.2   Matching
Test your understanding of terms and concepts presented in this chapter.

Concepts Check 3.3   Label It
Use the interactive tool to identify objects on a motherboard.

Concepts Check 3.4   Label It
Use the interactive tool to identify the parts of a computer.

Projects

Check with your instructor for the preferred method to submit completed work.

Project 3.1   Understanding Your Computer System and Performance

Project 3.1.1
Knowing the parts of your computer system will be helpful when you need to upgrade your system or buy a new computer. Using the following list of computer parts as a guide, create a table and include descriptions of the features of your current computer. If you don't own a computer, use a public computer or a friend's computer to perform this task. Note any hardware features that you want to upgrade for increased performance. (You can find information about the computer system in the Control Panel of Windows under the category of System and Maintenance; under System Preferences, General on a Mac; or by looking at your user manual or visiting your manufacturer's website and searching for your computer model.) Be prepared to discuss your findings in class.

CPU processor	Monitor type	Ports (types and numbers
CPU speed	Monitor size	of each)
RAM	Sound card	Size
Hard drive capacity	Video card memory	Weight
DVD drive	Speakers	Style (desktop/laptop/
		other)

Project 3.1.2   TEAM
Even though technology has improved and computers are more reliable than they were several years ago, they can still have problems. In assigned teams, search for two computer diagnostic tools that can help to resolve a potential computer issue. Compare and contrast the tools. Include in your summary, information about what the software will provide in solving issues related to hardware devices, operating systems and installed software, hardware, speed, performance benchmarks, and system stability.

Write a memo to your instructor discussing the advantages of using a diagnostic software utility to identify problems and enhance the performance of your computer.

Project 3.2   Purchasing a Computer

Project 3.2.1

You have decided to purchase a new computer to launch a home business. Because your current computer works fine, you would like to donate it to a charitable organization. Before making the donation, you know that your computer must be wiped clean of data. You realize that simply deleting files or reformatting your hard drive doesn't remove all the data, so you decide to research the proper way to permanently erase computer data. Based on your research, prepare a list of instructions for wiping your computer clean of data.

Project 3.2.2   TEAM

Your Introduction to Computers class has volunteered to help people in the community who need to buy new computers. Your instructor will divide the class into three groups:

- Group A is purchasing a computer for a senior citizen for personal use.
- Group B is purchasing a computer for a teenaged gamer.
- Group C is purchasing a computer for a business person who travels regularly and needs Internet access and basic business functionality.

Your group's task is to meet the needs of your assigned community member by researching a variety of computer options. To begin the process, consider the user's likely computer needs and cost limitations. Then investigate different computer systems that satisfy those requirements. Use the table format created in Project 3.1.1 to guide you in your research, and keep a list of your reference sources. Prepare a group presentation that shares your research findings and computer recommendation.

Project 3.3   Exploring Data Storage

Project 3.3.1

With an increased need for computer users to access information from any location, online data storage is becoming a popular service. Research several cloud storage companies, and examine the pros and cons of the service, the costs, and any security issues. Write a report about online data storage and include a recommendation for an online storage company. Be sure to provide your instructor with a list of references for your information.

Project 3.3.2   TEAM

As a help desk member of an information technology department, you observe some risky data handling practices. In particular, you have noticed that many employees have discs, flash drives, and external hard drives lying around on their desks. You have also observed some employees placing discs and flash drives in their pockets to carry them home, and posting files in the cloud to access while on the road. After speaking with your supervisor about the potential for damaged or lost data, your supervisor asks you to prepare a slide presentation about the proper use of data storage devices. As a team, select three storage devices and provide guidelines that address how to keep the devices and the data stored on them safe. Be prepared to present these guidelines to your class, and to submit a list of references to your instructor.

Project 3.4   How Much RAM Is Enough?

Project 3.4.1

Your classmate is having a hard time understanding RAM. To help your classmate, you have been asked by your instructor to research RAM and to create an outline covering its basic concepts. Your outline should include the definition of RAM, the types of RAM, the location of RAM, and the amount of RAM a well-equipped computer used by an average college student should contain. Keep a list of references that you used in your investigation. After you have completed the outline, work with a partner to review each other's outline and to solicit feedback on its usefulness. Record any comments on each other's outlines, and submit your outline and list of references to your instructor.

Project 3.4.2   TEAM

A local school has received a donation of computers that are in excellent shape but are operating slowly and need a new software suite installed. A school employee, Tony, has volunteered to install the software. Tony realizes that the computers need more RAM to run the new software and address the slow operating speed, but he has never installed RAM. To help Tony with this task, prepare a tutorial presentation (supported with text and screen captures) on the installation of RAM. Be sure to include a list of references for your information.

Project 3.5   Wiki—Exploring New Computer Technologies

Project 3.5.1

Research the Internet to find an article about a new computer device released in the current calendar year. If possible, focus your search on devices that use a new technology that wasn't available a year ago. Read the article and write a summary of the device, including a description of the device, its purpose and functions, the total cost of the device (including all components), and where you can buy it. Attach a list of references that you used to write your summary, and post the summary on the course wiki site.

Project 3.5.2   TEAM

You or your team will be assigned to edit and verify the content posted on the wiki site from Project 3.5.1. If you add or edit any content, make sure you include a notation within the page that includes your name or team members' names and the date you edited the content—for example, "Edited by [student name or team members' names] on [date]." Keep a list of references that you used to verify your content changes. When you are finished with your verification, include a notation at the end of the entry—for example, "Verified by [student name or team members' names] on [date]."

Project 3.6 Green Computing

Project 3.6.1

The increasing use of computer technology has had a significant impact on the environment. As a result, many companies have implemented policies that support green computing. Research the term "green computing" and the major initiatives behind this environmental movement. Write a report that discusses the definition and main concepts of green computing. Address the measures being taken by companies to support this movement and their positive impact on the environment. Be sure to offer a recommendation in your report as to how computer users can support the green computing movement. Submit your report and a list of your references to your instructor.

Project 3.6.2 TEAM

Your information technology team has been assigned to prepare a slide presentation on green computing for the board of directors of your school. This presentation should provide the broad definition and purpose of green computing as well as specifically define and address the major concepts of this environmental initiative: green use, green design, green disposal, and green manufacturing. Be sure to include in your presentation a recommended green computing plan for your school to implement.

Class Conversations

Topic 3.1   What happens to old computing devices?

The personal computer began to become a household fixture in the early 1990s. In the last twenty-five plus years, computer manufacturers are increasing productivity and are building computers that are faster, smaller, and continue to improve year after year. What happens to all the old computers, tablets, and smartphones? What impact will these old devices have on our environment in the next ten years?

Topic 3.2   Will technology go up, up, and away?

Technology changes rapidly. Amazon has proposed the concept of delivering packages by drones. (See the video about Amazon's plans to use drones for package delivery at http://ODW4.emcp.net/Octocopter.) What impact will this type of technology have on our economy? Will flying drones affect our quality of life? What are some other possible uses of drones?

Topic 3.3   How can you shop smart for a computer?

Computers are sold in a variety of settings, such as specialty computer stores, large discount retailers, or online at retail stores or auction sites. What are the benefits of purchasing a computer at a specialty computer store? How can you tell if a particular online store is secure when you are making a purchase from it? Is the support you can get for your computer better if you buy it at a bricks-and-mortar store? What support options do you think exist for a computer purchased online?

System Software

The Control Center of Your Computer

What You'll Accomplish

When you finish this chapter, you'll be able to:

4.1 List tasks performed by system software, describe the steps performed by the operating system in starting your computer, and outline the history of operating system development.

4.2 Explain platform dependency and differentiate the popular operating system packages in use today.

4.3 Describe tasks the operating system performs, list system maintenance utilities that are included in an operating system package, and explain how to send the computer to sleep or shut it off.

4.4 Explain the differences between an operating system for a PC and an operating system for a tablet or smartphone and list the common mobile operating systems in use today.

Why Does It Matter ?

Hardware without system software is like a powerful new car without a driver. The computer may have the latest gadgetry under the hood, but without system software, the gadgetry can't do anything. Every computer, from a small mobile device to a large mainframe computer, needs system software, which includes the operating system and various utility programs, to work. Understanding how an operating system package such as Windows manages the various devices, programs, and files on your computer will help you make choices when purchasing a computer, troubleshoot your system when things go wrong, keep your data secure, and perform regular maintenance to keep your computer running well.

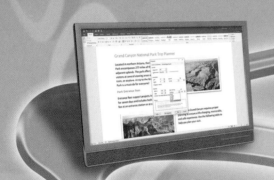

Routes data between applications and devices

Controls output devices

Controls input devices

Manages system performance and memory

94

Chapter 4 System Software: The Control Center of Your Computer

System software performs basic computing functions, including starting your computer and loading the operating system, which provides the interface between you and the machine. It also provides tools for configuring and maintaining your computer system and managing programs and files.

Provides a user interface

Creates and manages files

Configures hardware

Shuts computer off

Maintains computer

Provides search and help

Operating System

4.1 What Controls Your Computer?

The first instructions your computer uses when you turn on the power are stored in a ROM BIOS chip located on the motherboard (the circuit board that holds the various elements of your computer). These instructions are called *firmware*. **Firmware** in a computer system contains code that is used to start the computer and load system software.

System Software

System software includes your operating system and several types of utility software. The **operating system (OS)** provides you with an interface to work with your computer hardware and applications, while the **utility software**, or utilities, optimizes and maintains your computer. The OS and utilities are typically combined in an operating system package such as Windows, Linux, UNIX, Mac OS X, Android, or Chrome OS. More portable devices such as tablets and smartphones typically use a mobile operating system that provides similar functionality to the OS on your desktop or laptop computer.

The OS part of the system software allows you to organize and control your computer hardware and software. It's in charge of loading files, deciding which applications get to do what and when as you work, and shutting down your computer. The OS is essential for you to interact with your computer because software and hardware simply can't run without an OS in place. Your OS translates your commands and performs appropriate actions.

The utilities included in an operating system package such as Windows aren't *essential* to the functioning of the OS but are *useful* to the OS and to the user. **Disk Cleanup** in Windows, for example, helps the OS function by maintaining your computer and getting rid of unused or unusable files.

Figure 4.1 shows the devices and components that are managed by the OS.

FIGURE 4.1 Devices and Components Run by the OS

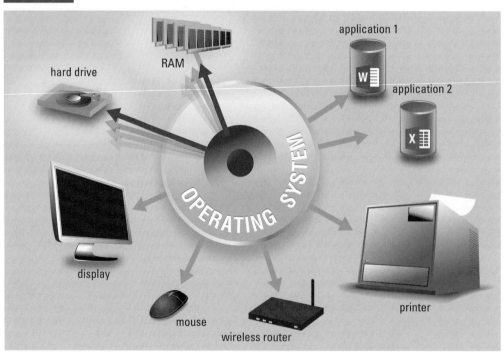

Mac OS X, though outsold by Windows, has a loyal and growing following. This is the Mac OS X desktop.

Starting Your Computer

The process of starting your computer, called **booting**, is handled by instructions that reside on the BIOS (basic input/output system) chip slotted onto the motherboard. These instructions load the OS, which then loads the remaining system and software files into RAM (memory). If you start a computer when the power is turned off, you're performing a **cold boot**; if you restart the computer (shut it down and then turn it on again without turning the power off), it is called a **warm boot**. A new specification for booting your computer, called **UEFI (Unified Extensible Firmware Interface)**, is just beginning to be adopted; UEFI is meant to eventually replace the aging BIOS firmware and could make booting computers a much speedier process. UEFI provides a layer of security called *Secure Boot* that prevents unauthorized code from being installed on your computer. UEFI can stop loading of malware before your operating system and its security features are loaded.

Figure 4.2 shows the steps in booting a computer. During this procedure the following components are involved:

- The motherboard, which holds the central processing unit (CPU) and other chips.
- The CPU, or microprocessor chip, which is the brains of your computer.
- The BIOS or UEFI chip on the motherboard with the embedded code (firmware) that your computer uses to load the operating system and communicate with hardware devices.
- **System files**, which run when you start up your computer and provide the instructions that the operating system needs to run.
- **System configuration**, a definition or means of defining your entire computing system, including the identity of your computer, the devices connected to it, and some essential processes that your computer runs.

> “Rebooting is a wonder drug—it fixes almost everything.”
>
> —Garrett Hazel, "Help Desk Blues"

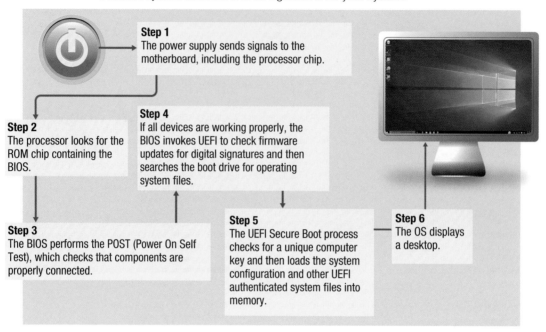

FIGURE 4.2 Steps in Booting a Computer

The process of booting your computer is actually a series of steps that load system software and configurations for your system.

Step 1
The power supply sends signals to the motherboard, including the processor chip.

Step 2
The processor looks for the ROM chip containing the BIOS.

Step 3
The BIOS performs the POST (Power On Self Test), which checks that components are properly connected.

Step 4
If all devices are working properly, the BIOS invokes UEFI to check firmware updates for digital signatures and then searches the boot drive for operating system files.

Step 5
The UEFI Secure Boot process checks for a unique computer key and then loads the system configuration and other UEFI authenticated system files into memory.

Step 6
The OS displays a desktop.

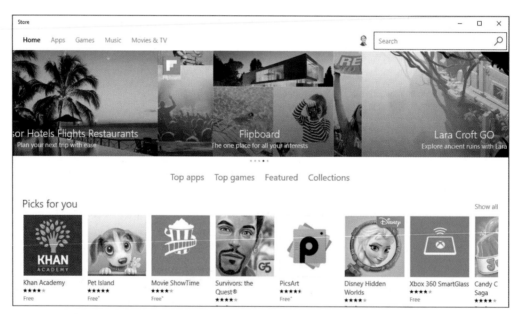

Operating systems make your computer work, but they also offer access to applications and games to entertain you. For example, the Windows Store app is where you can download your favorite new app or game. App stores offer new content often.

The Operating System Package

An **operating system package** such as Windows or Linux includes system software that runs and manages your computer's hardware and software resources; organizes files and folders containing your documents, images, and other kinds of content; and helps you perform maintenance and repairs when your computer has problems.

Operating system packages also offer security features such as password protection to keep others from using your computer and a firewall to prevent someone from remotely accessing your computer.

Operating system packages also include basic applications you can use to get your work done or be entertained, such as simple word processing programs like WordPad; games like Spider Solitaire; media players such as QuickTime Player to play music or videos; and tools such as a calculator, a calendar or address book, and an Internet browser.

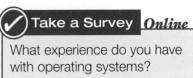

What experience do you have with operating systems?

A (Brief!) History of Operating Systems

There was a time when computers had no operating system. In this pre-OS time, every program had to have all the required **drivers** (software that allows an operating system to interface with hardware) and specifications needed to connect to hardware such as printers. In the early days of computing, functions in software were simple enough that this system worked. As programs became more sophisticated and hardware grew more complex, something was needed to orchestrate the interaction between software and hardware.

Mainframe computers—the pre-consumer computers that were often the size of a large desk or van—typically used an operating system created for them by their manufacturer. UNIVAC I, the first commercial computer produced in the United States, is an example. In the pre-personal computer period, names of the operating systems were not significant because the hardware drove the purchase decision.

UNIX, developed by AT&T Bell Laboratories in the 1970s, was an OS written with the C programming language, which became popular with corporations for running their workstations. It was usable across a variety of hardware and could be customized by the companies who licensed it. UNIX continues to be widely used by larger organizations today, and there are several versions of this OS.

With the development of microprocessors, small personal computers began to catch on, and by the 1980s it was clear a more standardized OS was needed. In 1980, Microsoft produced its first OS, MS-DOS, which eventually became known simply as **DOS** (an acronym for *disk operating system*). This and other early operating systems were **command-line interfaces**, meaning that you typed commands as text, but they were not in plain English—and not very intuitive.

A huge breakthrough in operating system development came in the

The Remington Rand Corporation introduced the first commercial computer produced in the United States, the UNIVAC I, in 1951.

1980s and 1990s when the **graphical user interface (GUI)** was introduced to the public by Apple and then by Microsoft. A graphical user interface added a much more user-friendly way to work with a computer because you could click icons and choose options from menus and dialog boxes, rather than typing commands. With Windows 8 and Windows 8.1 Microsoft expanded and improved touchscreen functionality in its operating system, representing a significant shift in how users provide input to their computing devices. Windows 8.1 and 10 are modeled after mobile device operating systems.

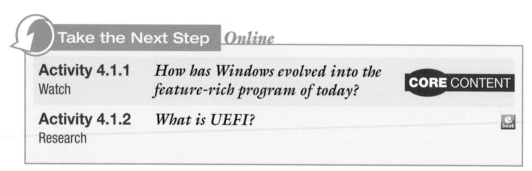

DOS sported white, amber, or green letters on a black background and required that you memorize commands to use it.

Take the Next Step *Online*

Activity 4.1.1 Watch	*How has Windows evolved into the feature-rich program of today?*	**CORE** CONTENT
Activity 4.1.2 Research	*What is UEFI?*	

PRECHECK → ## 4.2 Perusing the Popular Operating System Packages

The major operating systems used by individual consumers in the world today are Windows, for PCs (or personal computers); Mac OS X, for Apple computers; and Linux, an open source operating system available in different versions. (Open source means that the software was built with contributions by users and its source code is free to anybody to modify and use.) Smartphone and tablet devices use mobile operating systems such as the Apple iOS and Linux-based Android. All operating systems can take advantage of computing "in the cloud."

Understanding Platforms and Platform Dependency

The term **platform** is used to describe the combination of hardware architecture and software used to run applications. The platform's OS may be dependent on the hardware. For example, a Mac operating system isn't designed to run on a Windows computer. This is called **platform dependency**. Table 4.1 lists four common operating system platforms.

TABLE 4.1 Operating System Platforms

Platform	Operating Systems
PC/Windows	Windows 10, Windows 8.1, Windows 7
Mac/Mac OS	OS X in various versions: El Capitan, Yosemite, Mavericks, Lion, Snow Leopard
Tablets	Windows 10, Windows 8.1, Windows 7, Android, Chrome OS, iOS
PC to Mainframe/UNIX	New versions of UNIX are now released as open source software through the Open Solaris project, including SchillX, Belenix, and AIX
PC to Mainframe/Linux	Linux, being freely distributable, comes in many different distribution "flavors" such as Red Hat, SUSE, and Ubuntu, as well as a wealth of versions for specific languages such as Chinese (Sunwah Linux) and Norwegian (Skolelinux).

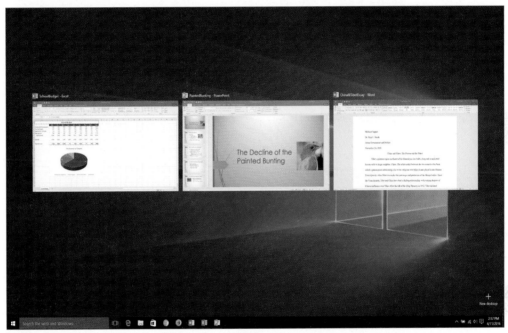

Multitasking demands that the OS handle several functions at once.

However, platform dependency is becoming less of an issue as consumers demand cross-functionality when they buy computers and software. Today, software such as Boot Camp, which is included with Mac OS X, allows you to run Windows on a Mac. Though there are still different versions of productivity software, such as Word for PCs, Word for Mac, and Open Office's Writer, you can typically save files in each version that are compatible with (able to be used by) any other platform.

Still, when you purchase application software such as a computer game or word processor, you should make sure that you buy programs that will work with the platform on which your computer is based. If you are using software in the cloud, the cloud service provides the latest or most compatible version for your computer.

> It does not matter which browser, operating system, program or service you use—it falls down to whether the job can be done or not. If it can, then continue. If not, by all means move on.
>
> —Zack Whittaker, ZDNet

Today's popular graphical operating systems: Windows 10, Mac OS X El Capitan, and Linux Ubuntu.

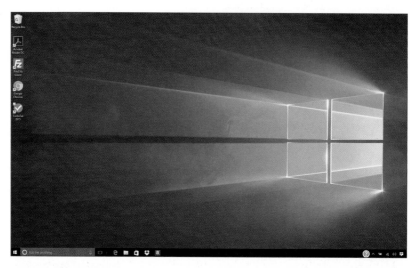

Windows **Microsoft Windows** was initially a graphical interface layered on top of the DOS operating system. Eventually, it became a true GUI OS with a robust feature set, and today Windows is the most widely used operating system in the world. It can be used on computers from a variety of manufacturers and there are thousands of software products available to run on Windows. Regular updates keep the Windows OS current as issues become known or new security fixes are required.

The latest Windows OS is **Windows 10**, which provides an intelligent assistant and search tool named **Cortana**. Users can interact with their desktop, laptop, or tablet computer using a touchscreen, and on the **Start menu** live tiles that represent apps such as Weather, People, or Finance update on the fly.

 Ethics and Technology Blog *Online*

Ethical Choices in Device Manufacturing

It seems like whenever there's a new technology, whether it be a new way to deliver videos or music or a breakthrough in mobile phone or computer hardware, companies scramble to produce the winning version and consumers end up the losers, lost in a sea of incompatible technologies. Should device manufacturers be forced to work together to establish common standards for new technologies? Is that feasible in a free market?

Mac Those who swear by Macs and the Mac operating system, **Mac OS X**, have several reasons to do so. Macs have sophisticated graphics-handling capabilities and clear, crisp screens. Their computer designs are unique, and include models such as the iMac, which incorporates the CPU into the monitor, and the sleek MacBook Air notebook computer, which weighs less than three pounds.

In their early days, Mac computers were heavily marketed to the educational world, though PCs have since made significant inroads in that environment. Creative industries such as graphic design and photo imaging have also been historically strong markets for Macs because of the computers' ability to handle advanced graphics-related tasks. Today, the growing popularity of iPhones, iPads, and the iTunes online store have convinced many more people to adopt Apple's hardware, software, and services. At the time of writing, Apple's newest version of Mac OS X, El Capitan, added features to help you manage your workspace when using multiple windows. The Spotlight search feature was improved, and several apps such as Photos, Safari, and Mail were updated.

> "For years, OS X has followed the nomenclature set forward by Steve Jobs, of naming OS X releases after different felines. Well, they were starting to run out of really cool-sounding cats, so they're going on a decidedly different tack [with Mavericks, Yosemite, and El Capitan]."
>
> —Adriana Lee, TechnoBuffalo

Mac's increased popularity comes with a downside, however. Once thought to be a less virus-prone system, the Mac OS X has been receiving more attention from programmers of malicious software. For example, in March 2016, there was the first instance of ransomware being targeted to Mac users. Although Mac PCs are still less susceptible to certain types of malware (such as drive-by trojans), Mac users must practice malware prevention just like their Windows counterparts. Luckily, antivirus programs can combat malicious software on both Mac and Windows systems.

UNIX **UNIX** is primarily a server operating system. Created by a handful of AT&T Bell Labs employees, UNIX was designed to run servers that support many users. UNIX uses a command-line interface and because it is written in the C programming language, it is more portable across platforms—meaning that it can run on all types of computers including PCs and Macs. UNIX is a popular choice for web servers that support thousands or millions of users. Several other server operating systems exist, such as Open Enterprise Server, as do many other specialized server operating systems, such as those used to run web applications and email.

Linux **Linux**, first developed by Linus Torvalds in 1991, is, to a great extent, based on UNIX. In fact, some people believe it may eventually take over UNIX's market. Linux can be used as either a network operating system or a personal computing OS.

The Windows 10 Start menu provides access to various apps through graphical tiles.

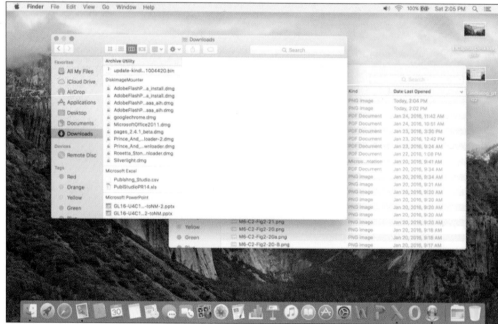

An OS controls the interface you see, as with the Mac OS X desktop shown here.

Linux is an **open source** operating system, meaning that its source code is freely available so that anyone can use or modify it. Modifications contributed over the years have resulted in various distributions or versions of Linux, such as Red Hat, Ubuntu, Mandriva, and SUSE.

Linux can run on multiple platforms and users state that the OS is highly stable and flexible. When it first appeared, Linux was seen as the rebel's OS and was supported by lots of people who were against Microsoft and the general dependency on their products. Though Linux hasn't toppled Windows, it has definitely found its place in the OS world. Linux is not just for personal computers and servers.

The Linux logo is a penguin, which has been known to appear in many costumes and versions.

Other computing environments such as mainframe computers and supercomputers used by larger organizations and governments also require an operating system. These operating systems are often based on Linux or UNIX and are highly customized to suit the hardware architecture and special purposes that the computers are designed to serve. IBM also uses z/OS on many of its established mainframe systems.

The Future of the OS

It is possible that operating system packages could become less important, or at least, less visible to the average user in the not-too-distant future.

Google's **Chrome OS** is a Linux-based operating system meant to appeal to people who work primarily in web-based applications. In June 2011, Chromebooks—PCs running the Chrome operating system—manufactured by Samsung and Acer were released, and in 2013, Toshiba, HP, and Google entered the market, expanding the Chromebook choices. Chromebooks boast an 8-second startup time with all settings, applications, and documents stored in the cloud. Using the web to deliver the majority of the user experience makes Google Chrome a cross-platform OS, because it works on any computer that supports browsers (which is essentially all computing devices in use today, including smartphones).

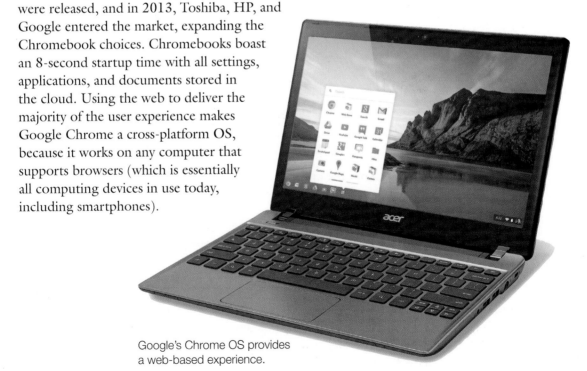

Google's Chrome OS provides a web-based experience.

While the Chrome OS is currently only available on the Chromebook platform, new consumer-oriented operating systems give you choices that span other platforms. While primarily an operating system for mobile phones (currently laying claim to just over 80 percent of that market), Google's **Android** is also offered as an operating system on tablets and some netbook models. Similarly, the **iOS** from Apple powers some iPod models, iPhones, and iPads.

In a sense, Chrome OS, Android, and iOS all function as web operating systems, providing access to services online. Android and iOS also allow users to customize their experience by downloading and installing apps on a device, while Chrome OS offers web apps. These modern operating systems allow consumers to take advantage of a variety of mobile computing platforms and customize them to work wherever and whenever they are needed. With its Windows 10 operating system, Microsoft is betting that a touchscreen approach to input and a continuously updated OS will be the wave of the future.

Take the Next Step *Online*

Activity 4.2.1 Watch	*What types of tasks does network operating software handle?*	**CORE** CONTENT
Activity 4.2.2 Research	*Are Windows and the Mac OS X all that different?*	
Activity 4.2.3 TEAM Research	*What does it take to run the Mac OS X on Windows (and vice versa)?*	
Activity 4.2.4 TEAM Discuss	*What's the story of Linux?*	
Activity 4.2.5 TEAM Present	*Will Chromebooks succeed?*	

PRECHECK

4.3 The Tasks of the Operating System Package

Although there are different operating system packages out there, they have similar basic functions in common. The following sections provide a rundown of those functions and what they help you do with your computer.

Providing a User Interface

A **user interface** is what you see when you look at your computer screen. Most operating systems provide a graphical user interface; this means that icons and pictures are used to represent the text that dominated operating systems of the past.

Your computer's **desktop** is like home base for your computer, from which you use a text or graphical interface or menus to run applications and work with files. As illustrated in Figure 4.3, GUIs use graphical tiles, buttons, and panes or windows that display operating system settings or open documents. You can open more than one window at a time; for example, one window may show your web browser at the same

FIGURE 4.3 **Some Customizable Settings for Windows PCs**
Operating systems allow you to customize their environment with different backgrounds, resolution settings, and tools.

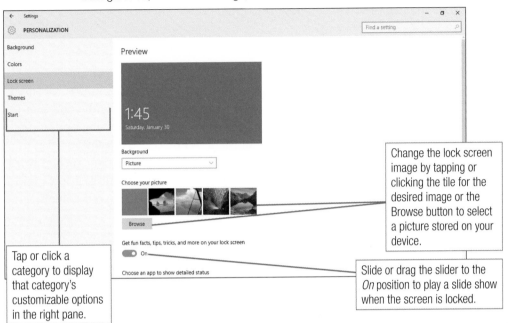

Tap or click a category to display that category's customizable options in the right pane.

Change the lock screen image by tapping or clicking the tile for the desired image or the Browse button to select a picture stored on your device.

Slide or drag the slider to the *On* position to play a slide show when the screen is locked.

time that another window displays a photo editing program. You can also customize your Start screen and/or desktop to use a different background image or color, or change the color scheme for all of your screen elements, including window borders and title bars.

Configuring Hardware

As previously defined, a driver is a small software program that provides the instructions the OS needs to communicate with a piece of hardware, such as a printer or keyboard. You may notice when you first plug in a new device, such as a wireless mouse receiver into a USB drive, that the OS has to find the driver before you can use the mouse. If your system has the wrong driver for a device, you may have problems; for example, a printer may print garbage text if you're not using the correct driver.

When you buy hardware and take it home, there will usually be a CD in the package that contains the necessary device driver software. In addition, most operating systems today come packaged with many common device drivers, or offer a way for you to download a driver from the web. Most devices today work with **Plug and Play**, a feature that recognizes devices you plug into your computer, for example, into a USB port. Once the Plug and Play feature identifies the hardware, the OS can install the necessary driver if the driver is available.

Most operating systems don't require a CD to install drivers for peripheral hardware, but it's a good idea to keep the disc in case of problems or to access additional software features for the device.

You may have to update drivers now and then—especially when you upgrade your OS. Your OS may be set up to perform regular system updates that download and install newer drivers for hardware automatically and the hardware manufacturer may alert you to updated drivers if you have registered your computer.

Controlling Input and Output Devices

Your operating system also controls input and output devices. Commonly used input devices include your keyboard, mouse, finger or stylus on a touchscreen, joystick (used for gaming), or microphone. These devices provide a way to interact with your computer, telling it what to do through typing, clicking, speaking, or selecting options in menus and dialog boxes (Figure 4.4). In addition, input devices (typically your keyboard) allow you to enter text into documents you create using programs such as word processors or spreadsheet software. Output devices include your monitor, printer, and speakers. These generate visual, printed, and audio information from your computer.

Input and output devices may be wired, which means you connect to them by plugging them into your computer, typically through a USB port; or they may be wireless, which means you connect to them by plugging a transmission device into your computer, leaving your input device free from restrictive wires. Your operating system uses device drivers to set up and control input devices. Each input and output device has a unique driver.

Some computing devices, such as tablets and smartphones, allow you to use a touchscreen to communicate with the OS. Your finger or a stylus becomes the input device, rather than a mouse or keyboard.

FIGURE 4.4 **Microsoft Word Input Options**
The most common input options for interacting with your operating system and applications are a touchscreen, the keyboard, and the mouse.

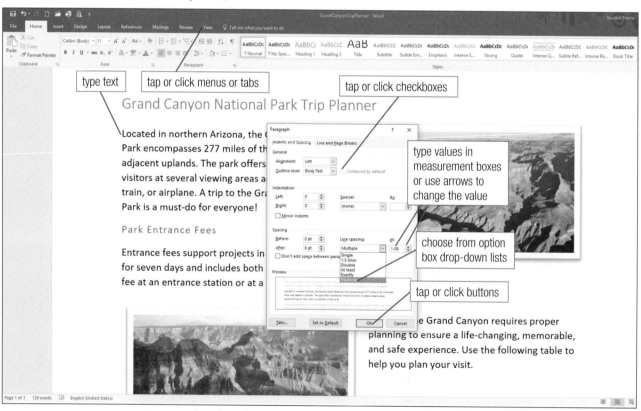

Our Digital World

Ethics and Technology Blog *Online*

Why Should I Conform?

My company is upgrading all PCs to Windows 10, but I prefer Windows 8.1. Why should I conform?

Managing System Performance and Memory

The speed with which your computer functions, called its **performance**, is largely determined by the computer processor, available cache, bus, and the amount of memory installed in the computer. All of these are orchestrated by system software.

Utilities in your operating system package monitor system performance and provide information about system resources. This allows you to troubleshoot performance and adjust settings, change which programs the OS loads when you start up, and so on.

The following is a brief rundown of the four most significant factors controlling system performance.

Memory Memory refers to the capacity for storage in a computer. One kind of memory is permanent—for example, read-only memory (ROM), which holds information such as the BIOS and start-up instructions for the operating system. Another kind of memory is temporary—for example, random access memory (RAM), which stores data while your computer is operating, but loses that data when you shut down your computer. **Virtual memory** is the part of your operating system that handles data that cannot fit into RAM when you are running several programs at once. Figure 4.5 shows how, when RAM is used up, data is stored or "swapped" into virtual memory (the file moved into virtual memory is called a **swap file**). As each program is loaded and data fills RAM's "bucket," it spills over into virtual memory.

Cache Cache memory is a dedicated holding area in which the data and instructions most recently called from RAM by the processor are temporarily stored. The process of caching allows your computer to hold a small amount of recently used data

---

FIGURE 4.5 **Using Up RAM**
RAM is used up quickly, and virtual memory supplements RAM.

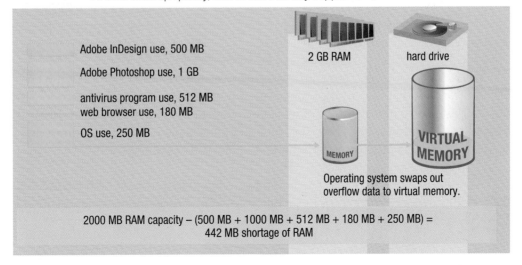

Adobe InDesign use, 500 MB

Adobe Photoshop use, 1 GB

antivirus program use, 512 MB
web browser use, 180 MB

OS use, 250 MB

2 GB RAM   hard drive

MEMORY   VIRTUAL MEMORY

Operating system swaps out overflow data to virtual memory.

2000 MB RAM capacity − (500 MB + 1000 MB + 512 MB + 180 MB + 250 MB) = 442 MB shortage of RAM

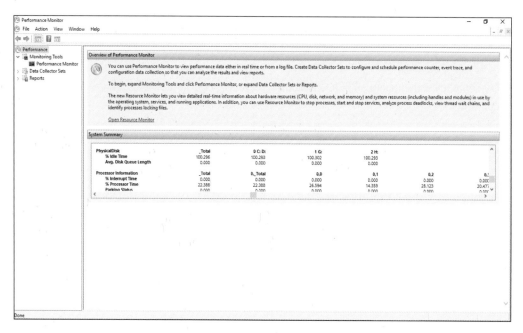

System performance monitoring tools on Windows 10 (top) and Mac (bottom) computers.

in memory so that, when you ask for something again, the OS doesn't have to run around in RAM looking for it. This is similar to the function of RAM, but because the cache sits on the microprocessor, it can be accessed more quickly than RAM, which is stored on another chip. The larger the cache size, the more data can be held and quickly retrieved, though cache always has a maximum size to keep the process of searching of the cache efficient.

Processor The CPU, sometimes referred to as the computer's processor, is an electronic circuit that runs your computer's hardware and software. The OS coordinates the use of a processor's resources by scheduling and prioritizing tasks. In systems with more than one processor core (dual or quad core systems, as shown in Figure 4.6), the OS manages tasks between or among processors.

Bus A **bus** is a subsystem that moves instructions and data around between the components in your computer (for example, between RAM and the processor and between the processor and the cache). The faster the bus, the faster the computer.

FIGURE 4.6

FIGURE 4.6 **Sending a Task to the Processor**
In dual processor configuration, the OS determines which processor completes a task.

One measurement of bus speed is how much data can move at one time. Another is the speed at which the data can travel. A bus with a larger capacity to move data and a faster speed helps your computer complete tasks faster.

Routing Data between Applications and Devices

It's midnight, and you've just finished a lengthy homework assignment and want to print a copy to submit to your instructor the next morning. You click the Print button in your word processor program and grab the pages as they come out of the printer. Ever wonder what your operating system is doing in the background?

Figure 4.7 shows how this routing of data between an application and a printer works and what role the OS plays. Your OS may also route data to and from your network or other devices such as a scanner.

FIGURE 4.7 **The Role of the Operating System in Routing Data among Applications**

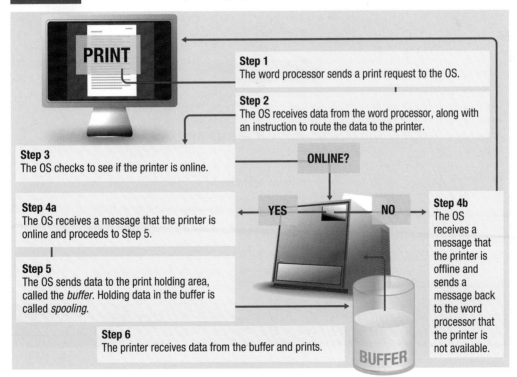

Step 1
The word processor sends a print request to the OS.

Step 2
The OS receives data from the word processor, along with an instruction to route the data to the printer.

Step 3
The OS checks to see if the printer is online.

ONLINE?

Step 4a
The OS receives a message that the printer is online and proceeds to Step 5.

YES

NO

Step 4b
The OS receives a message that the printer is offline and sends a message back to the word processor that the printer is not available.

Step 5
The OS sends data to the print holding area, called the *buffer*. Holding data in the buffer is called *spooling*.

Step 6
The printer receives data from the buffer and prints.

BUFFER

Managing File Systems

The operating system provides the features used for storing and retrieving files. The OS has to keep track of the physical location where a document is saved on your hard disk; to do this, it maintains the **file allocation table (FAT)**. Because the bits that make up a file may be stored all around your hard disk and not in a contiguous group, this table provides an index of data locations the OS can reference, helping to speed up the time it takes to open a file.

The OS also provides the commands you use for naming, organizing, and maintaining files, such as Rename, Delete, Move, and Copy.

You can create and organize your own hierarchy of file folders to store related files in one spot. This hierarchy provides a so-called **path** to the file that starts with the name of the drive where the files are stored. All drives in your computer, including your hard drive, USB drives, CD/DVD drive, and network drives, are designated with drive letters on Windows-based computers.

For example, a word processing file named *Acton Engineering Invoice.docx* might be filed in your Documents folder (Figure 4.8). The file location might have a path of This PC → Documents → Acton Engineering Invoice, where

- *This PC* is the entire contents of your computer and any external storage devices that are attached.
- *Documents* is the documents folder created for your user account name.
- *Acton Engineering Invoice* is the word processing file.

FIGURE 4.8 **Windows File Management**
The path name, shown in File Explorer, identifies the location where you stored a document.

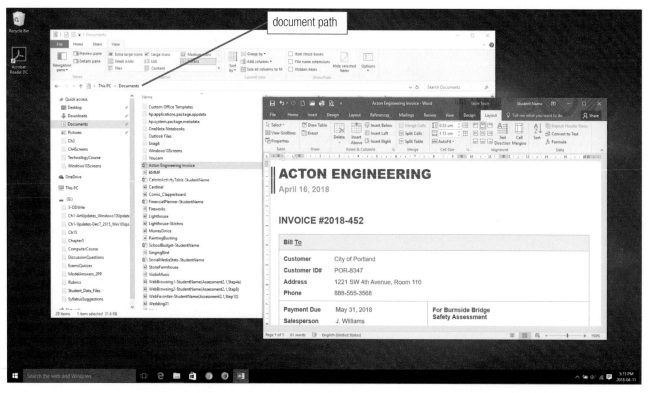

Providing Search and Help Capabilities

All operating systems provide a method of searching your computer for the files you need, and a help system you can use to look for information about how to use your computer.

Search features allow you to enter information about a file, such as the date it was last saved, a word contained in the file name, or the actual contents of the file, and the operating system helps you locate the file. Features such as Finder on a Mac and File Explorer on a Windows computer also help you search through hierarchies of folders and files to find what you need.

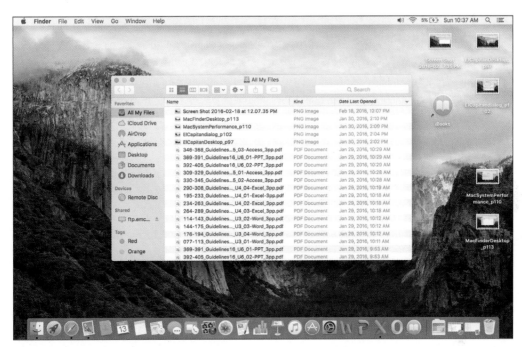

The Mac Finder window helps you locate files in a hierarchy of folders.

Windows 10 provides help in the new Get Started app and access to online help and support using a browser as shown here.

Help features provide searchable support information and troubleshooting tools for the operating system, some of which are located on your computer and some of which you can access online. Windows even provides a remote assistance feature that allows another person to take control of your computer to pinpoint your problem and fix it for you.

Computers in Your Career

Computer support specialists may work in a small, local computer repair store, a larger national chain store, or an expansive technical support call center for a large software or hardware corporation. To become a computer support specialist, you must have a solid grounding in a computer-related field (at least an associate's degree or certification in a topic such as servers or databases) and be able to communicate well and deal with the public. Because many computer problems require troubleshooting within the OS, being comfortable with operating system settings, configurations, and utilities will help you succeed in your work.

Maintaining the Computer with Operating System Utilities

System maintenance is an important task for system software. This process is similar to taking your car into the shop on a regular basis for tune-ups to keep it running efficiently. There are several utility programs included in your operating system package that you can use to perform system maintenance tasks, scan drives and files for problems, and otherwise help protect your system and troubleshoot problems. Typical utility program functions include those listed in Table 4.2.

Sending the Computer to Sleep or Shutting It Off

The operating system is in charge of shutting down your computer. The way you shut down your computer is important, because following the proper procedure prevents the loss of unsaved data and properly saves system settings. In addition to shutting down your computer, you can use features with names such as Sleep or Hibernate to save computer power but still be able to return to your desktop and any running programs quickly, without having to reboot.

Playing It Safe

If you use a remote assistance feature in an operating system be sure that you trust the person to whom you are giving access, and that you remove access privileges after a short period of time to prevent unwanted access to your files.

Optimizing the power options for your computer or mobile device is an important strategy for green computing. Laptops and mobile devices are preset to enter a power saving state after a period of inactivity. You can shorten or lengthen the time before a power saving mode kicks in. If you're not going to use the computer for a while, the Shut Down option ensures power consumption will be zero. Conserving power on your computing devices will not only save you money on your electricity bill but will also contribute to a greener environment.

TABLE 4.2 Utility Program Features

Function	Windows Feature Name	Mac Feature Name
Backing up or restoring damaged files	File History (Windows 8.1 or Windows 10); Backup and Restore (Windows 7)	Time Machine
Performing automatic updates to get updated drivers or definitions	Windows Update	Software Update
Cleaning up your hard drive to get rid of temporary files or files you haven't used for a long time	Disk Cleanup	Repair Disk
Defragmenting your hard drive so that scattered bits of files are reorganized for efficiency in retrieving data	Optimize Drives (Windows 8.1 or Windows 10); Disk Defragmenter (Windows 7)	
Restoring your system to an earlier date to remove new settings that may have caused problems	System Restore	Time Machine
Scheduling regular maintenance tasks such as backing up and downloading updates	Task Scheduler	Time Machine
Uninstalling unwanted programs	Uninstall or Change a Program	Uninstaller
Providing security features such as a firewall or spyware protection	Windows Firewall and Windows Defender	Security

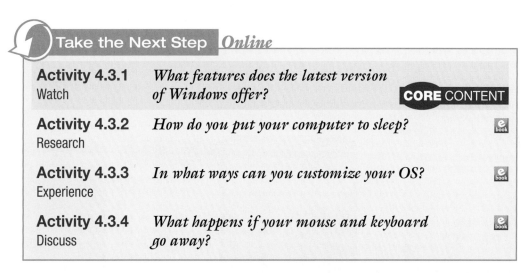

Take the Next Step *Online*

Activity 4.3.1 Watch	*What features does the latest version of Windows offer?*	**CORE** CONTENT
Activity 4.3.2 Research	*How do you put your computer to sleep?*	e book
Activity 4.3.3 Experience	*In what ways can you customize your OS?*	e book
Activity 4.3.4 Discuss	*What happens if your mouse and keyboard go away?*	e book

PRECHECK

4.4 Going on the Road with Mobile Operating Systems

A **mobile operating system** (also known as a mobile OS or mobile platform) is the brains behind mobile **smartphones** such as the Samsung Galaxy, HTC One, Sony Xperia, and iPhone. These devices contain a rich feature set that essentially makes them into small computers.

What Makes a Mobile OS Different?

A mobile OS, which is stored in ROM, is not nearly as robust as a personal computer operating system, because a phone simply doesn't have a great deal of memory and most users don't need as much functionality from their phones as they do from their personal computers.

A mobile OS also uses and accesses smaller resources so it can run quickly and efficiently, with an emphasis on conserving battery life. The OS also manages touchscreen functionality and wireless broadband connections.

A Wealth of Mobile OS Choices

Stroll through an electronics store and you'll notice dozens of mobile phone models, including smartphones that include an operating system. Different phone manufacturers adopt different operating systems for their various smartphones. Each mobile operating system also has an online store where users can download applications (called *apps*) for their mobile phones.

Smartphones come with several popular apps already installed. However, people love downloading new apps as they discover various ways to use their smartphones. Applications that users download to their phones typically only work with that phone's OS. If you buy a new phone with a different operating system, you need to buy new apps.

According to Strategy Analytics, the leading mobile operating system is Android with over 80 percent of the North American market. Next in line is Apple's iOS, which powers the popular iPhone and iPad devices. Windows Phone has been gaining traction and experienced a surge in 2013 when Nokia, a popular handset manufacturer, adopted Windows Phone for its devices. The remainder of the mobile OS market is split between BlackBerry OS and others. The market for mobile devices changes rapidly and varies by geographic location. What is popular today may be outdated a year from now. Table 4.3 lists today's most common mobile operating systems.

A wealth of mobile operating systems run on phones from different phone manufacturers.

TABLE 4.3 **Common Mobile Operating Systems in Order by Market Share**

OS	Description
Android	An open source, cross-platform OS supported by Google used by many manufacturers; even Blackberry adopted Android in 2016
iOS	Apple-developed iPhone and iPad OS based on Mac OS X
Windows 10 Mobile	Microsoft's mobile OS based on Windows 10
Ubuntu Touch	An open source OS based on Linux

With so many different mobile operating systems, the variety of options and incompatibilities between them can prove confusing and inconvenient for consumers to manage and difficult for wireless companies to support.

The widespread use of mobile devices such as tablets has resulted in employees bringing their own devices into the workplace and connecting the devices to company networks. This is referred to as **BYOD (bring your own device)** and is also used to refer to an employee connecting his or her personally owned smartphone or laptop to the company network.

> 66 [BYOD is] one of the single most important steps in motivating business productivity. 99
>
> —Adriana Karaboutis, CIO, Dell

 Spotlight on the Future *Online*

Control through Voice and Gesture

The operating systems that we use to control our devices in the future are likely to be very different, according to a recent survey from the Pew Research Center.

"It will become less deliberate, less typing on keyboards and moving a mouse around with your hand, and even punching and swiping at a screen, and more built around voice and gesture," says Lee Rainie, director of the project.

Even further out in the future, there are predictions of new, very advanced interfaces in which we might have a direct brain-to-computer connection, where anticipatory algorithms know what we're thinking.

It's hard to know what implications this will have, although the experts generally think these advances "are going to give us a lot easier time navigating the world," Rainey says.

Talk about It

1. Compare the operating systems we use today with some changes we may see in them in the future.

2. What are some of the improvements that could come with systems built around voice and gesture?

3. In the more distant future, what do some visionaries think we could see in terms of direct brain interfaces?

4. Discuss the atmosphere at the time the Internet was first developed, in terms of a small group of people who all knew one another, to the worldwide connections of today and the future.

5. What is meant by "iteration" of a system or application and how can that help or hinder those who use it?

Computers in Your Career

Web designers that specialize in responsive web design are in demand. When people started browsing the web from their tablets and smartphones, web designers' initial strategy was to create a mobile version of each website with content adjusted to minimize the need to expand the display or pan from side to side. Eventually, web designers realized a responsive design, which adjusts the website layout based on the device's screen size, was a better solution. In this approach, a web developer creates code that allows a website to query each device's screen size and then adjust the web content accordingly. For example, on a restaurant site, menus are just as readable on a 4-inch smartphone screen as they are on a 27-inch desktop monitor. Successful responsive web designers have knowledge and experience in the latest versions of JavaScript, HTML, and CSS, as well as media queries.

Computers in Your Career

When new versions of an operating system or application appears and companies upgrade, there are a few key jobs to be handled. If you provide network support in a corporation, you will help to *roll out* new versions of software to all necessary employees by installing and customizing the software. If you are a trainer, you may be called upon to provide instruction in the new software features. Other IT (information technology) workers may run a help desk, answering technical questions and troubleshooting problems that come up in the first few weeks or months of use.

Take the Next Step *Online*

Activity 4.4.1 *What is 4G?*
Watch

CORE CONTENT

Activity 4.4.2 *What's the best deal for a 4G smartphone?*
TEAM Present

Review and Assessment *Online*

An interactive Summing Up with audio, a Study Notes document, slide presentations with audio, and Terms to Know flashcards with audio are available from the links menu on this page in your ebook.

Summing Up

What Controls Your Computer?

System software contains an **operating system (OS)**, which you use to interact with hardware and software, and **utility software** to maintain your computer and its performance. An operating system package—for example, Windows 10—contains the operating system plus certain utilities.

Starting your computer, called **booting**, is carried out by instructions located on a chip on your computer's motherboard. If you start by turning the power on, you're performing a **cold boot**. If you restart the computer (shut it down and then turn it on again without turning the power off), that's called a **warm boot**.

Early computer manufacturers used their own operating systems. Microsoft's first OS, MS-DOS, which eventually became known simply as **DOS**, was a **command-line interface**, meaning that you typed in text commands.

A huge breakthrough in operating systems happened in the 1980s when the **graphical user interface (GUI)** was introduced by Apple.

Perusing the Popular Operating System Packages

The major operating systems used by individual consumers today are **Microsoft Windows** for PCs; **Mac OS X** for Apple computers; and various versions of **Linux**, an **open source** operating system. **UNIX** is an OS used by larger organizations to run their networks. Other operating systems such as Google's **Chrome OS**, **Android**, and **iOS** allow for computing on smaller devices such as netbooks, tablets, and smartphones, and enable the user to buy apps, either online through a browser or by downloading to the device.

The term **platform** identifies the architecture of a computer and the OS intended to run on it. **Platform dependency** is becoming less and less important as consumers demand cross-functionality when they buy computers and software.

The Tasks of the Operating System Package

Operating system packages have certain basic functions in common:
- Providing a **user interface**, including a **desktop**.
- Configuring hardware using device **drivers**.
- Controlling input and output devices.
- Determining the speed at which the computer functions (its **performance**), which involves the processor, available cache, bus, and memory.
- Providing information about system resources to enable the user to troubleshoot performance, adjust settings, change which programs the OS loads upon startup, and so on.
- Routing data between applications and devices—for example, when you send a document to a printer or scan an image from hard copy using a scanner.
- Managing folder and file systems to store and retrieve information.

- Providing search capabilities for locating files and a help system for information about how to use your computer.
- Performing system maintenance tasks through utility software included in your operating system package.

Going on the Road with Mobile Operating Systems

Mobile operating systems are used to power **smartphones** (phones with a rich feature set that emulate some of the power of computers) and tablets. A mobile OS is stored in ROM and uses smaller resources to make sure that it runs quickly and efficiently.

Terms to Know

What Controls Your Computer?

Perusing the Popular Operating System Packages

The Tasks of the Operating System Package

Going on the Road with Mobile Operating Systems

Concepts Check

Concepts Check 4.1   Multiple Choice
Take this quiz to test your understanding of key concepts in this chapter.

Concepts Check 4.2   Matching
Test your understanding of terms and concepts presented in this chapter.

Concepts Check 4.3   Label It
Use the interactive tool to identify the standard components found in a Windows 10 This PC window.

Concepts Check 4.4   Label It
Use the interactive tool to identify the standard components found in a Mac OS X desktop.

Concepts Check 4.5   Arrange It
Use the interactive tool to order the steps in the booting process.

Projects

Check with your instructor for the preferred method to submit completed work.

Project 4.1   To Upgrade or Not to Upgrade

Project 4.1.1
You work as an intern at a small restaurant consulting business. The owner employs five restaurant consultants who each have a laptop. While in the office, each consultant connects to a wireless network for printing and accessing the Internet. The company laptops all use the Windows 8.1 operating system. The consultants primarily use their computers for the following tasks:

- Track time and expenses
- Prepare new menu proposals for clients
- Cost food inputs for menu recipes
- Design new restaurant layouts using a CAD/CAM program

The owner is considering an upgrade from Windows 8.1 to Windows 10. To help the owner make the best decision for her business, research and compare the features of Windows 8.1 and Windows 10. Before you begin your investigation, prepare a list of questions you would ask or facts you would gather to analyze whether the owner should upgrade or not. Next to each question or fact, explain why you need to investigate the item. Based on your research, prepare a brief summary of the main points that the owner would be interested in knowing about Windows 10. Be sure to include a list of references for your information.

Project 4.1.2 `TEAM`

The owner of the restaurant consulting business has agreed to listen to a ten-minute sales presentation on converting her business PCs to Macs. As a team, prepare a slide presentation that highlights the features and functions of Macs and their applications to the needs of the business owner. In addition to presenting your arguments, your slide presentation should address usability, reliability, compatibility, and cost issues.

Project 4.2　Mobile Mania

Project 4.2.1

Your school's alumni committee has assigned you the task of purchasing a smartphone complete with a one-year service contract that includes unlimited talk, text, and data to be given as a door prize at the alumni dinner. You have narrowed down the choices to the latest offerings of the Samsung Galaxy and Apple iPhone. Research these smartphones on the Internet, and prepare a table listing the pros and cons of each phone. Aside from the benefits and drawbacks, consider the costs associated with purchasing the phone along with the one-year contract. After a careful review of all factors, write a summary of your research including your recommendation for the door prize.

Project 4.2.2 `TEAM`

The manager of the school's alumni office has asked your team to prepare a list of items that will be given to a mobile app programming team to create a new app for the school's alumni office. The free app will be available for download on Android, Apple, and Windows Phone smartphones. To help you get started, the manager has already said she wants alumni to be able to access news and upcoming alumni event information. Research your school's alumni association to see what activities and/or benefits the association offers alumni. If possible, interview a few alumni to find out what they would want in a mobile app. Brainstorm with your team the types of activities that a user would want the new app to provide. Prepare a brief presentation for the alumni office manager with your team's recommendation for the mobile app programming team.

Project 4.3　Housekeeping 101

Project 4.3.1

Using utility programs to perform system maintenance tasks is important to the efficient operation of a computer, yet many people neglect these tasks. For example, we have all experienced or know of someone who has lost a file on his computer. If all of us maintained daily backups, losing data from a computer malfunction or user error would not be a problem because we could simply restore the data from our backup copy.

Consider five maintenance tasks that every computer user should perform on a regular basis to avoid data loss and keep his or her computer running efficiently. Create a survey checklist with your five maintenance tasks. Next, choose a representative sampling of ten friends and/or relatives who use the computer for a variety of functions. Provide them with a copy of your checklist and ask each person to check off the tasks he or she performs routinely. Prepare a spreadsheet that displays the survey data results identifying the tasks that are and are not routinely performed. Write a summary with anecdotal information about data losses from your survey participants as they filled out your checklist. In your summary, write your conclusion as to the importance of computer maintenance among your survey participants. Provide an explanation as to whether the survey is or is not reasonably representative of the general population of computer users.

Project 4.3.2 `TEAM`

Read the article at http://ODW4.emcp.net/ComputerChecklist for a list of 29 tasks a technical support technician performs to keep a computer running smoothly. (As you are reading, keep in mind that this list is geared toward computer maintenance in a corporate setting by a dedicated IT staff.) Then, within your team, discuss the tasks on this list that would be useful for home computer users, and select the 10 most important tasks. As a group, design a Top 10 Maintenance Task Checklist that could be printed and distributed to home computer users. For each task on the checklist, note the frequency with which the task should be performed—for example, weekly, monthly, or annually. Also, be sure to include a tip for each task that provides users with the location of the system tools needed within the operating system software.

Project 4.4   Accessibility Options

Project 4.4.1

You work as a volunteer with senior citizens at a local community center. These individuals have asked for your assistance with customizing their settings to make their computers more user-friendly. Specifically, the seniors have mentioned difficulties with reading small type, seeing the mouse pointer, and hearing system sounds during certain activities. Research and experiment with various Windows Ease of Access options. Experiment with various settings until you find a group of Ease of Access options that you think will address the seniors' needs. Prepare a handout with instructions on how to set up the Ease of Access options you have decided to recommend. Include screenshots where appropriate.

Project 4.4.2 `TEAM`

Many senior citizens at the community center have arthritis, making it difficult for them to type on a computer. To help them with this task, you would like to set up speech recognition on their computers. Research the speech recognition technology that is included with the operating system. Determine the key features of the program and whether any special hardware is needed for the program to work. Also, find out if the speech recognition feature has support for Spanish, the first language of several of the senior citizens. Prepare a presentation that summarizes the results of your research and evaluates the adequacy of the program for the needs of these individuals.

Project 4.5   Wiki—File Management Tips and Tricks

Project 4.5.1   TEAM

You or your team will be assigned to address one or more of the file management questions listed below:

- What is the distinction between a file and a folder? How is each one visually represented?
- What are the default folders provided with the operating system?
- What is a file extension? Should file extensions be displayed?
- How do I browse the folders on my computer or other storage device?
- How can I search for a file?
- How do I perform common file management tasks?
- What can I do with deleted files that have been sent to the Recycle Bin (Windows) or Trash (Mac)?
- What are the pros and cons of using cloud storage (such as OneDrive for all my data?

Prepare a post to the course wiki site for your assigned topic. Write the post as if it were going to be used as a help document for people unfamiliar with file management.

Project 4.5.2   TEAM

You or your team will be assigned to edit and verify the content posted on the wiki site from Project 4.5.1. If you add or edit any content, make sure you include a notation within the page that includes your name or team members' names and the date you edited the content—for example, "Edited by [student name or team members' names] on [date]." Keep a list of references that you used to verify your content changes. When you are finished with your verification, include a notation at the end of the entry—for example, "Verified by [student name or team members' names] on [date]."

Project 4.6   Wiki—Troubleshooting Tips

Project 4.6.1   TEAM

You or your team will be assigned to one or more of the following topics related to troubleshooting computer problems:

- Help! My printer is not working.
- Help! My Internet is not working.
- Help! My file will not open.
- Help! My computer keeps freezing up.
- Help! I need to create a PDF of my document and I don't know how.
- Help! No sound is coming out of the speakers.
- Help! I don't know how to attach a file to an email message.
- Help! I don't know how to share pictures between my smartphone and my computer.

Prepare a post to the course wiki site for your assigned topic. The goal is to provide the average computer user with simple, precise instructions to follow to resolve the problem or answer the question without calling in an expert. When writing your instructions, use clear, concise language and avoid technical jargon that might confuse your audience.

Project 4.6.2 `TEAM`

You or your team will be assigned to edit and verify the content posted on the wiki site from Project 4.6.1. If you add or edit any content, make sure you include a notation within the page that includes your name or team members' names and the date you edited the content—for example, "Edited by [student name or team members' names] on [date]." Keep a list of references that you used to verify your content changes. When you are finished with your verification, include a notation at the end of the entry—for example, "Verified by [student name or team members' names] on [date]."

Class Conversations

Topic 4.1   Are the latest Windows or Mac OS X editions worth the time, effort, and cost to upgrade?

Windows and Mac OS X have been around for several years and have been used successfully by millions of people who are satisfied with the products they have. In the past operating systems such as Windows were updated every few years with small updates delivered through service packs a few times during that interval. Today, however, Microsoft is following Apple's lead by producing a major upgrade every year or so with small updates delivered regularly over the Internet. Sometimes upgrading to a newer OS may involve a lot of time and effort to install the operating system and learn how to use it. The upgrade may also involve a fee for the new software. Some versions involve major design changes such as upgrading from Windows 8.1 to Windows 10. Other upgrades involve a shorter learning curve such as mastering the changes from Windows 8 to Windows 8.1. Are upgrades to operating systems really worth the time, effort, and cost? How do you feel about software companies automatically updating your system to add new features or apps every few weeks or months with little or no fanfare?

Topic 4.2   What more should a smartphone do?

With 4G smartphones and tablets becoming more commonplace, many consumers are becoming used to pulling out their smartphones to watch a movie or their favorite television show, video message a friend, or video call a friend or relative across the world using Skype or FaceTime. Thousands of apps are available for smartphones for just about any purpose. What features should the next generation (5G) of smartphones provide that offer functionality that you lack with your current smartphone?

Topic 4.3   How is a file naming standard developed?

A large amount of the time that a user spends interacting with the OS involves file management tasks. Browsing the content of a USB drive, a hard drive, or your cloud storage account, looking for that elusive file that you created last week, the name of which you can no longer remember, is something that has happened to everyone. A file name that seemed clever and memorable last week will no longer be memorable three months down the road. The search ability of an OS has improved with each new release over the years but one can still spend an inordinate amount of time looking for a file. Assume you have been hired by a company to devise a standard file naming system for all employees to use when naming new files. Consider how you would go about developing such a standard. For example, what questions would you need to ask end users before you attempted to develop a set of "rules" to use when assigning new file names so they can be easily retrieved? Consider elements that should be included in file names (such as names or revision dates) for workplaces where employees save different versions of files to shared network folders. How would the file folder hierarchy be developed so that each department has similar folders and subfolders? What challenges do you foresee in developing a file naming standard?

Application Software
The Key to Digital Productivity

What You'll Accomplish

When you finish this chapter, you'll be able to:

5.1 State the role of application software.

5.2 Discuss the role of major categories of application software with examples of products in each category.

5.3 Describe how software is created, obtained, and priced.

5.4 Explain how software products can use content created in other software products.

Why Does It Matter

Your computer exists largely to run application software—the software you use to get things done. In your personal life and on the job you will use software that helps you accomplish tasks, and you will learn how to use new programs to help you complete your work more efficiently. Understanding the different types of software that exist and how they are used will help you take advantage of a wide variety of tools to increase your productivity.

Chapter 5 Application Software: The Key to Digital Productivity

We use application software to get our work done, from writing and calculating to analyzing and presenting information. But we also use application software for fun, to play games, listen to music, view photos, and read books. We can use software on a computer, tablet, or even a mobile phone.

5.1 Software's Role in the World of Computing

System software, specifically the operating systems described in Chapter 4, enables your computer to function and run **application software**. You use application software to make your computer work for you. Application software helps you do many things such as get your work done, learn something new, communicate with others, create art, or play games.

Application software started out providing basic functions. Products such as VisiCalc, the first spreadsheet application for personal computers, were basically glorified calculators. Early word processors, such as WordStar, offered little more than the ability to enter and edit text to create simple documents. When using these products, you had to key command codes to enter or delete text and even to scroll (move up and down the page) through a document.

In the next section, you will discover what major categories of software exist today and how each is used.

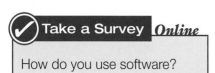

Take a Survey *Online*

How do you use software?

With primitive interfaces and functionality, early software such as VisiCalc (right) and WordStar (below) provided the foundation for today's software applications.

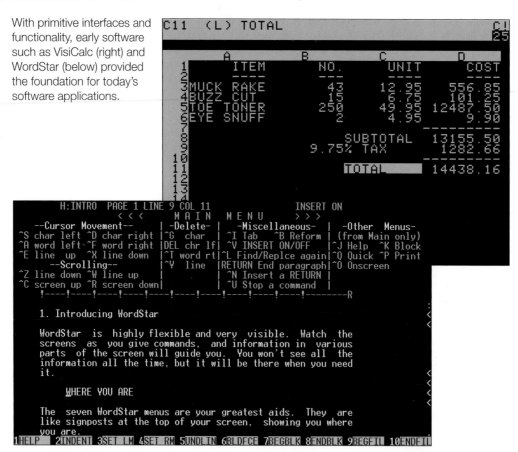

5.2 The Many Types of Application Software

From the early days of consumer software, which consisted mainly of basic business tools and simple games, software application development has exploded for computers and all varieties of mobile devices. A huge number of categories of software applications now exist, each with sophisticated feature sets. Using application software you might:

- Produce business documents such as reports, memos, budgets, charts, presentations, product catalogs, and customer lists.
- Manage massive amounts of data for student, patient, or employment records.
- Complete a learning exercise, a course, or even an entire degree without ever entering a classroom.
- Create works of art, including photos, drawings, animations, videos, and music.
- Organize content such as photos, appointments, contacts, home inventories, and music playlists.
- Manage your personal finances, deposit and withdraw money from a bank, handle your tax reporting, or generate legal documents.
- Play games or pursue hobbies such as sports or interior design.
- Stream music or video for entertainment.
- Communicate with others individually or in large online conferences.
- Perform maintenance or security tasks that help keep your computer functioning and your data secure.

In fact, software is so much a part of our lives that it's difficult to categorize modern application software products by work or personal use. For instance, word processors aren't just used for business and design software isn't just used by artists. Financial software is used for creating department budgets and invoices as well as to track personal finances.

In this section we have categorized software applications by what they help you do. As you read through the following sections, consider how many categories of software you use.

Productivity Software

Productivity software includes software that people typically use to get work done, such as a word processor (working with words), spreadsheet (working with data, numbers, calculations, and charting), database (organizing and retrieving data records), or presentation program (creating slideshows with text and graphics). Software suites such as Microsoft Office, OpenOffice, and Apple iWork combine productivity applications into one product, because many people use two or more of these programs to get their work done. Software suites often include a word processor, a spreadsheet application, presentation software, and database management software. Suites also allow users to easily integrate content from one program into another, such as including a spreadsheet in a report created with a word processor. Productivity software and suites are also available for many smartphones and other mobile devices so you can be productive from anywhere. Productivity suites available in the cloud—notably Office 365 and Google Docs—and the ability to store data files in the cloud enable you to work wherever you have Internet connectivity.

Word Processor Software **Word processor software** certainly does "process" words, but today it does a great deal more. With a word processor such as Microsoft Word, Pages for Mac, and Writer from OpenOffice, you can create documents that include sophisticated formatting: for example, you can change text fonts (styles applied to text); apply effects such as bold, italics, and underlining; add shadows, background colors, and other design treatments to text and objects; and include tables, photos, drawings, and links to online content. You can also use templates (pre-designed documents with formatting and graphics already in place for you to fill in) to design web pages, newsletters, and more. A mail merge feature makes it easy to take a list of names and addresses and print personalized letters, envelopes, and labels. Figure 5.1 shows some of the word processing features and tools Microsoft Word offers.

Spreadsheet Software With **spreadsheet software**, such as Microsoft Excel, numbers rule. Using spreadsheet software, you can perform calculations that range from simple (adding, averaging, and multiplying) to complex (estimating standard deviations based on a range of numbers). In addition, spreadsheet software offers sophisticated charting capabilities. Formatting tools help you create polished looking documents such as budgets, invoices, schedules, attendance records, and purchase orders. With spreadsheet software such as Microsoft Excel, Numbers for Mac, and Calc (part of OpenOffice), you can also keep track of data such as your holiday card list and sort that list or search for specific names or other data. Figure 5.2 shows a typical spreadsheet using several key features.

FIGURE 5.1 **A Word Document**
Sophisticated word-processing tools allow you to create attractive documents.

FIGURE 5.2 **An Excel Worksheet**

This worksheet in an Excel workbook tallies expenses automatically with formulas and includes an embedded chart to present the information visually for the reader.

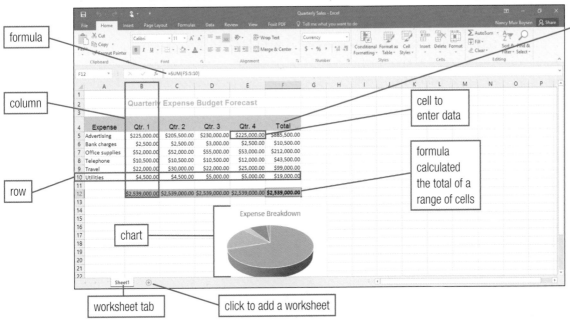

formula

column

row

formatting applied to cells and text

cell to enter data

formula calculated the total of a range of cells

chart

worksheet tab

click to add a worksheet

 Computers in Your Career

Spreadsheet software isn't just used by accountants. Managers use spreadsheets to compile and track department and project budgets. Statisticians and people working in marketing use the charting features of spreadsheets to map trends and summarize survey findings. Salespeople may use a spreadsheet to keep track of sales by customer or region. An administrative assistant in a small company may use the data functions to manage customer lists. The calculation, data manipulation, analysis, and charting features of spreadsheet software can be useful in many, many occupations.

Database Software **Database software**, such as Microsoft Access and Base (OpenOffice), can manage large quantities of data. The software provides functions for organizing the data into related lists and retrieving useful information from these lists. For example, imagine that you are a salesperson who wants to create a list of customers. Of course you want to include fields to store the name, address, and company name for each person. However, you might also want each customer record to include the customer's birthday, his or her spouse's name, and his or her favorite hobby as well as a record of purchases in the past year. You can also set up fields to look up data in tables in the database. For example, you can use the zip code field to look up the name of a city that is stored in a different table. Using look-up fields saves time by eliminating the need to enter a city name over and over. Reducing redundant data also helps improve the accuracy of the database. Once that data is entered into a table you can view information in a tabular list or as individual customer record forms. You can create queries that let you find specific data sets. For example, say you want to find every customer with a birthday in June who is interested in sports and has purchased at least $2,000 of products in the last year so you can invite them to a company-sponsored sports event. With a database, you can generate a list of those records quickly. Figure 5.3 shows some of the features of Microsoft Access.

Presentation Software **Presentation software**, such as Microsoft PowerPoint, KeyNote for Mac, or Impress from OpenOffice, uses the concept of individual slides that collectively form a slideshow. Slides may contain bulleted lists of key concepts, graphics, tables, animations, hyperlinks to web pages, and diagrams and charts. A slideshow can provide visual support for a presenter's comments during a talk, run continuously on its own (at a trade show booth, for example), or be browsed by an individual. Presentation software, including some newer programs or online services such as Prezi and PointDrive, helps users create attractive slides by allowing them to use templates containing background art and placeholders for objects such as titles and bulleted text. Presentation programs also make it easy to

FIGURE 5.3 **A Microsoft Access Database**
Access offers several useful tools for managing data.

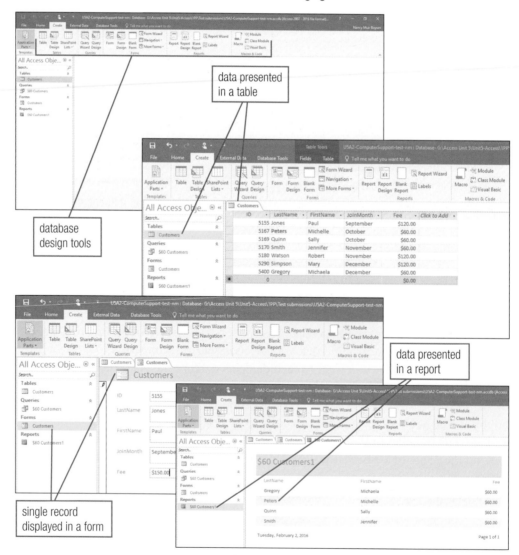

add graphics to slides. Figure 5.4 shows a presentation slide created in Microsoft PowerPoint and Figure 5.5 shows a different slide created in KeyNote, which is designed for the Mac operating system.

FIGURE 5.4 **A Microsoft PowerPoint Presentation**

Several available views in PowerPoint help you see your presentation as individual slides, an outline of the content, as speaker's notes, or as a set of slides you can easily reorganize.

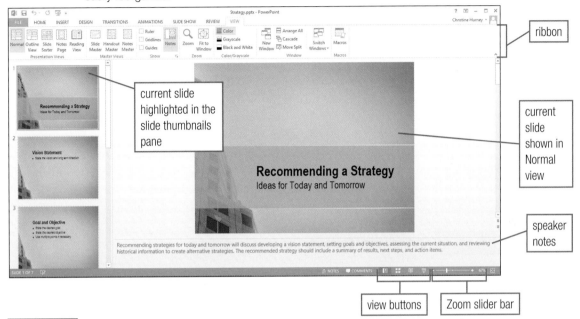

FIGURE 5.5 **A KeyNote Presentation**

Presentation software offers templates to provide design elements for a polished look.

Software to Keep Us Organized

Several software products help you organize your life by keeping track of the people you deal with and your personal and work schedules.

You can use **calendar software** to schedule appointments or events and set up reminders. The web-based Google Calendar, for example, lets you schedule events, invite others to your appointments, and share your calendar with others. **Contact management software** helps you store and manage information about the people you work or otherwise interact with. You might keep track of information for clients, family members, or people in your book club, for example. Microsoft's Outlook.com is an online program that includes email, calendar, contact management, and storage features in one place. These applications share data; for example, sharing of data allows you to easily address your email message. The Calendar and People features of Outlook are shown in Figure 5.6. Windows and the operating systems for most mobile devices include application software that has an address book function for storing contact phone numbers, email addresses, and the like.

Data sharing also allows you to share calendar event and contact information with your other computers and mobile devices. For example, when you leave the office for the day, you may want to make sure that all your appointments for the next day have been copied from your PC calendar to your smartphone calendar, so you'll have

FIGURE 5.6 **Outlook.com Calendar and People Features**
Use Calendar to schedule, edit, and view events and use People to manage contacts.

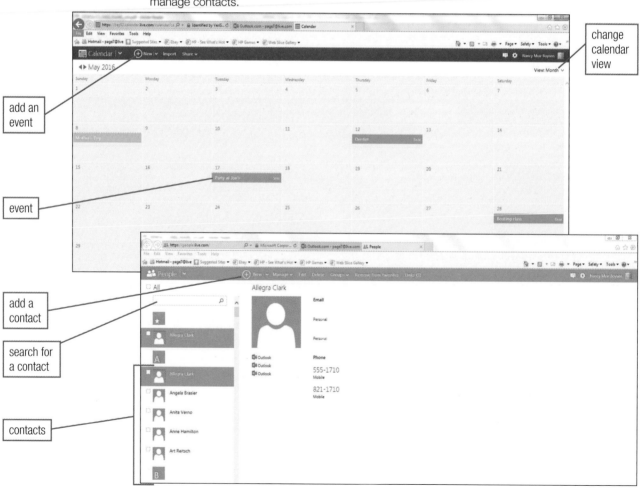

your schedule with you. You sync (synchronize) devices to make sure that data on one device is updated based on changes made to the data on another device.

Microsoft Windows is working to keep your calendar and contact manager software connected. Computers running Windows 10 include three apps called *Mail*, *People*, and *Calendar*, which work together and with Outlook online. The People app for Windows 10 includes an address book and provides access to social apps. You can use it to add and edit contacts, view posts on Facebook and Twitter, and communicate digitally using Skype. The People, Mail, and Calendar apps in Windows share data, so if you add a contact in one app, that contact will be available in the other two apps as well.

Still other applications and services, such as salesforce.com or ACT!, expand on contact management and function. These suites of programs are known as **customer relationship management (CRM) software**. CRM suites contain software and online services that are used to store and organize client and sales prospect information, as well as automating and synchronizing other customer-facing business functions such as marketing, customer service, and technical support. This type of software can be useful for those who have to keep track of many customers or a lengthy sales or product implementation process.

Graphics, Multimedia, and Web Pages

If you like to work with drawings, photos, or other kinds of images, you may have used **graphics software**, which is software that allows you to create, edit, or manipulate images. Though most types of productivity software, such as word processors and presentation software, include several graphics features, design professionals work with products that are much more feature-rich. These products include:

- **Desktop publishing (DTP) software**, which is used by design professionals to lay out pages for books, magazines, brochures, product packaging, and other print materials. Adobe InDesign, CorelDraw, and QuarkXPress are three of the most popular DTP products. These software applications allow a great deal of precision and control over the placement of objects and text on a page by using grids and columns, a large variety of fonts and text formatting tools, and the ability to insert, rearrange, and modify images.
- **Photo editing software**, which is used by design professionals to enhance photo quality or apply special effects such as blurring elements or feathering the edges of a photo. Photo editing software such as Adobe Photoshop and GIMP can also be used to edit content out of a picture or combine photo content into a more comprehensive composition.
- **Screen capture software** is useful for those writing software documentation or books about software, programming, or other technology. You can use this software to capture all or a portion of the contents of the computer screen. You can then use the resulting image to demonstrate how to use a particular software feature. Recent Windows versions include a basic screen capture application called

Design professionals can choose from a variety of sophisticated software products.

Snipping Tool. However, if you need more advanced capabilities, such as the ability to change the image resolution or add annotations or other edits to screen capture images, then an inexpensive third-party program such as Snagit or HyperSnap-DX might be a better choice.

 Computers in Your Career

Even if you don't intend to become a professional designer, you are still likely to use design software in your personal or work life. Simpler desktop publishing software, such as Microsoft Publisher, is useful for designing flyers to advertise a yard or garage sale, find a lost pet, or create a home business brochure or business card. Windows Live Movie Maker is an entry-level video editing software program that is simple to learn and might be useful in creating a video promoting your company's newest product on YouTube, for example. Many jobs, including teaching and sales, require that you give presentations and you can enhance the presentations by adding animations or music. No matter what your career path, consider exploring graphics and multimedia products to keep your work creative and current.

Still images aren't the only medium you can work with from your computer. **Multimedia software** enables you to work with media such as animations, audio, and video. The following are a few popular categories of multimedia software:

- **Animation software** enables you to animate objects and create interactive content (content the viewer can manipulate and control) that is sometimes combined with music or narration. Animations are like sophisticated cartoons that can be used in presentations and on the web to educate, advertise, or entertain. Popular animation software includes Anime Studio for 2-D animation and Autodesk Maya for 3-D animation.
- **Audio software** such as Audacity or Sony Creative helps you work with music files and record and edit audio to create a **podcast** (an audio presentation that can be posted online) or other types of audio files to be shared with others.
- **Video editing software** such as Adobe Premiere Elements, Pinnacle Studio, and Movie Maker are entry-level programs used to create and edit videos. Videos might include an audio track with voice or music, or a variety of special effects. Another product, Camtasia Studio, can record video of activity on your computer screen, which is useful for creating training videos for users. Professional level video editing programs can cost more than $1,000 and take significant time and training to master.

Another popular type of application software for personal and business use is **web authoring software**. Programs such as RapidWeaver for Mac developers and Adobe Dreamweaver provide advanced tools for creating web pages. Some of these products require knowledge of HTML (hypertext markup language) and advanced scripting technologies; others allow you to use a word processor–like interface to create text and add links, animations, and graphics to web pages. The current generation of web authoring programs are designed to adhere to or follow current standards for implementing HTML. These standards, established by the World Wide Web Consortium (W3C), define how to create pages that will display correctly in most web browsers. Rather than forcing you to work in code, most web authoring tools offer a **WYSIWYG (what you see is what you get)** interface. WYSIWYG (pronounced wiz-e-wig) simply means that the way the contents look as you are designing the web page in the software is the way they will look in a browser.

Major multimedia program suites often include a web authoring program. For example, Adobe's Creative Cloud, depending on which version you use, can include more than ten programs for working in print, interactive, audio, video, and web media.

Entertainment and Personal Use

Software isn't limited to the workplace. Huge industries are built around entertainment, gaming, and personal use software products.

Entertainment software is a category of software that includes games you play on your computer or game console. According to the Entertainment Software Association's 2015 Essential Facts about the Computer and Video Game Industry, more than 150 million Americans play computer and video games. The average age of gamers is 35 years and 42 percent play at least 3 hours per week. Sixty-two percent of gamers play games with others. But gaming software isn't just for fun; it's also used in educational settings, to improve physical fitness (as with Nintendo's Wii Fit), and to communicate about social causes (as with Food Force from the United Nations World Food Programme).

Hobby-related software covers almost any kind of interest, including genealogy, scrapbooking, sports, home design, and gardening. In some cases, what is a hobby to one person is a job to another, so you may end up using one or more of these products in your work.

If you want to organize your legal affairs or finances, many software products can help you. You can use specialized software to create your own legal documents such as wills, living trusts, or real estate leases. You can use tax software such as TurboTax to help you prepare your taxes. Personal financial packages such as Quicken allow you to track checking account activity, create and print checks, download checking account statements from your bank's website, reconcile your balance, and export information to tax software. In addition, you can track credit card accounts and investments.

Products such as TurboTax help individuals and small businesses prepare yearly tax returns.

🔒 Playing It Safe

If you download software such as games or media players, be sure you get them from a trusted source. If the source is questionable, you could be downloading viruses or spyware along with your game. Use antivirus and antispyware software such as McAfee or Norton, or a free product such as Windows Defender (built into Windows 10), AVG Antivirus Free or Avast Free Antivirus. Run updates and scans often.

You can help to address a major crisis and feed millions of hungry people with Food Force from the United Nations World Food Programme.

Software Gets Professional

Some types of application software address specific business needs, such as bookkeeping, project management, or the processes used in industries such as hotel management or banking.

Financial Applications

Financial software used by accounting professionals includes programs such as QuickBooks and Sage 50 Accounting. These accounting applications offer business-oriented features such as payroll, general ledger (the main accounting method for a business), invoicing, and reporting.

Business Processes

Some software applications used in business address specific processes that are useful in a variety of industries. The following list describes a few such products:

- Project management software such as Microsoft Project or the open source program OpenProj is used in many settings, from construction to space flight, to plan the timing of tasks, resources, and costs. With sophisticated tools and algorithms to calculate schedules and costs, project management software can help track the many factors that can cause delays or cost overruns. Project management software can help a business save thousands of dollars, especially when it comes to large projects that can take years to complete.

QuickBooks is an example of financial software used by accounting professionals. Financial software is used to keep track of information about a company's customers and the transactions that take place with those customers.

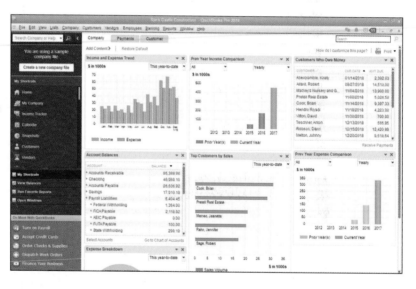

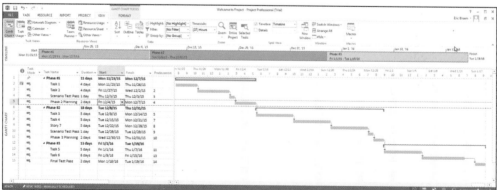

Microsoft Project is used in various industries to plan, track, and report on projects.

- CAD/CAM stands for computer-aided design/computer-aided manufacturing. This category of software is used to create complex engineering drawings and geometric models and to provide specifications for the manufacture of products. CAD/CAM software is used extensively in industries such as automotive manufacturing, bridge and factory construction, and architecture. An example of CAD/CAM software is AutoCAD from AutoDesk.

- Purchasing software is used by people in any industry where a sophisticated purchasing process must be managed. That process begins when a purchasing agent seeks quotes for a particular item, generates a purchase order, tracks that the item has been received, and submits an invoice to accounting for payment. Purchasing software is also used to track inventory and place new orders so a company's supply of a vital part or material never runs out.

- Document management software and systems enable a business to better store and manage critical business information including electronic or scanned documents such as contracts, images, email messages, and other forms of data. These systems not only replace bulky physical storage such as filing cabinets, but also enable people to search for and retrieve documents without regard to physical or geographic location. Because these systems reduce paper usage, they are also more environmentally friendly than traditional filing systems.

Industry-Specific Software Many industries have specific software needs based on the day-to-day tasks their employees perform. For example, hotels, medical offices, travel businesses, real estate offices, and banks have different functions that require different specialized software packages.

If you ran a large hotel, for example, you would need software such as Guest Tracker, which handles guest registrations, tracks charges such as room service and movies viewed, and generates a final bill. In the medical industry, specialized software handles insurance forms and billing, drug prescriptions for pharmacies, and electronic health record (EHR) management. Real estate professionals use property management software to keep track of rental properties and real estate sales software to analyze property values and track listings.

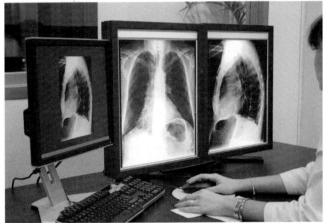

Many industries have their own unique computing needs that industry-specific software can accommodate.

Custom and Enterprise Software Larger companies (often referred to as enterprises) sometimes create their own software to handle the specific processes of their businesses. However, custom software is expensive to create and maintain, so many large companies adopt enterprise software such as SAP ERP, which addresses common business processes but is highly customizable. ERP stands for enterprise resource planning, which is a category of software that deals with standard business processes such as managing customer information (Customer Resource Management or CRM), product inventories (Supply Chain Management or SCM), and employee records and benefits systems (Human Resources Management or HRM).

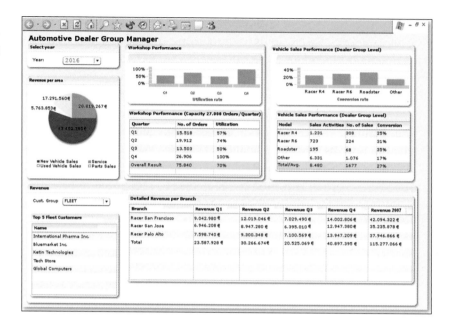

SAP enterprise products help track business activity and generate sophisticated analyses and reports.

Companies such as German-based SAP and US-based Oracle produce software modules that address these common business functions, building in best-practices and standard forms and features. They then work with individual companies to customize those product features to the organization's specific procedures.

In recent years enterprise software companies have broadened their offerings to include small and mid-sized business products, but depending on the degree of customization and training required, implementing an enterprise software product or suite of products at a company can be a very costly proposition. Still, when such products streamline and improve company procedures, the payoff in productivity and profit can be huge.

 Computers in Your Career

Computer forensics is used by law enforcement agencies. In a computer forensics career, you solve mysteries as you find hidden or deleted information on computers that helps law enforcement solve crimes. You might specialize in cryptography, which uses software to decode information hidden in pictures or text. Some computer forensics specialists use utility software to recover deleted files that can be used as evidence in crimes from child pornography rings to embezzlement.

Mobile Applications

Today everybody is mobile, so applications have come to your cell phone or smartphone in a big way. In the past, mobile applications were typically not as full-featured as their non-mobile counterparts because of the limitations of memory and screen size, but today's smartphones and tablets feature much more power and storage than earlier hardware. As a result, more applications are being created for mobile devices, allowing you to perform a variety of activities while on the go. In addition, web designers are taking advantage of new technology standards to design sites that work well on many devices. So-called responsive design allows web pages to sense the device being used and reformat content for optimum display on all screen sizes.

For example, some productivity software is available in simpler versions for use on smartphones, such as Word, Excel, PowerPoint Mobile, and various apps to help us stay organized. Google has an entire suite of applications that includes calendar, mapping, and news/weather software for mobile phones.

Other mobile software options include:

- Games
- Tools such as calculators, currency convertors, and music players
- Mobile banking
- WikiMobile (Wikipedia's mobile app)
- Browsers
- Instant messaging
- GPS navigation applications

In addition, you can access and upload content to sites such as Facebook and YouTube from your phone by installing a mobile application. The list of mobile applications is huge and growing all the time. In 2015, the number of apps in the Apple App Store exceeded 1.5 million. Apps in the Google Play store exceeded 1.35 million in 2014. There were 79 billion downloads from mobile apps stores in 2015 and this number is estimated to more than double to almost 269 billion by 2017.

Take the Next Step *Online*

Activity 5.2.1 Watch	*How can databases make a difference in our lives?*	CORE CONTENT
Activity 5.2.2 Watch	*How can software help you learn?*	CORE CONTENT
Activity 5.2.3 Experience	*Can you identify different types of software applications?*	e book
Activity 5.2.4 Research	*What software will you use in your career?*	e book
Activity 5.2.5 Research	*How do you read?*	e book
Activity 5.2.6 Research	*What makes an effective slideshow presentation?*	e book

5.3 Developing and Delivering Software

The way that software is developed and delivered to you has changed dramatically over the last several years. This is mainly due to the Internet and the ability to download software applications quickly to your computer or use software hosted on the web. Other changes, such as the development of open source and shareware applications, have also had an impact on the cost of software for the consumer.

Developing Software

The **software development life cycle (SDLC)** has evolved over time. This procedure dictates the general flow of creating a new software product. As illustrated in Figure 5.7, the SDLC involves:

- Performing market research to ensure there is a need or demand for the product and then completing a business analysis to match the solution to the need.
- Creating a plan for implementing the software, which involves creating a budget and schedule for the project.
- Building the software, which is the phase where software engineers and programmers create the actual program code.
- Testing the software, which involves having users work with the **alpha version** (the first stage of testing of the software) and then one or more **beta versions** (the second and subsequent stages of testing of a software product). Once all tests are complete and the product seems stable, a final **release to manufacturing (RTM) version** is produced.
- Deploying the software to the public, either by selling the product in a package or online, or by installing it on a company network or workstations if it is a custom software product. Some software is entirely cloud-based, which means that users never install it but instead work with it online.
- Performing maintenance and bug fixes (a **bug** is a problem or malfunction in a program) to keep the product functioning optimally. During this phase, updates to the software may be released to resolve several maintenance or bug fixes at one time. The software release may be applied automatically or be offered as a service release that a user may choose to update or not.

Today, software is often updated several times before a new version is released. These updates happen automatically over the Internet.

> ❝ Software undergoes beta testing shortly before it's released. Beta is Latin for 'still doesn't work.' ❞
>
> —author unknown

 Ethics and Technology Blog *Online*

When Is It OK to Use Trial Software?

I recently needed to use a desktop publishing product to create a flyer for a fundraiser for my music club's trip to England. I was only going to use it once, so I downloaded a trial version, made the flyer, and then deleted the software. Is there anything wrong with that?

FIGURE 5.7 The Software Development Life Cycle (SDLC)

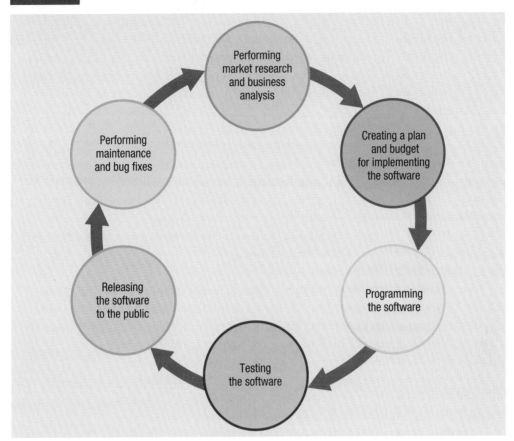

How Software Is Delivered to You

There was a time when software only came in boxes that contained several floppy disks (thin magnetic discs in either flexible or rigid cases) and large, printed manuals. You might have been required to insert almost a dozen floppy disks into your computer to install a large program such as an operating system. Free technical support came with most products to help users install the software and troubleshoot problems when they arose.

Packaged and Downloaded Software Today, software is typically downloaded from a website directly to your PC. **Packaged software** (software sold in boxes) still exists, but the software is often contained on a single DVD. Printed documentation has virtually disappeared. Instead, help files in the product itself or on the manufacturer's website are available, and free technical support has been replaced with tutorials and blogs on manufacturer and other sites, largely supported by user comments and suggestions.

Software products can be purchased individually, or they may be available in a **software suite**, which bundles several products together. Key benefits of suites include a common user interface among programs, the ability to easily share data among the products, and shared features that make certain functionalities, such as graphing, available to all the products.

> **Playing It Safe**
>
> When installing software, read prompts carefully before clicking OK or Continue. Some software installation programs will automatically install additional software and/or toolbars on your computer unless you deselect the options when they are presented.

A significant development in recent years is the ability to buy and download software online, from either the manufacturer or an online retailer. Before faster Internet connections came along, transmitting huge application files was impractical, but today, with fast broadband connections, downloading a program can take just a few minutes. Smaller downloadable programs called *apps* are popular with smartphone and tablet users. Software can be free, cost a few dollars, or come with a hefty price tag. Often, when you purchase software online you are given a product key you can use to install the software.

Cloud Computing The latest development in software delivery and access is **web-based software**. The process of using web-based software is referred to as **cloud computing**. With cloud computing, software is hosted on an online provider's website and you access it over the Internet using your browser—you don't have to have software installed on your computer to get work done. Google, IBM, Microsoft, and Oracle are names you might be familiar with in the list of companies that offer cloud computing. For example, Office 365 includes a word processor, a spreadsheet program, and a presentation program online.

Today, more software applications are available in the cloud, so users can often select if they wish to use cloud-based software or install software. When using cloud-based software, users have access to the data and applications they need, all hosted on a remote computer server. This is referred to as **software as a service** (SaaS, pronounced "sass"). A provider licenses an application to customers to use as a service on demand. Office 365 from Microsoft is an example of SaaS. Office 365 offers online applications for personal, professional, and business needs for a subscription fee.

The cloud computing model has several advantages over installed software programs:

- There is no need to download a large application or take up room on your hard drive.
- Updates to the software product can be made frequently by the provider and are transparent (invisible) to the user.
- There is less danger of a conflict with another software product or driver on your computer.
- Applications can be accessed from any compatible device.
- Some cloud applications are free, while you may have to pay for the installed versions.

Google Docs is a free, web-based software that includes a spreadsheet app.

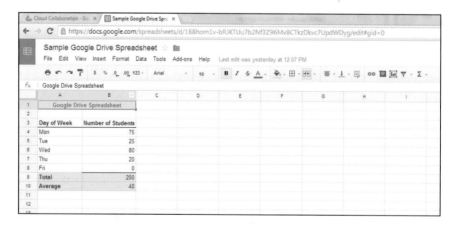

Popular shareware site tucows.com has been around for many years, offering a wide assortment of shareware and freeware.

How We Pay for Software

Software prices range from free, to being available for a small fee, to high costs for some sophisticated business applications.

Freeware and Shareware Generous programmers sometimes share software products for free (**freeware**) or for a small payment (**shareware**). In recent years the amount of free software available online has grown, and today you can probably find a free or shareware version of just about any type of application. Some of these free software products are quite sophisticated and feature-rich; others are a greatly simplified version of a similar software product you can purchase. Free products may also come with a hidden price: the company may capture and sell your information when you download the product, or they may use email and pop-up messages to attempt to upsell you to a more feature-rich product.

Open Source Software The open source movement makes **source code** (the programming code used to build the software) available to everyone in an effort to continue to build and improve the functionality of **open source software**. The open source movement has produced applications that are contributed to by individuals and are free to all. For example, the White House uses Drupal, an open source web development system. Since there is no ownership of open source software, users with technical questions often have to rely on blogs and forums for answers. Service companies that charge a fee for technical support are sometimes formed to support open source software.

Mobile Apps There are thousands of mobile apps for use on smartphones and tablets. The apps follow one of two pricing structures; they can either be used for a fee or for free. Purchased apps are available for a fixed cost at the time of download. Although free apps may seem like a good deal at first, they do have a price, as they are often ad-supported or will encourage the user to make in-app purchases.

Licensed Software When purchasing a software product, you will find a wide range of pricing, from lower costs for upgrading to a new version of a program, to higher, yet competitive, pricing for the full product at retail sites, auction sites, and manufacturers' sites.

Companies that wish to buy software for many employees enter into software licensing agreements that allow them to install a product on multiple workstations or on their network for individual computer users to access.

Cloud-Based Software With the cloud computing model, vendors can charge a subscription fee. They host the application on their servers. They can then disable access to the service when the user's contract expires. In some cases use of the products is free, as with Google Docs, Microsoft Office Online, some Adobe products, and Amazon Cloud Player. Microsoft offers Office 365 by license with separate pay scales for students, single or multiple users, and corporate customers.

 Spotlight on the Future *Online*

There's an App for That

"There's an app for that"—it's a catchphrase that sums up the explosion in application software for mobile devices, and we're likely to see even more in the future.

Technology journalist Dwight Silverman sees growth in software beyond desktop and mobile devices even to home appliances, fulfilling the predictions about the Internet of Things.

For example, you could walk up to your refrigerator and ask it to find a recipe using the ingredients you have inside. The fridge will use application software to go to the Internet and find your recipe seamlessly, running in the background. "Increasingly, we'll see more and more of this software running in the cloud," Silverman says. "Software will become simpler for the user, and what happens under the hood will be more complex. The end result is that you will have to do less work as a human."

Talk about It

1. What do we mean when we say "software"?

2. How have applications (apps) changed the way we live our daily lives?

3. What are some of the ways that application software may expand in the future?

4. What opportunities may there be for individuals to create their own apps aside from those offered by large companies?

5. Discuss the paradox of simplicity versus complexity in the application software of the future, from the point of view of the user and the creator.

Take the Next Step *Online*

Activity 5.3.1 Watch	*How do I access my software using cloud computing?*	**CORE** CONTENT
Activity 5.3.2 Watch	*How did the open source movement evolve?*	**CORE** CONTENT
Activity 5.3.3 Watch	*How does software work?*	**CORE** CONTENT
Activity 5.3.4 Research	*Do you get what you pay for when using free software?*	e book
Activity 5.3.5 **TEAM** Experience	*How do I schedule a team meeting using an online scheduler?*	e book
Activity 5.3.6 **TEAM** Experience	*How can collaborating online make project planning more efficient?*	e book

PRECHECK ⇒ # 5.4 Software Working Together

Today, many applications can use content created in other applications by importing or embedding the content. In addition, products within software suites often include shared features that provide functionalities such as diagramming or drawing.

Importing and Exporting

Many software applications allow you to **export** (send data to another application) and **import** (bring in data from another application). This works seamlessly within software suites such as Corel's WordPerfect Office suite and Microsoft Office. For example, PowerPoint includes an option to export a PowerPoint presentation to Word as handouts.

Other means of exporting and importing involve saving text in certain file types, such as **rich text format (RTF)**, which allows you to exchange data with many other applications. Saving as an RTF file reduces a document to a more rudimentary, commonly useable format that another software product is more likely to be able to open or import. Some software applications reduce the need for RTF files as they can directly open files that were created using a competing application.

Comma-separated-values (CSV) format, which separates each piece of data with a comma, is another widely used file type for importing and exporting. Using this format you might, for example, export all of your contacts from an Excel spreadsheet into a contact management application, such as Sales Cloud from Salesforce.

Converting Handwritten Notes and Speech to Text

Using **handwriting recognition software**, you can take content such as notes you handwrite on a tablet screen and convert them to a text file. That text file can then be further edited and finalized using a word processor or other program. Some mobile devices have built in handwriting recognition software to turn notes written with your finger or using a stylus into text. Some scanners can also recognize what you write on paper and convert it to text.

With **speech recognition software**, you speak into a microphone connected to or built into your computer. The software turns the sounds into text that you can then edit in a word processor. Speech recognition is built into Microsoft Windows, for example, and can be activated from within Microsoft Word.

Accuracy can be an issue with any handwriting or speech recognition system, as there are many variables in each person's handwriting, voice inflections, and accents. Generally speaking, handwriting recognition has advanced more rapidly than speech recognition software and can recognize nearly anyone's writing.

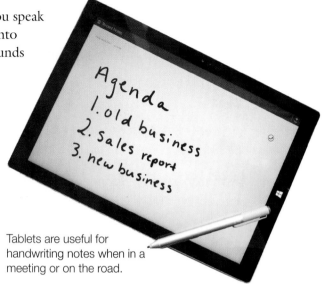

Tablets are useful for handwriting notes when in a meeting or on the road.

Embedding and Linking Content

Microsoft Office products use a technology called **object linking and embedding (OLE)** that allows content to be treated as objects that can be inserted into different software files, even if they were not created using that software. For example, you can place either a linked object or an embedded object, such as a graph from Excel, into a word processed document. A **linked object** maintains a link to the source; when the source is updated the linked item is also updated (if the source file is available). An **embedded object** resides in the file you've inserted it into along with information required to manage the object, but there is no connection to the object in the source file.

Embedding may also be familiar to you from using web pages, where a designer might embed a video or audio clip on a page. The embedded video was not created with the web authoring software, and in fact may play using a media player installed on your computer.

Using Shared Features

A **shared feature** is a small application that cannot run on its own but can be used with other software products. Shared features contain a particular functionality, such as the ability to build diagrams, and sometimes libraries of images that are useful to several kinds of software products. By allowing multiple products to draw on the feature, you save space on your computer and have a consistent procedure for getting that work done.

Some common shared features used by Microsoft Office products are:
- WordArt, which allows you to add shape, dimension, and color to text.
- SmartArt, which helps you diagram processes and work flow.
- Chart, which helps you build charts and graphs.
- Online Pictures, which is a library of artwork you can organize and insert into documents.
- Shapes, which is a collection of shapes you can draw in a document.

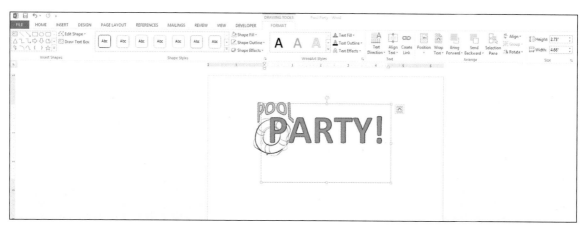

WordArt is a popular text enhancement feature that is shared by all Microsoft Office applications.

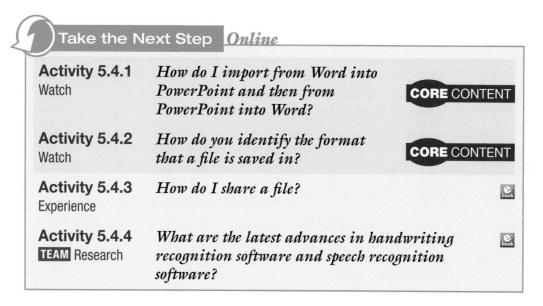

Take the Next Step *Online*

Activity 5.4.1 Watch	*How do I import from Word into PowerPoint and then from PowerPoint into Word?*	CORE CONTENT
Activity 5.4.2 Watch	*How do you identify the format that a file is saved in?*	CORE CONTENT
Activity 5.4.3 Experience	*How do I share a file?*	ebook
Activity 5.4.4 TEAM Research	*What are the latest advances in handwriting recognition software and speech recognition software?*	ebook

Review and Assessment *Online*

An interactive Summing Up with audio, a Study Notes document, slide presentations with audio, and Terms to Know flashcards with audio are available from the links menu on this page in your ebook.

Summing Up

Software's Role in the World of Computing

Application software includes the software you use to get things done, from producing reports for work to creating art or playing games.

The Many Types of Application Software

Productivity software includes software that people typically use to get work done such as a word processor, spreadsheet, database, or presentation software. This type of software is often compiled into suites of applications, such as Microsoft Office, OpenOffice, and Apple iWork. Productivity suites available in the cloud—notably Office 365 and Google Docs—also enable you to work wherever you have Internet connectivity. Four major categories of productivity software are:

- **Word processor software**, which you can use to create documents that include sophisticated text formatting, tables, photos, drawings, and links to online content. You can also use templates to design web pages, newsletters and more.
- **Spreadsheet software**, which allows you to perform calculations that range from simple (adding, averaging, multiplying) to complex (estimates of standard deviations based on a range of numbers).
- **Database software**, which organizes data. Once that data is entered into relational tables, you can view information in a spreadsheet-like list or as individual records using forms. You can then create queries that let you find specific data sets.
- **Presentation software**, which uses the concept of individual slides that form a slideshow. Slides may contain bulleted lists of key concepts, graphics, tables, animations, hyperlinks to web pages, or diagrams and charts. A slideshow can support a presenter's comments during a talk, run continuously on its own (at a trade show booth, for example), or be browsed by an individual.
  Other categories of software include:
- **Calendar software** and **contact management software** that help you organize your time and professional or personal contacts, and **customer relationship management (CRM) software** that helps coordinate client-focused business functions.
- **Graphics software**, **web authoring software**, and **multimedia software** including **desktop publishing (DTP) software**, **photo editing software**, and **animation software** used by many professionals.
- **Entertainment software** such as games and special-interest programs related to genealogy or sports.
- Personal finance software for managing your spending and saving goals.
- Professional software, which handles professional financial or business tasks, software written for specific industry needs, and custom or enterprise software that packages business best practices and procedures in a customizable format.

- Software for mobile devices, which may be simpler versions of full-featured computer software. With the increasing power of smartphones and tablets, the variety and capabilities of mobile software continue to increase rapidly.

Developing and Delivering Software

Software delivery venues have changed dramatically over the last several years, mainly due to the Internet and its ability to download software applications to your computer or allow you to use web-based software.

The process of developing software is described as the **software development life cycle (SDLC)**. Software typically comes out in new versions every few years. As it is being created by software engineers who write the source code, the new version goes through various development and testing phases—first an **alpha version** or very initial draft is released, and then one or more **beta versions**. When the software is in a final version, called the **release to manufacturing (RTM) version**, it is then duplicated or made available for download and sold to the public.

Today, you can buy **packaged software**, which is typically downloaded but can also be purchased on storage media (typically a DVD).

The latest development in software delivery is **web-based software**, generally referred to as **cloud computing**. With this model, software is hosted on an online provider's website and you access it over the Internet using your browser. Software updates are usually done in the background as you work, over the Internet. You typically access online software for free or by paying for a subscription.

In recent years the amount of free software available online has grown, and today you can probably find a **freeware** or **shareware** version of just about any type of application. The **open source software** movement has produced many applications that enable the users to study the source code of programs, change and improve their designs, and distribute their updates.

Companies that wish to buy software for many employees enter into software licensing agreements that allow them to install a product on multiple workstations.

Software Working Together

Many software applications allow you to **import** and **export** data to other applications. This works seamlessly in software suites such as Corel WordPerfect Office and Microsoft Office. By saving files in certain formats, such as **rich text format (RTF)** and **comma-separated-values (CSV)** format, you can access data with many other applications.

Using **handwriting recognition software**, you can take notes you handwrite and convert them to a text file that can then be used by word processors or other software. **Speech recognition software** turns words (sounds) spoken into a microphone into text that you can then edit.

Microsoft Office products and many other programs use a technology called **object linking and embedding (OLE)** to insert content created in one software application into different software files. Using linking, you can update the **linked object** and see those updates automatically reflected in the source file. With embedding, you insert the **embedded object** into a file and can edit it, but no link to the source content exists.

Shared features are small applications that cannot run on their own, but can be used from within other software products. Allowing multiple products to draw on the shared feature saves storage space on your computer and provides a consistent procedure for accomplishing certain tasks.

Terms to Know

Software's Role in the World of Computing

application software, 130

The Many Types of Application Software

productivity software, 131
word processor software, 132
spreadsheet software, 132
database software, 133
presentation software, 134
calendar software, 136
contact management software, 136
customer relationship management
  (CRM) software, 137
graphics software, 137
desktop publishing (DTP) software, 137
photo editing software, 137
screen capture software, 137
multimedia software, 138
animation software, 138
audio software, 138
podcast, 138

video editing software, 138
web authoring software, 138
WYSIWYG (what you see is what you
  get), 138
entertainment software, 139
query, Activity 5.2.1
table, Activity 5.2.1
record, Activity 5.2.1
field, Activity 5.2.1
entry, Activity 5.2.1
relational database, Activity 5.2.1
primary key, Activity 5.2.1
Structured Query Language (SQL),
  Activity 5.2.1
edutainment, Activity 5.2.2
web-based training, Activity 5.2.2
MOOC, Activity 5.2.2

Developing and Delivering Software

software development life cycle
  (SDLC), 144
alpha version, 144
beta version, 144
release to manufacturing (RTM)
  version, 144
bug, 144
packaged software, 145
software suite, 145
web-based software, 146

cloud computing, 146
software as a service (SaaS), 146
freeware, 146
shareware, 146
source code, 147
open source software, 147
software on demand, Activity 5.3.1
GNU General Public License,
  Activity 5.3.2

Software Working Together

export, 149
import, 149
rich text format (RTF), 149
comma-separated-values (CSV)
  format, 149
handwriting recognition software, 149
speech recognition software, 149

object linking and embedding (OLE),
  150
linked object, 150
embedded object, 150
shared feature, 150
file extension, Activity 5.4.2

Concepts Check

Concepts Check 5.1   Multiple Choice
Take this quiz to test your understanding of key concepts in this chapter.

Concepts Check 5.2   Matching
Match the software application to the primary use of the software.

Concepts Check 5.3   Label It
Use the interactive tool to label the elements in a Microsoft Excel worksheet.

Concepts Check 5.4   Arrange It
Use the interactive tool to arrange the phases in the software development life cycle.

Projects

Check with your instructor for the preferred method to submit completed work.

Project 5.1   Spreadsheet Analysis

Project 5.1.1
You have been assigned to create a spreadsheet that shows how your friends spend their days. Survey ten friends and ask them how much time they spend on the following activities: in school, doing homework, sleeping, eating, socializing, spending time with family. When you have finished collecting the information, set up the categories on a spreadsheet and enter your friends' responses. On the same spreadsheet, summarize the data. Submit the spreadsheet to your instructor.

Project 5.1.2
Using the data from the spreadsheet you created in Project 5.1.1, create a bar chart that displays your survey results. To complete this task, use the charting tools to select the type of bar graph you want to design. Format the chart and submit it to your instructor.

Project 5.2   Using Web-Based Tools

Project 5.2.1
Learning organizational and time management skills is important in today's busy society. As a student, you know firsthand the difficulties in balancing your classes, assignments, and possibly a job and family responsibilities. At times, you may forget assignments, appointments, or upcoming events. One tool that can help you stay organized is a Google Calendar. Create a school calendar to record all appointments, assignments, tests, and so on for the next two weeks. When you have finished scheduling your information, export the calendar and submit it to your instructor.

Project 5.2.2 `TEAM`

Your company's executive board is considering using Google tools such as Gmail and Google Drive to organize their communications and documents. The board members have asked your IT team to prepare a slide presentation that outlines the advantages of using these Google tools. Using Google Docs, create a collaborative presentation that discusses these Google tools and their applications. When complete, share the presentation with your class.

Project 5.3   Graphics and Multimedia

Project 5.3.1 `TEAM`

You have been asked to create a podcast overview of software applications. Choose two applications and create a podcast describing the purpose, cost, useful features, and the types of documents the application produces. You will also include the rationale for purchasing the application. Begin by downloading Audacity from http://ODW4 .emcp.net/Audacity and the Lame MP3 converter from http://ODW4.emcp.net /Lame to record and convert your podcast to an MP3 format. Create an audio file and export it as an MP3 file. Finally, create an account on Podbean (http://ODW4 .emcp.net/Podbean) where you can post your podcast. Share the link with your instructor and classmates.

Project 5.3.2 `TEAM`

The public relations director of your school has asked the students in your Introduction to Computers class to create a flyer promoting the course. With your teammates, select a desktop publishing or word processing software application, such as Publisher or Word, to design your flyer. As you develop the content for the flyer, consider the basic information your flyer should provide: a general course description, the time and location of the class, the cost of the course, any course prerequisites, and the instructor's name. In addition to this general information, provide specific course objectives, learning tools, student projects, and activities that might serve as incentives for students to register for the course. To add visual interest, incorporate graphics by using tools such as WordArt.

Project 5.3.3 `TEAM`

Use the free Gmail photo sharing tool, Picasa (http://ODW4.emcp.net/Picasa), to create a photo album scavenger hunt for your classmates. Have your team prepare a photo album of landmarks or sites in your local area. Ask each member of your team to contribute either an existing digital photo that they have or to go on location to take a new photo. Try to find photos that show enough detail to provide clues as to the photos' locations. Upload the individual photos to the team's Picasa album. When complete, share your team's album with the class. Ask other teams to post their responses as to the locations of the photos.

Project 5.4   Word Processor and Presentation Software

Project 5.4.1

You need to explain to a colleague how to change a font in Microsoft Word. In order to do this, you have decided to create a series of screen captures with callouts (descriptive labels). Use the software program Jing (available at http://ODW4.emcp.net/Jing) or the Windows Snipping tool to capture the screen images. After creating the images, insert the screen captures in a text document and add callouts.

Project 5.4.2 `TEAM`

You are a college student and a part-time employee of the IT department of a local business. Your manager recognizes your knowledge of current technological advances and would like you to share your insights with other members of the department. In particular, your manager would like you to explain cloud computing, the latest development in software delivery and access. Working with a team of colleagues, create a PowerPoint presentation explaining cloud computing. Post the presentation to Microsoft OneDrive or to a course website to share with your class and instructor.

Project 5.5   Wiki—Collaborative Use of Software

Project 5.5.1 `TEAM`

Businesses today prefer to use software applications that allow their employees to collaborate on the creation of documents. To model that practice, your class will create a document for the class wiki on the advantages and disadvantages of buying a PC or a Mac. The document's content should include an analysis of features and applications available for each platform, the costs of components and any upgrades, and so on. Your instructor will divide you into three teams. Each team should post their content on the class wiki.

Project 5.5.2 `TEAM`

You or your team will be assigned to edit and verify the content posted by one team on the wiki site from Project 5.5.1. If you add or edit any content, make sure you include a notation within the page that includes your name or team members' names and the date you edited the content—for example, "Edited by [student name or team members' names] on [date]." Keep a list of references that you used to verify your content changes. When you are finished with your verification, include a notation at the end of the entry—for example, "Verified by [student name or team members' names] on [date]."

Project 5.5.3 `TEAM`

You or your team will be assigned to format and add visuals to one team's document posted on the wiki site from Project 5.5.2.

Project 5.6   Learning about Application Software

Project 5.6.1

As a help desk employee of a large insurance company, you often receive calls about how to use a variety of software applications. You have begun to keep a list of the most frequently asked questions and have decided to prepare a reference guide for employees that you will post to the company intranet. To help you with this task, go to Microsoft Office Online Help and find the answers to the following questions:

1. The data for my report is slightly confusing. I think that it would be better communicated in a table. How can I insert a table in Word to make my data more reader-friendly?
2. How do I create a chart for the current year's sales data?

3. Is there a way to create a formula using Excel to total the values of the range A1:A7?

4. I have to give a PowerPoint presentation to the Board of Directors, and I need to know how to export my Excel spreadsheet and import it to my PowerPoint presentation. Is this possible?

5. I want to run a query in my Access database showing all my customers in the United States. How do I run an Access query?

6. I have two tables in Access, and I want to join the tables so that I can run a query with data from both tables. How do I join tables in Access?

7. All my colleagues use a variety of animations in their PowerPoint presentations. I have an object that I would like to animate. How do I apply a custom animation to an object?

8. One of my colleagues uses the Outline View to create PowerPoint presentations. I am unable to locate how to create a presentation in Outline View. Are there specific steps that need to be followed?

9. I have two new customers that I would like to add to my contact list in Outlook. Is there a way to add contacts?

Project 5.6.2 TEAM

You are a member of the IT department in a company about to adopt an enterprise software solution. The vice president of information systems has assigned your group to create a PowerPoint presentation for training customer service employees on enterprise customer relationship management (CRM) software. Research enterprise CRM software, and create a slide presentation that describes the software and its benefits and uses sound and animation. Submit the presentation along with a reference list of sources to your instructor.

Project 5.7 Preventing Software Failure

Project 5.7.1

You are the project leader for a new software application. The coding is nearing completion and you are investigating ways to ensure you do not encounter a major software failure. You decide to research other software products that have encountered failure and consider preventative measures that your project team can use. Read the article "Top software failures 2015/2016" at http://ODW4.emcp.net/SoftwareFailures. Choose one of the examples mentioned in the article. Consider the steps in the software development cycle and identify what you think went wrong with this particular product and what could have been done differently to prevent the failure from happening. Create a presentation that lists your recommended preventative measures along with the rationale for the recommendations. Be prepared to share the presentation with your class.

Class Conversations

Topic 5.1 Is it OK to share software?

You have recently purchased the newest version of a cloud-based web authoring software application which costs over $700. You are excited about using all the great features. Your friend also wants to use the same software but can't afford it. Your friend asks you if he/she can log into the software using your credentials. You check the software terms of use and find that this is illegal. What would you do?

Topic 5.2 Should I fix the photo to tell a better story?

Photo editing dates back to the 1860s. Manipulating photos can be done to misrepresent products, sensationalize something in the press, or cause somebody embarrassment. There have been several controversial photos that have been edited and placed in magazines or newspapers, such as a 1982 National Geographic cover photo of the pyramids in Egypt and a 2008 picture of vice presidential candidate Sarah Palin. Do you think that manipulating photos is ethical? Why or why not?

Topic 5.3 Should we take responsibility for our mistakes?

Spell check is a feature available in many software applications. Most of you probably have grown up using spell check and grammar check. Are you dependent on spell check to proof your documents? Do you believe that features such as spell check and online calculators are causing our population to be overly dependent on them and unable to spell or calculate without those tools? What effect could this dependence have on the literacy of our society—or does it not matter how these things are checked, as long as the tools are available?

Communications and Network Technologies

Connecting through Computers

What You'll Accomplish

When you finish this chapter, you'll be able to:

6.1 Differentiate the use of networks to share data and computing resources in the workplace and at home.

6.2 List the components in a communications system and describe the types of signals and typical transmission speeds that travel over the system.

6.3 Recognize types of wired transmission media and list wireless transmission systems in use today.

6.4 Explain the role that network standards and protocols play in communications and give examples of commonly used wired and wireless networking standards.

6.5 Describe the three characteristics used to classify networks and give examples of typical network classifications.

6.6 Identify and differentiate among various networking devices and software that enable you to send and receive data.

6.7 State the reasons why network security is important and give an example of a security device.

6.8 Summarize trends that affect the future of networking.

Why Does It Matter

Your computers and mobile devices depend on a communications system to send and receive data over a network. Without such a system, you couldn't send emails and text messages, update your Facebook status, send a Tweet, download music, or share a printer with other computers. Whether you're downloading a new app, sharing a file or a device with other computers in your home or office, or tapping into the resources on the worldwide network that is the Internet, understanding how to use the power of networks to share with others can make your work easier and your life more satisfying.

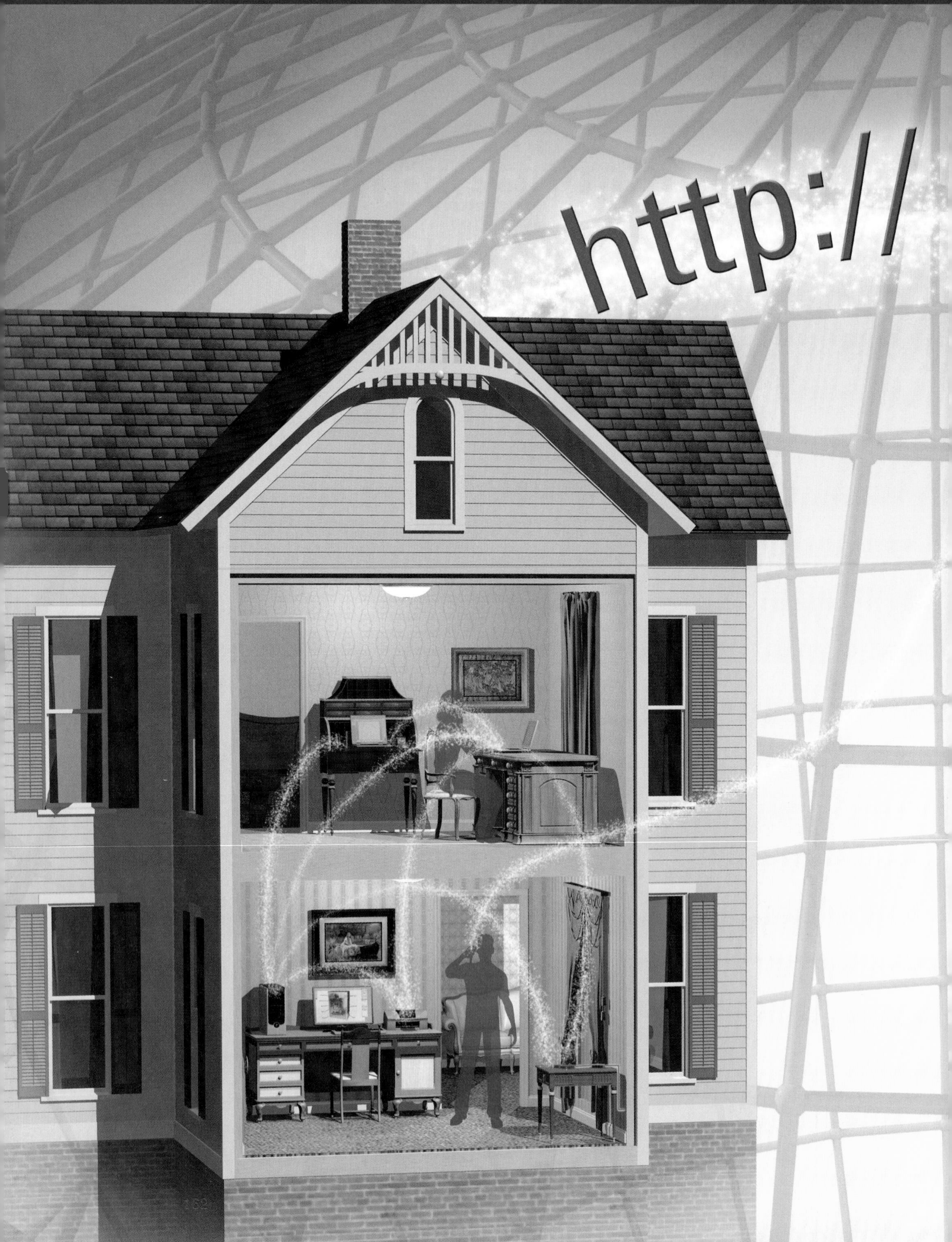
http://

Chapter 6 Communications and Network Technologies: Connecting Through Computers

Computer networks allow people to connect to share work, devices, and information. Whether wired or wireless, networks use various technologies, hardware components, and software to make the connection.

6.1 How Does the World Use Networking?

A **computer network** consists of two or more computing or other devices connected by a communications medium, such as a wireless signal or a cable. A computer network provides a way to connect with others and share files and resources such as printers or an Internet connection.

> "As network administrator I can take down the network with one keystroke. It's just like being a doctor but without getting gooky stuff on my paws."
>
> —Scott Adams, creator of *Dilbert*

In business settings, networks allow you to communicate with employees, suppliers, vendors, customers, and government agencies. Many companies have their own network, called an **intranet**, which is essentially a private Internet within the company's corporate "walls." Some companies also offer an extension of their internal network, called an **extranet**, to suppliers and customers. For example, a supplier might be allowed to access inventory information on a company's internal network to make sure the company does not run short of a vital part for its manufacturing process.

In your home, networks are useful for sharing resources among members of your family. For example, using a home network, you might share one printer or network storage among three or four computers.

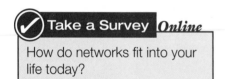

Take a Survey *Online*

How do networks fit into your life today?

The Internet is a global network made up of many networks linked together. If you consider all the applications, services, and tools the Internet allows you to access, as you discovered in Chapter 2, you can begin to understand the power of networking and how it opens up a new world of sharing and functionality.

6.2 Exploring Communications Systems

A computer network is one kind of **communications system**. This system includes hardware to send and receive data, transmission and relay systems, common sets of standards so all the equipment can "talk" to each other, and communications software.

You use such a networked communications system whenever you send/receive text or email messages, pay a bill online, shop at an Internet store, send a document to a shared printer at work or at home, update a social network, or download music or videos. Figure 6.1 shows some of the common communications system components in use today.

The world of a computer network communications system is made up of:

- Transmission media upon which the data travels to/from its destination.
- A set of standards and **network protocols** (rules for how data is handled as it travels along a communications channel). Devices use these protocols to send and receive data to and from each other.
- Hardware and software to connect to a communications pathway from the sending and receiving ends.

The first step in understanding a communications system is to learn the basics about transmission signals and transmission speed when communicating over a network.

FIGURE 6.1 | **Communications Systems**

Communications systems include computer hardware and communications software that allow computer users to exchange messages or other data around the house or around the world.

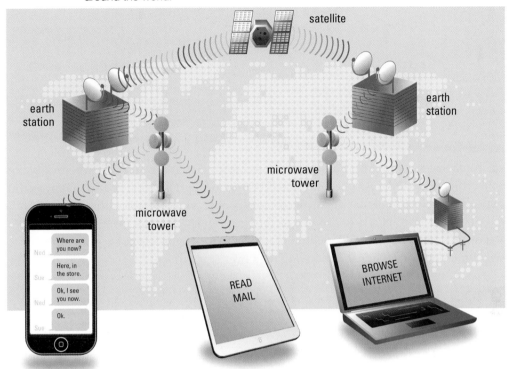

satellite

earth station

earth station

microwave tower

microwave tower

Where are you now?

Here, in the store.

Ok, I see you now.

Ok.

Ned

Sue

READ MAIL

BROWSE INTERNET

Types of Signals

There are two kinds of signals used in transmitting voices and other sounds over a computer network: analog and digital (Figure 6.2). An **analog signal** is formed by continuous sound waves that fluctuate from high to low. Your voice is transmitted as an analog signal over traditional telephone lines at a certain frequency. A **digital signal** uses a discrete signal that is either high or low. In computer terms, high represents the digital bit 1, and low represents the digital bit 0. These are the only two states for digital data.

Computers use a binary system of 1s and 0s, also called *digital signals* or *data* when processing and storing information. If you send data between computers using a medium that transmits data via an analog signal (such as older telephone and cable networks), the signal has to be transformed from digital, to analog (modulated), and back again to digital (demodulated) to be understood by the computer on the receiving end. The piece of hardware that connects your computer to a transmission source such as your telephone line or cable television line to send and receive data is a **modem**. The word *modem* comes from a combination of the words *mo*dulate and *dem*odulate.

Modems convert analog signals to digital signals and vice versa. Newer communications technologies use digital signals.

FIGURE 6.2 **Analog and Digital Signals**

A change in an analog wave represents a change in sound. Computers send and receive data using digital signals.

analog signal

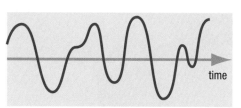

digital signal

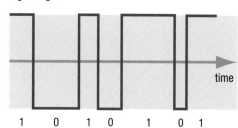

time

time

1 0 1 0 1 0 1

Today most communications technologies use a digital signal, saving the trouble of converting transmissions. The demise in 2009 of analog television transmissions as the industry switched to digital signals sent some people scrambling to either buy a more recent TV set or to purchase a converter box to convert digital transmissions back to analog to work with their older equipment. Computer networks use a pure digital signal method of sending and receiving data over a network.

Transmission Speed

If you've ever been frustrated with how long it takes to download a file from a website, you're familiar with the fact that, in a communications system, data moves from one computer to another at different speeds. The speed of transmission is determined by a few key factors.

The first factor is the speed at which a signal can change from high to low, which is called **frequency**. A signal sent at a faster frequency provides faster transmission (Figure 6.3).

The other factor contributing to the speed of data transmission is bandwidth. On a computer network, the term **bandwidth** refers to the number of bits (pieces of data) per second that can be transmitted over a communications medium. Think of

FIGURE 6.3 **Faster and Slower Frequencies**

A signal that changes from high to low quickly travels faster.

short wavelength

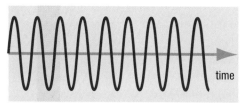

high-frequency signal

time

long wavelength

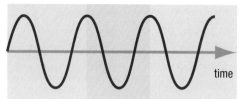

low-frequency signal

time

Our Digital World

bandwidth as being like a highway. At rush hour, with the same amount of cars, a two-lane highway accommodates less traffic and everybody moves at a slower speed than on a four-lane highway, where much more traffic can travel at a faster speed. Table 6.1 lists communications bandwidth measurements.

If you have plenty of bandwidth and your data is transmitted at a high frequency, you get faster transmission speeds. Any communications medium that is capable of carrying a large amount of data at a fast speed is known as **broadband**, such as cable, DSL, or fiber-optic.

Though transmission speeds at any moment in time may vary depending on network traffic and other factors, each of the common communications media has a typical speed. Table 6.2 lists typical transmission speeds. Providers continue to improve transmission speeds, and for some forms of connections, you can purchase plans offering much faster connections than those listed in Table 6.2. Some very high-powered connections being tested today provide transmission speeds of as much as 100 gigabits (one billion bits) per second, which allows you to download a high-definition movie in 2 seconds.

Most people quote connection speeds based on download speeds. Be aware that upload transmission speed is different from download transmission speed, and in many cases the upload speed is significantly slower. Some companies even put restrictions on upload speeds.

Of course, everybody wants high-speed Internet transmissions, but the higher the speed, the higher the cost. When you think about the type of connection you need for your computer, consider what you typically do when you're online. Do you send or receive many pictures or videos, which are typically very large files? Do you want to stream music or video, or play online games? In those instances, you need a broadband connection such as cable or DSL. On the other hand, if most of your transmissions are simply text messages or text documents, then a lower speed connection will probably work for you.

TABLE 6.1 Bandwidth Measurements

Term	Abbreviation	Meaning
1 kilobit per second	1 Kbps	1 thousand bits per second
1 megabit per second	1 Mbps	1 million bits per second
1 gigabit per second	1 Gbps	1 billion bits per second
1 terabit per second	1 Tbps	1 trillion bits per second
1 petabit per second	1 Pbps	1 quadrillion bits per second

TABLE 6.2 Comparison of Network Connection Speeds

Type of Connection	Typical Speed Range
dial-up	56 Kbps
satellite	6 or more Mbps
DSL	6 to 40 Mbps
cable	20 to 100 Mbps
fiber-optic	Up to 1 Gigabit per second

Take the Next Step *Online*

| Activity 6.2.1 Watch | *What happens when you send a message over a network?* | **CORE** CONTENT |
| Activity 6.2.2 Experience | *How fast is your network connection?* | e book |

PRECHECK

6.3 Transmission Systems

The signals that are sent in a communications system might be transmitted via a wired medium (a cable) or wirelessly, using radio waves.

Wired Transmissions

At one time, all networks were wired. Long strings of wire connected each workstation to the network. Though they have lost popularity in the age of wireless, wired network models are still in use.

Wired transmissions send a signal through various media, including (Figure 6.4):

- **Twisted-pair cable**, which is used for an analog, wired telephone connection. This type of cable consists of two independently insulated wires wrapped around one another. Twisted-pair cable is used to transmit over short distances. It is used in many homes because signals can travel over the built-in telephone system. Cat 5 is an example of twisted-pair cable used in many wired networks.
- **Coaxial cable**, which is the same cable used to transmit cable television signals over an insulated wire at a fast speed—in this case, millions of bits per second.
- **Fiber-optic cable**, which uses a protected string of glass that transmits beams of light. Fiber-optic transmission is very fast, transmitting billions of bits per second.

Many businesses lease T-lines (such as T1 or T3), developed by long distance telephone companies, to carry multiple types of signals (voice and data) at very fast speeds over fiber-optic or older copper-wired lines.

Wireless Transmissions

There are several wireless transmission systems in use today, including cellular, microwaves, and satellite. All use radio waves to transmit data, but each system handles these transmissions in different ways, and the systems vary in signal strength and frequency.

A **cellular network**, like those used by your cell phone, transmits signals, called **cellular transmissions**, by using cell towers (Figure 6.5). Each cell tower has its own range (or cell) of coverage. Cellular systems are used to transmit both voice and data in every direction. There are several generations of cellular transmissions, from the first generation (1G) that was used for analog transmissions to the fourth generation (4G) which transmits digital data at speeds up to 100 Mbps. (Speed performance varies by carrier.)

A **microwave** is a high-frequency radio signal that is directed from one microwave station tower to another. Because the signal cannot bend around obstacles, the towers have to be positioned in line of sight of each other as in Figure 6.6. Microwave transmission might be used, for example, to send a signal from towers located on top of several buildings in a school or company campus. If it's not possible to place

FIGURE 6.4 | Three Types of Cables

Wired transmissions send signals over coaxial, twisted-pair, or fiber-optic cables.

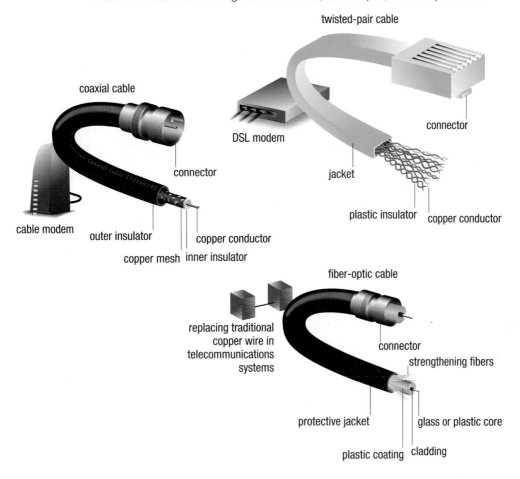

FIGURE 6.5 | Cellular Technology

A smartphone sends a signal that travels along a series of cell towers until the data reaches the intended recipient.

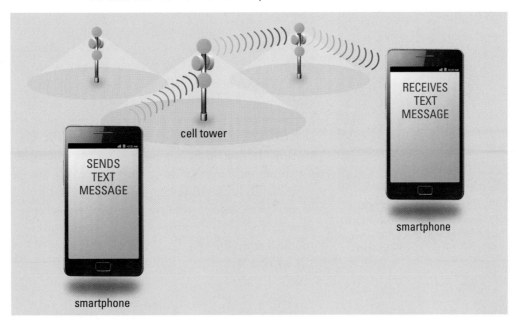

FIGURE 6.6 **Microwave Technology**

Radio signals travel through the atmosphere from one microwave tower to another. These towers have to be relatively close to each other because radio signals can't bend around the earth or around objects such as buildings. Alternatively, they can be bounced off a satellite.

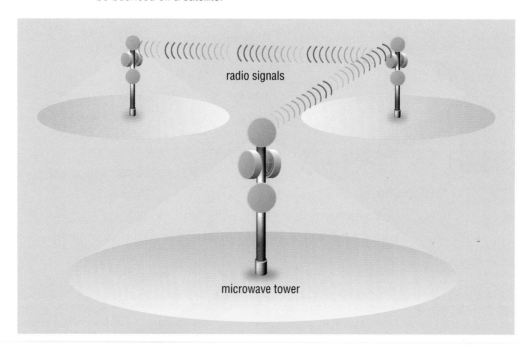

radio signals

microwave tower

To avoid physical obstructions between them, some microwave towers send signals up to a satellite to be bounced down to the target tower.

towers within sight of each other, signals can be sent upward where there are no obstructions. The signal is then bounced off the atmosphere or a satellite and then sent back down to another microwave tower.

Satellite communication uses space-based equipment, and is typically used for longer range transmissions, for international communications, and for connectivity in rural areas where cellular or microwave towers aren't available. A satellite receives microwave signals from an earth-based station and then broadcasts the signals back to another earth-based station or dish receiver (Figure 6.7). Video conferences and air navigation control are typical uses of satellite communication.

In January 2016, NASA launched a satellite as part of a research project to monitor sea levels worldwide to help in our understanding of global warming and improve our ability to predict hurricanes. TDRS satellites have also been used for several years for services such as linking doctors in urban areas to monitor surgeries or providing medical assistance to people in remote areas of the world.

Our Digital World

FIGURE 6.7 **Satellite Communications**

Communications satellites are solar powered. They use transponders to receive signals from the ground, then retransmit them to a specific location on the ground.

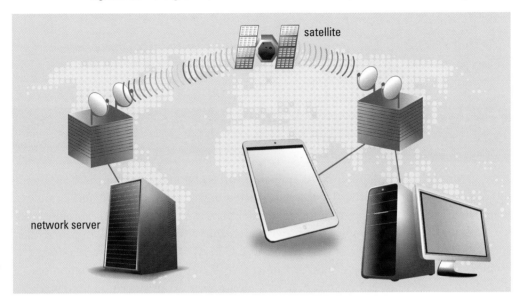

satellite

network server

 Spotlight on the Future *Online*

Networking Your Life

Networking has evolved dramatically from when you always needed cables, routers, and a fair bit of know-how.

Today, "networking means Wi-Fi for the most part, and you don't really worry about wiring a simple home network," says technology journalist Dwight Silverman. He predicts it will become even more integrated in the future, aligning with the Internet of Things. For example, you might bring a new device like a streaming TV box home and it will automatically know your network and connect to it securely.

Silverman says increasingly, consumers will have to make a networking choice: Google's Android or Apple's iOS/OS X. And that could affect decisions as broadly as what car you drive. "The idea that I would choose a car based on whether I have an iPhone seems bizarre, but 10 years from now, it may not be so bizarre," he says.

Talk about It

1. How has networking changed over the past 10 years?

2. What might networking look like in the future and how will it be different from today?

3. Discuss some ways that networking could make consumers' lives easier in the future.

4. Do you think the networks of the future will be more secure than today, and why or why not?

5. How could your choice of a technology today affect what networks you use in your home, office, and mobile devices in the future?

Take the Next Step *Online*

Activity 6.3.1 Watch	*How do our wireless gadgets work?*	 CORE CONTENT
Activity 6.3.2 Discuss	*Is a landline still relevant in today's home?*	

 PRECHECK

6.4 Communications Standards and Protocols

Browse through any computer store, online or off, and you'll find that there are many models of computers or other Internet-connected devices made by many different manufacturers. These different hardware models have to have a way to communicate with one another. For example, you may want to send a text message from your Nokia smartphone to your friend who uses a Samsung Galaxy. Or, you may attach a document to an email message and send it from your HP laptop to a customer who uses a Mac. You may even want to send data or a picture from your smartphone to your computer.

To allow all these different devices to talk to each other, the computer industry has developed **standards** that address issues of compatibility among these devices. Organizations such as the **American National Standards Institute (ANSI)** and the **Institute of Electrical and Electronics Engineers (IEEE)** (pronounced "eye-triple-e") develop and approve these standards, which specify how computers access transmission media, speeds used on networks, the design of networking hardware such as cables, and so on.

A standard that specifies how two devices can communicate is called a **protocol**. A protocol provides rules such as how data should be formatted and coded for transmission.

Hardware manufacturers design their devices to meet network standards that relate to the types of tasks their devices handle. Data sent from one device to another travels across a wired system, a wireless system, or a combination of both wired and wireless using a variety of standards.

Wired Networking Standards

The way that data is transported within a network relates to the standard that is used. Two standards you should know about are Ethernet and TCP/IP.

Ethernet is a common wired media standard. The Ethernet standard specifies that there is no central device controlling the timing of data transmission. With this standard, each device tries to send data when it senses that the network is available. Ethernet networks are fast, inexpensive, and easy to install. With Ethernet speed capable of 1 Gbps, it is the standard most commonly used for wired networks in the workplace. If you have a high-speed cable modem or DSL modem at home, chances are you use an Ethernet cable to connect a wired computer to the networking equipment.

TCP/IP is a protocol that specifies the order in which data is sent through the network. With the TCP/IP standard, instructions are given to divide data into small units called *packets* that are passed along the network. A **packet** is simply a smaller piece of data combined with information about the sender and intended receiver of the data. The process of breaking data into packets, sending, and then reassembling the original data is called **packet switching**. TCP/IP is the network standard upon which Internet communications are based.

Wireless Networking Standards

Getting rid of wires gives people the freedom to move around and get their connections on the go. This process is important whether you're part of a mobile workforce, or just like to use Twitter or email from your local coffee shop. Improvements in wireless technologies continue to enable mobile users to increase their access to different types of data, but just how do they work?

Wireless transmissions can use a variety of networking standards, including Wi-Fi, WiMAX, Long Term Evolution (LTE), Bluetooth, and Radio Frequency Identification (RFID).

Wi-Fi refers to a network that is based on the **802.11 standard** in its various versions such as 802.11 a, g, n, or ac. Wi-Fi is a popular choice for setting up a wireless home network. This standard tells wireless devices how to connect with each other using a series of access points and radio frequencies to transmit data. Table 6.3 lists the differences among various Wi-Fi standards.

> **🔒 Playing It Safe**
>
> Networks can be secured or unsecured. When you're logged on to a free wireless hotspot such as the one in a local coffee house, your connection is not secure because public networks typically do not have security features turned on. Never perform financial transactions online using a hotspot, such as checking your bank account balance or providing your credit card or checking account information to an online store. Always secure your home wireless network with a strong access password.

Table 6.3 **Differences Among Various WiFi Standards**

STANDARD	RELEASED	FREQUENCY	BANDWIDTH	HIGHEST DATA-RATE
802.11 (Legacy)	1997	2.4 GHz	20 MHz	2 Mbps
802.11b	1999	2.4 GHz	20 MHz	11 Mbps
802.11a	1999	5 GHz	20 MHz	54 Mbps
802.11g	2003	2.4 GHz	20 MHz	54 Mbps
802.11n	2009	2.4 GHz, 5 GHz	20 MHz, 40 MHz	Up to 450 Mbps OR maximum capability of 450 Mbps
802.11ac	2013	5 GHz only	20 MHz, 40 MHz, 80 MHz & 160 MHz (opt)	Up to 1733 Mbps OR maximum capability of 1.7 Gbps

Source: Adapted from *The Future of Next-Generation Tablets and Smartphones* by Partha Murali, Redpine Signals, Inc. on the Embedded Intel Solutions site at http://www.embeddedintel.com.

Computers and portable computing equipment come equipped with built-in Wi-Fi capability. Many public spaces, such as libraries, airports, coffee shops, restaurants, and malls, are now being equipped with Wi-Fi access points so you can connect with the Internet from your laptop, tablet, or smartphone. A location, such as a coffee shop, that makes Wi-Fi access available is called a **hotspot**. Operating systems such as Windows and Mac OS X are capable of automatically detecting hotspots and connecting to them.

WiMAX stands for Worldwide Interoperability for Microwave Access (also known as 802.16) and uses the 4G standard that is faster and can work over a longer range than Wi-Fi. WiMAX-capable computers or devices use radio waves and a WiMAX tower to connect with other devices. Some of the 4G networks used by cell phone or smartphone providers use WiMAX. **WiGig** is based on the 802.11ad standard and promises speeds of up to 7 Gbps. Operating in the 60 GHz range, it has range limitations.

Long Term Evolution (LTE) is touted as the true 4G network. LTE is offered under a variety of banners by carriers such as LTE, LTE-Advanced, and LTE-A to name a few. LTE networks encompass a set of standards that involves changes to the wireless infrastructure to improve data speeds. LTE networks offer better high-speed coverage with more bandwidth than WiMAX. To accomplish this standard, the transmitters function on different frequency bands to avoid interference. LTE is generally expected to replace WiMAX networks in the future. For example, Sprint has rolled out its LTE network and has stopped selling WiMAX devices. When Sprint's contract with its WiMAX operator expired in 2015, Sprint stopped offering WiMAX service.

Bluetooth is a network protocol that offers short-range connectivity (3 to 300 feet, depending on a device's power class) via radio waves between devices such as your smartphone and car. Bluetooth-enabled devices can communicate directly with each other. Many cars now come with Bluetooth connectivity integrated into their car systems for hands-free phone operation. This is partially the result of more and more states and provinces enacting laws against talking on a handheld phone while driving. A variety of devices today contain a Bluetooth chip, such as laptops, smartphones, mice, keyboards, and even digital cameras.

Bluetooth LE (BLE), which stands for Bluetooth low energy (also referred to as **Bluetooth Smart**), is a new Bluetooth standard that uses much less power to communicate within the same range as what is now called "Classic" Bluetooth. The Bluetooth Special Interest Group estimates that more than 90 percent of smartphones will support Bluetooth LE by 2018.

Smartphone users may be able to share the Internet connection of their device via a cable, Bluetooth, or Wi-Fi with another device such as a tablet or laptop. This process is known as **tethering**, and it is useful when access to the Internet via other means is not available for your laptop or tablet. In this case, your mobile phone basically becomes

Wireless Bluetooth headsets are popular with smartphone users who want hands-free operation.

a modem and could possibly service several other computing devices. To be able to tether your mobile device's Internet connection you will need software installed on your mobile phone to support tethering.

Radio Frequency Identification (RFID) is a wireless technology used primarily to track and identify inventory or other items via radio signals. An RFID tag contains a transponder (the part that sends the signal) which is read by a transceiver or RFID reader. As the tag is read, inventory data is automatically updated on the network. The manufacturing and retail worlds track products from production line to the end consumer using RFID tags. This technology is also becoming more widely used as industries embrace the technology to track patients, pets, wildlife, access to parking gates, and toll payments, just to name a few applications.

Wireless Application Protocol (WAP) specifies how mobile devices such as smartphones display online information, including maps and email. Devices using WAP to display web content have to contain a microbrowser, a less robust version of a browser such as Internet Explorer.

Ethics and Technology Blog *Online*

Could RFID Tags Be Misused?

RFID tags can be embedded in animals. The same technology could allow these tags to be embedded in humans or planted somewhere on a human to track that person. Anybody with the correct data reader can read any data stored on a tag. Does anybody think that embedding RFID tags in animals or humans could be misused?

 ### Take the Next Step *Online*

Activity 6.4.1 Watch	*What are SMTP, POP, and IMAP?*	**CORE** CONTENT
Activity 6.4.2 Watch	*How does Bluetooth work?*	**CORE** CONTENT
Activity 6.4.3 Discuss	*How will RFID technology transform your shopping experience?*	e book
Activity 6.4.4 **TEAM** Present	*What is NFC and how can I use it?*	e book
Activity 6.4.5 **TEAM** Present	*What should proper protocol be when a call is dropped?*	e book

---

 PRECHECK

6.5 Network Classifications

Networks have three important characteristics that we'll look at in this section:
- The size of the geographic area in which the network functions.
- The role of computers in the network and how data is shared and stored on the network.
- How devices in a network are physically arranged and connected to each other.

Types of Networks

Networks can be set up to work in your house, your city, or around the world. There are three main types of networks categorized by the area they cover and identified by the catchy acronyms LAN, MAN, and WAN.

Local Area Networks A **local area network (LAN)** is a network where connected devices are located within the same room or building, or in a few nearby buildings (usually not more than a hundred or so feet apart) (Figure 6.8). One computer is designated as the server. In computing terms, a **server** is any combination of hardware and software that provides a service, such as storing data, to your computer. The server in a LAN houses the networking software that coordinates the data exchange among the devices. Shared files are generally kept on that server. A LAN can include a separate print server that manages printing tasks sent from multiple computers to a group printer. Small and home businesses are often networked in a LAN, which can be wired, or wireless. A **wireless LAN** is called (you guessed it) a **WLAN** (a local area network that uses wireless technology).

Metropolitan Area Networks A **metropolitan area network (MAN)** is a type of network that connects networks within a city, university, or other populous area to a larger high-speed network. MANs are typically made up of several LANs that are managed by a network provider. If you connect to a network through your phone or cable company, then you probably connect through a MAN.

Wide Area Networks A **wide area network (WAN)** services even larger geographic areas (Figure 6.9). WANs are used to share data between networks around the world. The Internet is, in essence, a giant WAN. WANs might use leased T1 or T3 lines, satellite connections, radio waves, or a combination of communications media.

FIGURE 6.8 **A Local Area Network (LAN)**
A switch or hub connects individual devices on a network.

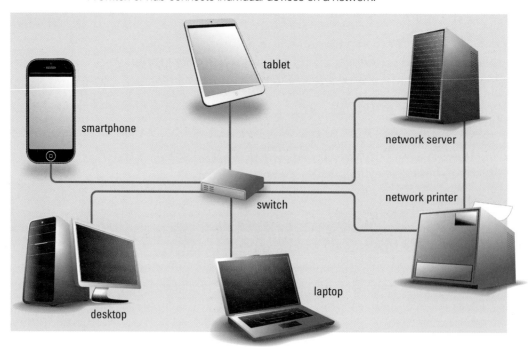

tablet

smartphone

network server

network printer

switch

desktop

laptop

FIGURE 6.9 **A Wide Area Network (WAN)**

Here three branches of a company located in different cities share resources through a WAN; a router directs network traffic to each city.

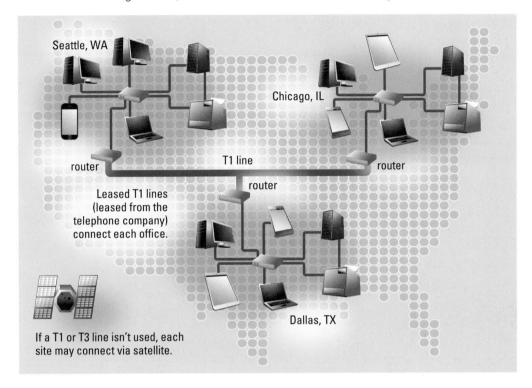

Network Architecture

In the noncomputer world architecture relates to the design of a building—where doors go, how walls connect to each other, and so on. **Network architecture** relates to how computers in a network share resources. The two major architectures are client/server and peer-to-peer.

In a **client/server network** (Figure 6.10), a computer called the *server* stores programs and files that any connected device (called a **client**) can access. Client/server is considered to be a **distributed application architecture** because it distributes tasks between client computers and server computers. For example, on the Internet, a typical client, such as your computer, makes a request of an email server. The sending and receiving of messages to and from your email account is handled on the mail server (not your client device).

In a **peer-to-peer (P2P) network** (Figure 6.11), each computer in the network can act as both server and client. Each computer can initiate requests of other clients and can act on requests initiated by others. A peer-to-peer network is simple to design and install, but won't function well in a network with heavy user demand. In a busier network, data flow becomes gridlocked like a busy traffic intersection because any computer on the network may request services of any other computer.

A modification of peer-to-peer used on the Internet to share files is **Internet peer-to-peer (P2P) network**. While users are logged onto a P2P connection, they can share and access files from their computers. Each user can both upload files (act as a server) or view uploaded files (act as a client).

FIGURE 6.10 **Client/Server Architecture**

A client sends information to or requests a service from a server. The server sends the information on to another client located on that same network or processes the service request.

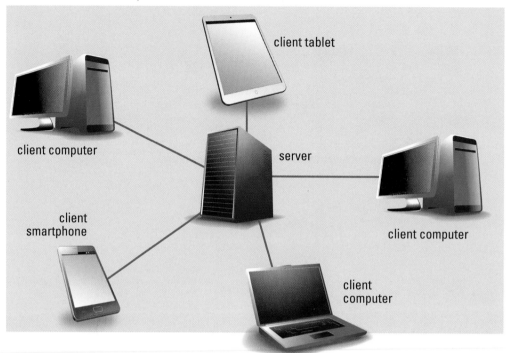

FIGURE 6.11 **Peer-to-Peer Architecture**

In a peer-to-peer network, any computer can be both a client and a server.

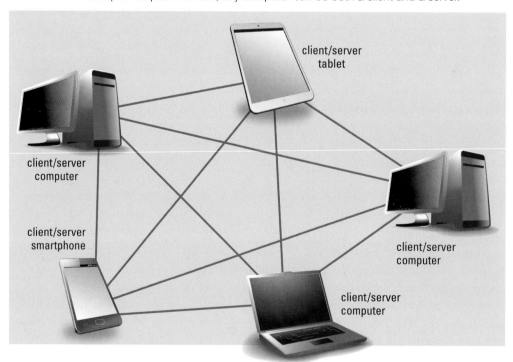

Network Topologies

Just as a floor plan describes the arrangement of furniture in a room, the arrangement of computers, servers, and other devices in a network is described as its topology. **Topology** relates to the physical layout but doesn't reflect how the data moves around the network.

Take the Next Step *Online*

Activity 6.5.1 Watch	*What is a network topology?*	CORE CONTENT
Activity 6.5.2 Watch	*What's the role of a hub and switch in a star network?*	CORE CONTENT
Activity 6.5.3 Research	*How can I find online music or movies that I can legally use?*	ebook
Activity 6.5.4 Research	*What is a virtual private network (VPN)?*	ebook

PRECHECK → ## 6.6 Networking Devices and Software

It's useful to understand the physical elements of a network in case you set up one yourself someday. Setting up a network involves several types of hardware and may involve a network operating system.

Network Devices

Each device connected to the network is called a **node**. Networking devices include hardware that facilitates the exchange of data from your computer to a transmission medium such as a cable connection, and hardware that enables various devices on a network to communicate with each other.

Modems to Send and Receive Signals As you learned earlier, a modem is the piece of hardware that sends and receives data to and from a transmission source such as your telephone line or cable television connection.

A **dial-up modem** works with phone transmissions. These devices change or manipulate an analog signal so that it can be understood by a computer or fax machine, which only understand digital signals. Dial-up modems typically take the form of adapter cards that are inserted in your computer motherboard.

A modem allows your computer to send and receive digital data via a broadband connection. Newer hardware combine a modem, router, and wireless access point in one piece of hardware.

According to figures from the Pew Internet & American Life Project, approximately 3 percent of US adults still access the Internet using a dial-up modem. This number has not changed since 2011.

Reasons for dial-up's continued existence include its low cost and lack of broadband options in rural areas.

A **DSL modem** also sends and receives data using lines on the telephone network. This modem modulates and demodulates data transmitted with analog signals, and filters out incoming voice signals. A DSL modem allows you to connect to your existing telephone system and separates voice from data traffic so you don't lose the use of your telephone while your computer is transmitting or receiving data.

A **cable modem** sends and receives digital data using a high-speed cable network based on the cable television infrastructure found in many homes.

A mobile broadband stick is a USB device that acts as a wireless modem to give your computer access to the Internet.

If your mobile device is not equipped with a wireless adapter, you may have a **wireless modem** in the form of a PC card that you slot into your device. This card provides the device with an antenna that can pick up an Internet connection. Mobile broadband sticks (also called *dongles*) have become popular for mobile users who want broadband flexibility while on the go. A **mobile broadband stick** is a USB device that acts as a modem to give your computer access to the Internet. These wireless modems can be moved easily between devices. Powered by the computer itself, a mobile broadband stick does not need to be recharged.

Hardware That Provides Access to a Network A **network adapter** is a device that provides your computer with the ability to connect to a network. A **network interface card (NIC)** (pronounced "nick") is one kind of adapter card. The NIC processes the transmission and receipt of data to/from the communications system.

In most recent computers, NICs take the form of a circuit board built into the motherboard. NICs enable a client computer on a LAN to connect to a network by managing the transmission of data and instructions sent by the server. At home, you plug one end of a cable into your desktop or laptop NIC card and the other into a DSL or cable modem.

"Describing the Internet as the Network of Networks is like calling the Space Shuttle, a thing that flies"
—John Lester

A **wireless interface card** functions in the same way as a NIC, except that a wireless interface card uses wireless technology to make the connection.

Hardware That Connects Devices to Each Other on a Network There are several devices that help other devices on a network to communicate with each other.

A **wireless access point** is a device that contains a high-quality antenna (Figure 6.12). This antenna allows computers and mobile devices to transmit data to each other or to exchange data with a wired network.

A router (top left), switch (top right), repeater (bottom left), and bridge (bottom right) are devices that networks may use to connect and send data.

FIGURE 6.12 **Wireless Access Point in a Network**

A wireless access point sends the data to computers or other devices equipped with wireless adapters. Newer hardware combines the cable modem, network router, and wireless access point into one device.

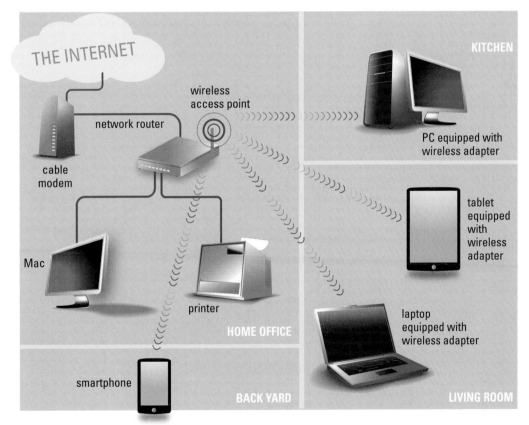

A **router** is a device that allows you to connect two or more networks in either a wired or wireless connection (in which case it is referred to as a **wireless router**). In a home, for example, a router allows you to connect multiple devices on a home network to the Internet using one high-speed connection. Routers used to connect business networks have many ports and are faster and more sophisticated than the routers you use in a home network. A mobile hotspot combines cellular network access with a wireless router, enabling multiple computers or devices to have wireless Internet access. Older models worked on 3G networks, while the newer models support 4G LTE mobile broadband.

A **repeater** is an electronic device that takes a signal and retransmits it at a higher power level to boost the transmission strength. A repeater can also transmit a signal to move past an obstruction, so that the signal can be sent further without degrading, or losing quality.

A **hub** is used on older LAN networks to coordinate the message traffic among nodes connected to a network.

A **switch** has a similar role to a hub. Switches join several nodes together to coordinate message traffic in one LAN network. However, a switch can check the data in the packets it receives, which helps to deliver each packet to the correct destination.

Gateways and bridges are devices that help separate networks to communicate with each other. A **gateway** is used when the two networks use different topologies, and a **bridge** is used to connect two networks using the same topology.

Network Operating Systems

Networks use a few different types of software to function, one of which is a network operating system.

A network uses a network operating system to add features that are essential to managing the network. In a network, a **network operating system (NOS)** is installed on the central server. A network operating system includes programs that control the flow of data among clients, restricts access to resources, and manages individual user accounts.

Some popular network operating systems are Microsoft Windows Server in various editions, Open Enterprise Server (OES), Linux Server in various editions, and Mac OS X Server. Another open source network operating system is ReactOS. Note that an NOS typically isn't required for a peer network. Current Windows operating system versions and Mac OS X have networking capabilities built in, making it easy to set up a basic wireless peer network in your home or office.

Take the Next Step *Online*

Activity 6.6.1 Watch	*How do I set up a wireless home network?*	CORE CONTENT
Activity 6.6.2 Research	*What will the smart home of the future be like?*	e book
Activity 6.6.3 Research	*What does a network administrator do?*	e book

6.7 Securing a Network

Whether on a home network or large company network, security is a vital concern today. That's because criminals and malicious hackers can find ways to break into a network to steal data and cause problems. They may locate sensitive financial information, plant viruses that destroy data, or modify settings in ways that cost you time and money.

Network security is managed through a combination of techniques involving hardware and software such as a **firewall**, which stops those outside a network from sending information into it or taking information out of it (Figure 6.13). On your home network, you may be the administrator (operating systems such as Windows allow you to set up administrator privileges) and set up your own firewall. In business, network security is an in-demand career specialty.

Chapter 8 explains computer security in more detail.

FIGURE 6.13 **How a Network Firewall Works**

In this intranet, all the devices containing company data are protected behind a firewall, which blocks unauthorized access. Access is controlled by the system administrator.

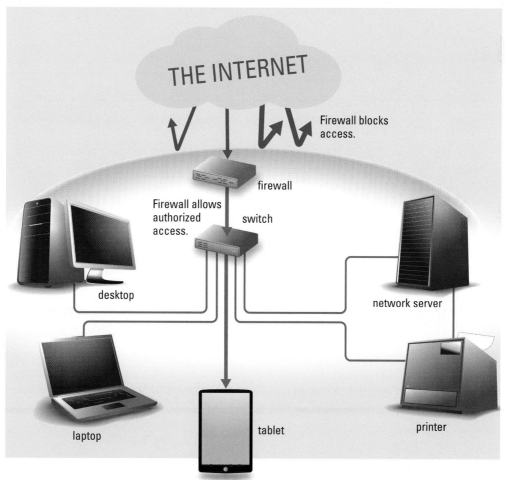

Ethics and Technology Blog *Online*

Is Stealing Time Online OK?

I hear a lot of companies crack down on employees who use the company network to conduct personal business. What's all the fuss about?

 Computers in Your Career

Computer security is a hot field for those seeking a career working with computer technology. More and more companies understand that protecting their information and their customers' records and privacy is essential to their success, and those in the IT department who deal with security are seen as vital partners. Security specialists will be employed to assess a system's vulnerability and implement security measures. According to the Bureau of Labor Statistics' *Occupational Outlook Handbook*, Information Security Analysts' responsibilities are continually expanding as the number of cyberattacks increase. This job requires someone with a bachelor's degree for entry-level positions. Additionally, computer analysts and developers will develop new antivirus software, programs, and procedures.

 Take the Next Step *Online*

Activity 6.7.1 Watch	*What is the difference between a hardware and software firewall?*	**CORE** CONTENT
Activity 6.7.2 Research	*How can BYOD (bring your own device) threaten corporate security?*	
Activity 6.7.3 Research	*What network security do you have in place?*	
Activity 6.7.4 Discuss	*Do you get what you pay for with free virus and spyware programs?*	

PRECHECK # 6.8 Interesting Trends in Networking

Two key buzzwords in networking circles today are *mobility* and *the cloud*. In fact, the trends are complementary, as both allow computer users more freedom in accessing what they need to get their work done from anywhere and at a lower cost.

Mobility and VoIP

Many companies have built or are building Wi-Fi and Voice over Internet Protocol (VoIP) into their internal computer networks. This means that employees can use their cell phones or smartphones both inside the

> So therefore, what is your purpose? What are you supposed to do? How are you supposed to educate? How are you supposed to create jobs? I feel that that is what Cloud is, that is what social media is going to do.
>
> —Mark Benioff, CEO, Salesforce.com

company's building and in the wireless networks outside the building without dropping a call as they move from one environment to the other. Also, VoIP is being used by companies to save money by routing voice calls via the Internet rather than via the traditional telephone network.

Cloud Computing

In the past, elements of the network that were kept invisible to users were considered to be in the cloud—that is, software installed on a network server that you simply open and use without having to install it on your computer.

Web 2.0 has ushered in an online cloud where software and services are accessed on the Internet (Figure 6.14). In previous chapters you were introduced to cloud computing as a way to access storage and software applications as services online. This is part of cloud computing, which relies on the concept of Software as a Service, or SaaS. By having applications installed, maintained, and updated outside their walls in the "cloud," companies save money.

Some basic cloud services such as Office Online and Google Drive are free for individual users, but more advanced cloud services cater to larger organizations. In 2013, Microsoft released Office 365 to home and business customers, a subscription-based license to the full-featured Microsoft Office suite, indicating the future is subscription software in the cloud for home users. Such a cloud service has three features that differentiate it from software located on your computer or network:

- It is sold on demand and billed by the minute, by the hour, monthly, or annually.
- People can use as much or as little of a service as they want at any given time.
- The service is fully managed and maintained by the provider (the end user only uses a computer and his/her Internet access to work with the service).

FIGURE 6.14 **How Software and Data Can Be in the Cloud**
Accessing software and/or storing data in the cloud means your device is the tool that securely connects you to the services and data for which you have subscribed via an Internet connection. No longer are you tethered to a specific desktop, laptop, tablet, or smartphone.

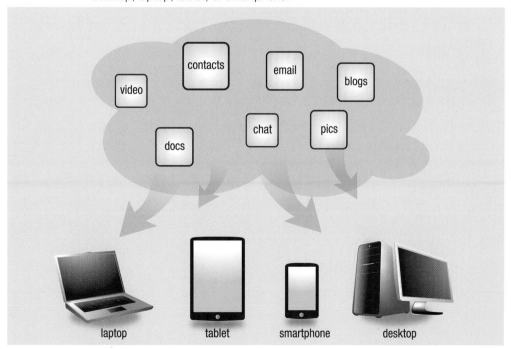

Cloud computing expenditures are a significant focus of IT budgets with a trend toward hybrid cloud deployments. A **hybrid cloud** is created when a company manages some computing resources and data in-house, but also has other services provided by outside vendors. For example, a company might use a cloud provider such as Amazon for storing archived data but maintain current data on internal systems. Gartner Research forecasts that nearly half of large enterprises will have hybrid cloud systems by the end of 2017.

The Evolution of 5G

Cisco's Global Mobile Data Traffic Forecast, updated in 2015, predicts that global mobile traffic will reach 366.8 **exabytes** by 2020. The driving force behind this forecast rests upon the expectation that the Internet of Things (IoT) will grow to 26 billion connected units by 2020. The Internet of Things excludes PCs, smartphones, and tablets, and represents everyday objects all interconnected and communicating with each other. For example, the coffee maker on your desk would brew your cup of coffee just in time for your arrival based upon updates transmitted from your car as you park in the company lot.

The wireless industry is generally expected to work on defining **5G standards** through 2019 with 5G deployments starting in 2020. No one knows for sure what 5G standards will be, but experts agree that more speed is the goal with a target of 1 Gbps to mobile devices. A survey of current news reveals the following 5G press releases:

- According to CNET, 5G is considered key to the Internet of Things (IoT), the name given to the notion of tying just about every and any thing into the Net. Billions of sensors will be built into appliances, security systems, health monitors, door locks, cars and wearables—from smartwatches to dog collars.
- The 5G Infrastructure Public Private Partnership, in short 5G PPP, has been initiated by the EU Commission and industry manufacturers, telecommunications operators, service providers, and researchers.
- As part of the evolution toward 5G, and to improve the performance and efficiency of today`s LTE technology while meeting the network demands created by growing data traffic, Ericsson is launching new Ericsson Radio System software and hardware. The launches support the world`s first commercial offering of LTE 1Gbps peak data rates.

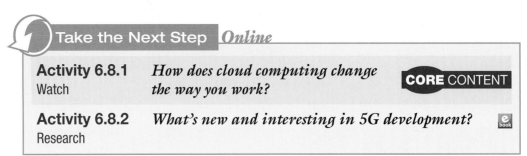

Take the Next Step *Online*		
Activity 6.8.1 Watch	*How does cloud computing change the way you work?*	CORE CONTENT
Activity 6.8.2 Research	*What's new and interesting in 5G development?*	e book

An interactive Summing Up with audio, a Study Notes document, slide presentations with audio, and Terms to Know flashcards with audio are available from the links menu on this page in your ebook.

Summing Up

How Does the World Use Networking?

A **computer network** consists of two or more computing devices connected by a communications medium, such as a wireless signal or a cable. A network provides a way to connect with others and share files and resources.

Many companies have their own networks, called **intranets**. Intranets are essentially a private Internet within the company's corporate "walls." An **extranet** is an extension of an intranet that allows interaction with those outside the company, such as suppliers and customers.

Exploring Communications Systems

A computer network is one kind of **communications system**. This system includes hardware to send and receive data, transmission and relay systems, common sets of standards so all the equipment can "talk" to each other, and communications software.

Two kinds of signals are used in transmitting data over a computer network: analog and digital. An **analog signal** is formed by continuous waves that fluctuate from high to low. A **digital signal** uses a discrete signal that is either high or low.

If you send data between computers using an analog medium such as a phone line, the signal has to be transformed from digital to analog and back again to digital. Today most new communications technologies simply use a digital signal, saving the trouble of converting transmissions.

The speed of transmission is determined by two factors: 1) **frequency**, which is the speed at which a signal can change from high to low; and 2) **bandwidth**, which refers to the number of bits per second that can be transmitted. Any communications medium that is capable of carrying a large amount of data at a fast speed is known as **broadband**.

Transmission Systems

Wired transmissions send a signal through various media, including:
- **Twisted-pair cable**, which is used for your wired telephone connection at home.
- **Coaxial cable**, the same cable used to transmit cable television signals over an insulated wire at a fast speed.
- **Fiber-optic cable**, a very fast system that uses a protected string of glass to transmit data as beams of light.

Wireless transmissions in use today include cellular, microwave, and satellite. All use radio waves to transmit data.

A **cellular network**, like those used by your cell phone or smartphone, transmits signals called **cellular transmissions**, by using cell towers. A **microwave** is a high-frequency radio signal that is directed between microwave station towers that are within sight of each other.

Satellite communication uses space-based equipment for longer range transmissions.

Communications Standards and Protocols

To allow different devices to talk to each other, the computer industry has developed **standards** that address issues of compatibility. A standard that specifies how two devices can communicate is called a **protocol**.

There are two primary wired standards: 1) **Ethernet**, which specifies that there is no central device controlling the timing of data transmission; 2) **TCP/IP**, in which **packets** are sent and reassembled by the receiver. TCP/IP is the standard upon which Internet communications are based.

Wireless networking standards include:

- **Wi-Fi**, which refers to a network that is based on the **802.11 standard**. A location that makes Wi-Fi access available is called a **hotspot**.
- **WiMAX** (Worldwide Interoperability for Microwave Access, also known as 802.16), which uses the 4G standard.
- **Long Term Evolution (LTE) standards** prepare mobile phone networks for new technologies, involving areas such as improved bandwidth efficiency and cost controls.
- **WiGig** offers faster connection speeds but with limited range.
- **Bluetooth**, a network protocol that offers short-range connectivity (3 to 300 feet, depending on a device's power class) via radio waves between devices such as your smartphone and car. **Bluetooth LE** (low energy) is designed to operate at a lower energy consumption level and a lower cost. Smartphone users may be able to share the Internet connection of their device via a cable, Bluetooth, or Wi-Fi with another device such as a tablet or laptop. This process is known as **tethering,** and it is useful when accessing the Internet via other means not available for your laptop or tablet.
- **Radio Frequency Identification (RFID)**, a wireless technology primarily used to track and identify inventory or other items using radio signals.
- **Wireless Application Protocol (WAP)**, which specifies how mobile devices such as smartphones display online information including maps and email.

Network Classifications

Networks are classified by three characteristics: 1) the size of the geographic area in which the network functions, 2) how data is shared and stored on the network, and 3) how devices in a network are physically arranged and connected to each other.

Types of networks include:

- A **local area network (LAN),** a network where connected devices are located within the same room or building, or in a few nearby buildings.
- A **metropolitan area network (MAN),** a network that connects networks within a city, a university, or other populous area to a larger high-speed network.
- A **wide area network (WAN),** which services even larger geographic areas.

Network architecture relates to how computers in a network share resources. The two major architectures are client/server and peer-to-peer. In a **client/server network**, a **server** computer stores programs and files that any connected device (**clients**) can access. In a **peer-to-peer (P2P) network**, each computer in the network can act as both server and client.

Networking Devices and Software

Networking devices include hardware that facilitates the exchange of data from your computer to a transmission medium such as a cable connection, or hardware that enables various devices on a network to communicate with each other. Each device connected to a network is called a **node**.

A **modem** is the piece of hardware that sends and receives data from a transmission source such as your telephone line or cable television connection. Types of modems include **dial-up**, **cable**, **DSL**, and **wireless**. A **mobile broadband stick** is a USB device that acts as a modem to give your computer access to the Internet.

A **network adapter** provides your computer with the ability to connect to a network. A **network interface card (NIC)** is one kind of adapter card. NICs support Ethernet.

A **wireless interface card** functions in the same way as a NIC, except that a wireless interface card uses wireless technology to make the connection.

Wireless access points contain a high-quality antenna that permits wireless devices to transmit data to each other or to exchange data with a wired network.

A **router** allows you to connect multiple networks (or multiple devices if used in a home) in either a wired or wireless connection.

A **repeater** is an electronic device that takes a signal and retransmits it at a higher power level to boost the transmission strength.

A **hub** is used on older LAN networks to coordinate the message traffic among nodes connected to a network.

A **switch** has a similar role to a hub, however, a switch can check the data in the packets to ensure delivery to the correct destination.

Gateways and **bridges** help separate networks to communicate with each other.

A **network operating system (NOS)** includes programs that control the flow of data among clients, restrict access to resources, and manage individual user accounts.

Securing a Network

Network security is managed through a combination of hardware and software such as a **firewall,** which stops those outside a network from sending information into it or taking information out of it.

Interesting Trends in Networking

Many companies are building Wi-Fi and Voice over Internet Protocol (VoIP) into their internal networks. The use of cloud computing is expected to continue to grow rapidly in the business world. Cloud computing is where software and IT services are accessed on the Internet and are usually billed as a service rather than by application license. By having applications installed, maintained, and updated outside their walls in the "cloud," companies save money. The wireless industry is generally expected to work on defining **5G standards** through 2019 with 5G deployments starting in 2020. No one knows for sure what 5G standards will be, but experts agree that more speed is the goal with a target of 1 Gbps to the mobile device.

Terms to Know

How Does the World Use Networking?

computer network, 164
intranet, 164

extranet, 164

Exploring Communications Systems

communications system, 164
network protocol, 164
analog signal, 165
digital signal, 165
modem, 165
frequency, 166
bandwidth, 166

broadband, 167
kilobit per second (Kbps), 167
megabit per second (Mbps), 167
gigabit per second (Gbps), 167
terabit per second (Tbps), 167
petabit per second (Pbps), 167

Transmission Systems

twisted-pair cable, 168
coaxial cable, 168
fiber-optic cable, 168
cellular network, 168

cellular transmission, 168
microwave, 168
satellite communication, 170

Communications Standards and Protocols

standards, 172
American National Standards Institute
    (ANSI), 172
Institute of Electrical and Electronics
    Engineers (IEEE), 172
protocol, 172
Ethernet, 172
TCP/IP, 173
packet, 173
packet switching, 173
Wi-Fi, 173
802.11 standard, 173
hotspot, 174

WiMAX, 174
WiGig, 174
Long Term Evolution (LTE), 174
Bluetooth, 174
Bluetooth LE (BLE), 174
Bluetooth Smart, 174
tethering, 174
Radio Frequency Identification (RFID),
    175
Wireless Application Protocol (WAP), 175
email server, Activity 6.4.1
webmail, Activity 6.4.1

Network Classifications

local area network (LAN), 176
server, 176
wireless LAN (WLAN), 176
metropolitan area network (MAN), 176
wide area network (WAN), 176
network architecture, 177
client/server network, 177
client, 177

distributed application architecture, 177
peer-to-peer (P2P) network, 177
Internet peer-to-peer (P2P) network,
    177
topology, 179
bus topology, Activity 6.5.1
ring topology, Activity 6.5.1
star topology, Activity 6.5.1

Networking Devices and Software

Securing a Network

Interesting Trends in Networking

Concepts Check

Concepts Check 6.1   Multiple Choice

Take this quiz to test your understanding of key concepts in this chapter.

Concepts Check 6.2   Matching

Test your understanding of terms and concepts presented in this chapter.

Concepts Check 6.3   Label It

Use the interactive tool to identify components in a local area network.

Concepts Check 6.4   Label It

Use the interactive tool to label two types of cables and their components.

Projects

Check with your instructor for the preferred method to submit completed work.

Project 6.1   Wi-Fi Know-How

Project 6.1.1

To familiarize yourself with how Wi-Fi networks work, watch the video at the web page titled *What Is Wi-Fi?* at http://ODW4.emcp.net/WhatIsWi-Fi and then read the article titled *How Wi-Fi Works* at http://ODW4.emcp.net/HowWi-FiWorks to learn more about Wi-Fi, including descriptions of the various 802.11 standards. Based on the information you learned from the video and article, prepare a document containing a bulleted list of key facts about Wi-Fi.

Project 6.1.2 `TEAM`

Have your team split into two groups. Each group should visit a place where free public Wi-Fi is available such as a library, coffee shop, or shopping center. See if you can spot the wireless access points mounted on walls, ceilings, posts, or other structures. How many did you see? (These devices should be apparent by the antennae on the device and are generally mounted high up in the space.) Using your smartphone or other mobile device, connect to the Wi-Fi network. Was it easy to identify and log on to the network? Did you need a password from an employee of the business? Did you have to agree to Terms of Service before continuing to your browser page? If yes, were the Terms of Service easy to read and understand?

Next, conduct a basic Internet search looking up a map or list of movies at local cinemas. Observe the speed as you navigate the Internet. Were you satisfied that the web pages loaded quickly or was there a few seconds lag? If the pages loaded more slowly than you like, look around the facility to see how many other people might be using the network. Is it possible the network is congested? Consider using a web-based speed measurement tool (such as speedtest.net) to measure the network speed. Meet back with the other half of your team and compare your experiences. Prepare a brief report that summarizes your Wi-Fi experience at each location.

Project 6.2   Public Connectivity

Project 6.2.1 `TEAM`

In June 2014, New York City launched *The Harlem Wi-Fi Network*. The network is the largest free outdoor public Wi-Fi network in the United States, covering 95 blocks in Harlem (a neighborhood within New York City) at the time of the announcement. Free public Wi-Fi is now made available to approximately 80,000 Harlem residents, as well as businesses and visitors. Within your team discuss the benefits of providing free outdoor public Wi-Fi in a city and the reasons why all city governments should provide free Wi-Fi. Assume your team has been hired by a local community organization to make a pitch to your city government to fund free outdoor public Wi-Fi to your entire city. Create a presentation with your team's sales pitch to your local city government.

Project 6.2.2 `TEAM`

Your team works at a local property management company that primarily leases commercial space for offices. The CEO of the company has been considering the idea of providing free wireless access in all of the buildings the company manages. To determine the feasibility of this plan, the CEO has asked your team to investigate the benefits and drawbacks of free and open wireless accessibility, including the cost, security, and other factors for its implementation. Prepare a slide presentation for the executive board that supports or discourages this plan, and provide a rationale for your team's position.

Project 6.3   Green Telecommunications Networks

Project 6.3.1

Watch the video titled *About the GreenTouch Consortium* at http://ODW4.emcp.net/ GreenTouch to learn about a non-profit group of leading telecommunications companies that is working on technologies to reduce the energy consumption of wireless networks. Find a recent article about green initiatives under way in the telecommunications industry. Prepare a document with a bullet-list summary of what you learned about the green initiatives in the wireless industry from watching the video and reading the article.

Project 6.3.2 `TEAM`

Did you know that supporting your smartphone takes lots of power? Telecommunications companies are huge consumers of energy. One of the factors involved in reducing the energy usage by telecommunications companies is the high cost to change their power source to a renewable form of energy, such as solar or wind energy. It is a difficult balance for executives to return a profit to shareholders while also conducting a socially responsible business. One suggested model is that governments should subsidize a green infrastructure in which businesses are rewarded for using green sources of energy. Within your team, discuss the problem of funding these high-cost investments for a greener future. Include in your discussions the problem of building a green wireless infrastructure in developing countries where the subscriber base could not provide enough revenue to support it. Who should pay for these projects? Create a brief presentation that summarizes the conclusions your team reached.

Project 6.4   RFID—Cure or Curse?

Project 6.4.1

Radio Frequency Identification (RFID) technology applications have exploded far beyond businesses using tags to track inventory through their supply chains. RFID tags are being used for safety practices, traffic monitoring, healthcare research and monitoring, food quality monitoring, and even tracking waste disposal. But, privacy concerns have arisen about the use of RFID technology. Find and read two articles about RFID from reputable sources. One of the articles should document the benefits of how RFID technology is being used. The second article should address privacy or other security concerns about the use of RFID technology. Create a document that summarizes in a bullet list what you learned from the two articles; include the URLs for the two articles.

Project 6.4.2 `TEAM`

Within your team, compile a list of the benefits of using RFID technology and a brief statement about privacy or security concerns. Each team member should present this information to three relatives or friends, ask each person the following two questions, and then record the answers.
- Do you have any concerns about widespread use of RFID technology?
- How should monitoring and use of data obtained from reading RFID tags be controlled?

As a team, discuss the responses you received to the two questions from all participants. Briefly summarize the participant responses and your team's conclusions about the future of RFID applications in a document or presentation.

Project 6.5   Wiki—Networking Devices and Terms

Project 6.5.1 `TEAM`

Your team will be assigned to research and write a brief explanation on one or more of the following devices or terms commonly associated with corporate networks: router, switch, bridge, repeater, gateway, firewall, wireless access point, wireless LAN controller, TCP/IP, T1 line, T3 line, T4 line, or VPN. Prepare a post to the course wiki site for your assigned topic(s). Include an explanation of the device or term along with examples or images, if possible, to aid comprehension. Be sure to compile a list of references for your sources of information.

Project 6.5.2 `TEAM`

Your team is assigned to edit and verify the content posted on the wiki site from Project 6.5.1. If you add or edit any content, make sure you include a notation within the page that includes the team members' names and the date you edited the content—for example, "Edited by [team members' names] on [date]." Keep a list of references that you used to verify your content changes. When you are finished with your verification, include a notation at the end of the entry—for example, "Verified by [team members' names] on [date]."

Project 6.6   Wiki—Acceptable Use of Computers and Networks at Work

Project 6.6.1 `TEAM`

Due to ongoing issues regarding the improper use of company-owned computing equipment, the executive board has asked you or your team to draft a new corporate policy on acceptable computer and network practices. You will be assigned to write a section for the new policy on one or more of the following topics:
- Gaming
- Personal email
- Social networking (Facebook)
- YouTube
- Blogging
- Access to high-quality color printers
- Company-provided computing equipment (laptop, tablet, smartphone)
- Internet surfing or shopping
- Texting and video chatting

When you have finished writing your assigned section, post your topic and its accompanying text to the course wiki site.

Project 6.6.2 `TEAM`

You or your team has been asked to comment on the content posted on the wiki site from Project 6.6.1. Post your commentary followed by a notation that includes your name or the team members' names and the date you commented—for example, "Comment by [your name or team members' names] on [date]."

Class Conversations

Topic 6.1   Can you see me now?

Location-Based Services (LBS) available for smartphones have opened new doors to managers who want to keep a watchful eye on their mobile workers. Service agreements are available with a company's cellular provider to log employees' movements, including enabling tracking when the employee has entered or exited a predefined region (called *GeoFencing*) and to send an alert when a specified speed limit has been exceeded. While LBS has obvious safety benefits (such as locating a mobile worker who may be lost or in need of assistance), is there a point at which an individual's right to privacy is at risk with this technology? If yes, where would you suggest this tracking technology has the potential to invade an employee's privacy? Assume you are a manager at a company that subscribes to LBS. How will you address any privacy issues raised by your employees about the data you will receive from the mobile device?

Topic 6.2   Should everyone open their wireless networks to everyone else?

"The Open Wireless Movement is a coalition of Internet freedom advocates, companies, organizations, and technologists working to develop new wireless technologies and to inspire a movement of Internet openness. We are aiming to build technologies that would make it easy for Internet subscribers to portion off their wireless networks for guests and the public while maintaining security, protecting privacy, and preserving quality of access."

—openwireless.org

The Open Wireless Movement wants a future in which the Internet is entirely open to everyone in urban environments. To achieve this goal, all Internet subscribers would have to allow open access to their own wireless networks. Visit openwireless.org and explore the reasons, myths, and facts about open wireless. Would you consider opening up your home Wi-Fi network to be accessed by strangers? Why or why not?

Topic 6.3   What happens when the network is down?

For some, being connected 24/7 can be both a positive and a negative influence in their lives. Have you ever logged in to your computer and become agitated because the network connectivity was slow or—even worse—down altogether? With increasing reliance on digital networks, what happens when the network goes down? If you try to contact someone over a network and receive no response, how do you react? Does work stop, or does work become more productive because employees are not distracted with constant online interruptions? How long would you be content with no connectivity in your day?

The Social Web
Opportunities for Learning, Working, and Communicating

What You'll Accomplish

When you finish this chapter, you'll be able to:

7.1 Explain the social web phenomenon and its impact on how our society functions.

7.2 Examine the past, present, and future of social technology and how our lives have changed through this development.

7.3 Identify a blog and explain the uses of blogs in today's workplace and personal settings.

7.4 Describe the development, growth, and trends of social networking.

7.5 Explain how social bookmarking works and identify three different services.

7.6 Identify the role of wikis and explain how people are using wikis in the social web.

7.7 Explain the role of media sharing and provide examples of how it is being used.

Why Does It Matter ?

Social networking sites, such as Facebook, have seen phenomenal growth in the past several years. In 2016, Facebook had more than one billion active users. Facebook has experienced a tremendous increase in mobile users of its site, growing to its current user base from only 750 million in 2011. If Facebook were a country, it would be the world's largest, with more than three times the population of the United States. But connecting with friends on social networking sites is only one aspect of a trend toward a more collaborative online environment. Social technologies are also being used by businesses to help employees connect with each other and communicate with customers, by nonprofit groups to document trends and promote social causes, by schools to involve students in collaborative projects and interactive learning, and in many other settings. You are part of a revolution in the way that people share and collaborate, and by choosing to embrace that revolution, you may reap benefits in many areas of your life.

Chapter 7 The Social Web: Opportunities for Learning, Working, and Communicating

From social networking sites that contain networks of friends to collaborative wikis, blogs, and media sharing sites, social websites represent a revolution in how people connect, learn, and work together.

7.1 The Social Web Phenomenon

You may belong to or have visited pages on websites such as Facebook, Twitter, YouTube, Pinterest, Google+, or Tumblr, or have read about these sites in the news. All of these are social sites, where people go to share their thoughts in text, video, or photos. Together with a wide variety of other social websites, these sites form the **social web**, a revolution in how people connect with each other, how news is delivered, and how our collective knowledge is formed. Social sites and the tools they offer create a vehicle for a two-way dialog between people and groups, rather than a one-way communication from the media to the public, stores to customers, or teachers to students.

> 66 Facebook was not originally created to be a company. It was built to accomplish a social mission—to make the world more open and connected. 99
>
> —Mark Zuckerberg, founder of Facebook

The social web is still evolving and defining itself, and as such is likely to include more types of websites and services than you think. Any site that allows users to interact with each other and share information or content can be considered, at some level, to be social. A website that allows you to share contacts and build a network of friends is a **social networking site**. Services that allow you to share media are **media sharing sites**. Online dating services and special interest sites, such as those about sports or genealogy, when they allow interaction and communication among members, are social sites. Social sites such as Pinterest also allow for sharing of visual images, articles, and collections of ideas related to travel, cooking, craft projects, and any other hobby or topic you may be interested in. The content of most of these sites is driven almost entirely by the members, though the site owners devise and maintain the infrastructure, communication tools, and rules for behavior.

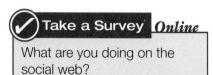

Take a Survey *Online*

What are you doing on the social web?

 7.2 Social Technology Comes of Age

In Chapter 2 you read about the concept of Web 2.0 as a phase of the development of the web associated with user involvement and collaboration. This collaboration happens through interactive web services, such as Wikipedia (an online encyclopedia) and Facebook (a social networking site that connects people to one another). These web services provide users with a way to share information, exchange ideas, and add or edit content in collaborative articles. The social web is one of the most publicized and successful examples of Web 2.0.

How the Social Web Was Born

Since the early days of the Internet, when it was used only by government and educational researchers, through the first few years after the Internet became available to the general public, people have been interacting online through tools such as discussion boards and email, but the social web took that interaction much further. The concept of Web 2.0 appeared in 2001, and understanding the trends it describes is important in understanding how the social web came to be. In the late 1990s, the open source

Social sites allow users to share ideas and content online.

movement allowed individuals to contribute to the source code of free software, such as the Linux operating system. **Open content** is to the social web what open source was to software development—it means that people can freely share their knowledge about topics in online collections, such as Wikipedia.

In 1997, at about the same time that the open source and open content movements were growing, one of the first true social networking sites, SixDegrees.com, appeared. Although other sites already existed that allowed users to create **profiles** with information about themselves and compile lists of friends, SixDegrees was one of the first sites that combined the use of profiles and searchable **friends lists** in one service: social networking was born.

SixDegrees failed, perhaps in part because its concept was ahead of its time. Meanwhile, in 1999, online journals called **blogs** (a term created from web + log) began to surface online, facilitated by blogging sites such as Open Diary and Blogger. Blogs became one of the key tools for online social interaction. A few more social networking sites appeared throughout the late 1990s, many incorporating a blogging component, until, in 2003, the phenomenon exploded with sites such as MySpace, Flickr, Facebook, and LinkedIn all launching within months of each other. Google+ was launched in 2011 and within the first two weeks had over 10 million users. Figure 7.1 presents the timeline of social networking sites.

FIGURE 7.1 Launch Dates of Social Networking Sites

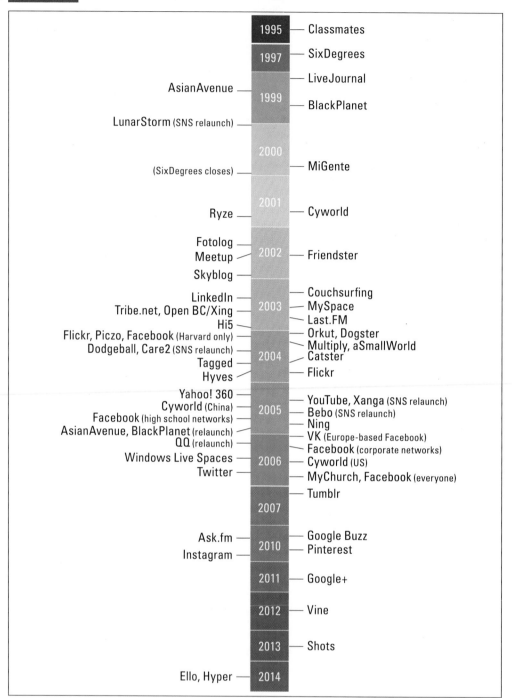

	1995 — Classmates
	1997 — SixDegrees
	LiveJournal
AsianAvenue — 1999	
	BlackPlanet
LunarStorm (SNS relaunch) —	
	2000
(SixDegrees closes) —	MiGente
Ryze — 2001	Cyworld
Fotolog —	
Meetup — 2002	Friendster
Skyblog —	
LinkedIn —	Couchsurfing
Tribe.net, Open BC/Xing — 2003	MySpace
Hi5 —	Last.FM
Flickr, Piczo, Facebook (Harvard only) —	Orkut, Dogster
Dodgeball, Care2 (SNS relaunch) —	Multiply, aSmallWorld
Tagged — 2004	Catster
Hyves —	Flickr
Yahoo! 360 —	
Cyworld (China) — 2005	YouTube, Xanga (SNS relaunch)
Facebook (high school networks) —	Bebo (SNS relaunch)
AsianAvenue, BlackPlanet (relaunch) —	Ning
QQ (relaunch) —	VK (Europe-based Facebook)
	Facebook (corporate networks)
Windows Live Spaces — 2006	Cyworld (US)
Twitter —	MyChurch, Facebook (everyone)
	Tumblr
	2007
Ask.fm — 2010	Google Buzz
Instagram —	Pinterest
	2011 — Google+
	2012 — Vine
	2013 — Shots
Ello, Hyper — 2014	

Adapted from "Social Network Sites: Definition, History, and Scholarship" by Boyd and Ellison, *Journal of Computer Mediated Communication*.

Ethics and Technology Blog *Online*

Design by Crowdsourcing

Crowdsourcing involves getting lots of people to contribute to a work online. If a graphic designer gets ideas from others using an app such as Thumb and then sells that work as his or her own, is it wrong? Maybe it's just "social" creativity?

The social net makes it possible for streams of information and connections to travel across the globe.

Overview of Social Technology Today

Today, the social web can be accessed by a variety of devices, such as smartphones and gaming devices. These devices allow people to connect with their social sites to post text, video, and photos and interact with their friends on the go. Certain social media services, such as Snapchat, are accessible only via apps on mobile devices—their content cannot be viewed using a browser.

If you perform a search using the terms "social web," you will see the incredible variety of social sites and applications available to you. The functions of these sites and applications are as varied as the people and organizations who use them. Social causes use the social web to muster support in times of crisis, such as raising money to help victims of natural disasters. Businesses use social marketing, driving their branding and sales messages to the public by participating in all kinds of social networking sites. Politicians hold online dialogs on political and social issues to gather votes and support. Artists create musical and visual pieces by sharing media and building new pieces of art collaboratively. Political demonstrators all over the globe have used social media to organize their efforts and communicate about incidents and developments.

The social web is growing and evolving rapidly, with changes happening daily. Functions and features of the different social websites overlap, making it challenging to define the technologies precisely. However, grouping them into the following broad categories provides a way to examine them and understand their value in our digital world:

- blogging
- social networking
- social bookmarking
- wikis
- media sharing

Each of these categories of social media is explored in this chapter in terms of how the technology works, who uses it, and for what purposes.

Khan Academy is just one example of a site that provides students with videos, practice exercises, and assessments for free.

The Future of Social Technology

By the time you read this chapter, social technology will have changed. That's one of the most exciting things about web content driven by the masses: it morphs very quickly because anybody can suggest an idea that becomes the next great trend, rather than having trends dictated by businesses or the media. Still, it's possible to speculate about some future directions for the social web that are already emerging.

One predicted trend is the ability to carry your **identity** (the profile you create when you join a service) with you from site to site. There will be a connection among all the social sites you now use separately. You will have one set of friends who have access to your page, and one set of **preferences** (such as privacy settings). Currently, you can see the potential of this kind of system in the ability to sign up for or into multiple sites using your Facebook credentials.

> " Social networking in the enterprise will break down . . . barriers and provide equal access to information across levels and job functions. "
>
> —Luosheng Peng,
> CEO, GageIn

Another trend is the ability to gather together content from a wide variety of services. For example, a service like HootSuite allows you to create categories of information and post updates on a variety of services, such as Twitter, Facebook, and more in one action.

It's been suggested that in the future all websites will have social networking features, and in fact that movement is already underway. For example, Outlook.com, which started as an email and calendar service, now allows you to build a friends network, as do some bookmarking sites. You may also be able to use your social media account to log in to interactive features of other media websites, such as the comments feature for online newspapers. Social media has become a real-time reporting tool. Recent changes in government regimes in the Middle East spread through the use of social media sites such as Google Crisis Response, which allows people to get news updates and share emergency-service data in critical times. What could that mean to the way we share knowledge, do business, become aware of global social causes, and report the news?

HootSuite is a social relationship platform that allows users to control their various social media profiles from one secure dashboard.

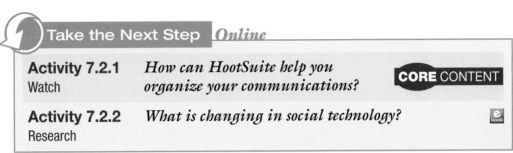

Take the Next Step *Online*

| **Activity 7.2.1** Watch | *How can HootSuite help you organize your communications?* | CORE CONTENT |
| **Activity 7.2.2** Research | *What is changing in social technology?* | ebook |

PRECHECK ➡ # 7.3 Blogging: The Internet Gets Personal

A blog is an online journal that anybody can use to express ideas and opinions online. A blog may be focused around a particular topic, such as animal rights, or simply be a random collection of personal thoughts. Blogs can contain text, images, videos, and links to other online content. Most sites that host blogs allow bloggers to set a level of privacy that determines who can view their content.

People who read blogs can post comments about blog entries. Blogs and responses to them are typically listed in reverse chronological order, with the most recent post at the top.

How Blogging Has Evolved

Blogging began on a small scale in the mid-1990s, but gained popularity in 1999 when blogging tools became more generally available to the public with blog hosting services, such as LiveJournal and Blogger.

Over time, blogging has moved into many online settings. Today you may create your blog on a blog hosting site, or you may post to a blog that is part of a social networking site, such as Facebook, Tumblr, or Bebo. Companies often host blogs on their websites where they can share information with their customers and listen to their customers' opinions through product reviews. Experts write columns on sites such as ZDNet and The Huffington Post, which allow them to discover new ways to build readership.

Blogs are incredibly popular, but it's interesting to consider some of the consequences of people posting their opinions and thoughts before millions of others. Blogs have been the subject of lawsuits when posts slander another person or organization.

Commenting on technology trends is a popular use of blogs.

Some governments have cracked down on political blogs that challenge government policy. Job seekers have begun to realize that employers often read personal information they have posted online and consider that content in their hiring decisions.

Computers in Your Career

If you have an interest in journalism as a career, you'll find that your chosen field is undergoing major changes. Journalism once provided a "one speaking to many" model, but blogging has brought a new dynamic of two-way communication. Old models of print newspapers and magazines are being challenged, but the Internet is also bringing new opportunities. For example, mobile phone journalism (MoJo) offers the ability to report instantly from the field via mobile phones. According to John S. Carroll, former editor of the *Los Angeles Times*, "Journalism…is now a conversation with millions of participants, which gives us access to new facts and new ideas. Thanks to hyperlinks, you can write accordion-like stories that can be expanded to match each reader's degree of interest. The journalism of the future will be flexible, making fluid use of video, audio, and text to tell stories as they can best be told." Journalism is certainly a career that is undergoing dramatic change; still, future opportunities to take advantage of new media and content choices continue to make this an intriguing career choice.

The Many Uses of Blogs

Many blogs are simply personal journals chronicling a person's day or opinions. But today, blogs have also taken on a role in reporting news stories and in providing a soapbox for experts—or *pundits*—on topics from politics to the environment. Governments of various countries host official blogs where citizens can voice their opinions. People who spot technology and social trends find huge audiences for their blogs, as do entertainers such as Bill Maher and other TV and movie stars. An interesting blog statistic is that, somewhere in the world, a new blog is created every half a second.

A fascinating aspect of blogging is the use of the social web during crises. In 2014, political demonstrations broke out in countries such as Ukraine and Venezuela, and social networking sites allowed people in these countries to share with the world the

Our Digital World

The Social Web

Machines will be an integral part of our social media networks in the future.

That's the prediction of experts from a recent report by the Pew Research Center, says Lee Rainie, director of the project.

"There will be nodes in our networks that will be algorithms, or bots, that are acting on our behalf, and hopefully are helpful to us," he said. "They're going to enhance and enrich our lives."

For example, say you've just been diagnosed with a rare medical condition. You'll still rely on your personal network of doctors, friends and support groups, "but there will be bots or agents that you can set loose in the world to help you find information that maybe your social network can't deliver to you," Rainie said.

Talk about It

1. How will the social web of the future be different than what we know today?

2. How will machines be able to help you expand and enrich your network of information?

3. Can you think of any instances where such changes will create problems or concerns?

4. Describe a situation where you might use this new machine-enhanced social web.

5. How do you think this vision of the social web will affect people's basic interaction and humanity?

Mobile use of social networks (so-called **social mobile media**) continues to grow. People are using mobile phones to access their social networking pages, upload pictures and videos they capture with their phones, tweet thoughts, and comment on friends' posts. Over 40 percent of smartphone owners use a social networking site on their phones. In addition, 28 percent use their smartphones daily to access their social networks to update their statuses, post videos or pictures, or comment on a post from a connection or friend. As shown in Figure 7.3, time spent on social media sites is most often spent on mobile devices.

Social networks are reaching beyond online communication to connect with events in our offline lives. Sites such as Socializr, Punchbowl, and Evite have become popular for organizing social events. People post events, send RSVPs, and later post event photos, which they can pull onto the event site from sites such as Facebook or Flickr.

A trend that continues to expand, involving services such as Groupon and Living Social, provides users with discount coupons/vouchers that may be delivered through a mobile device. These services also provide users the opportunity to share these coupons with friends and receive benefits for doing so.

More people are using their cell phones to communicate with others through social networks.

FIGURE 7.3 **Time Spent on Social Networks in the United States**
A large percentage of time spent by adults on social networks is done using mobile devices.

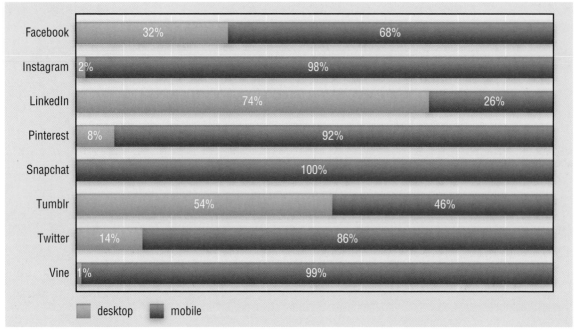

Network	desktop	mobile
Facebook	32%	68%
Instagram	2%	98%
LinkedIn	74%	26%
Pinterest	8%	92%
Snapchat		100%
Tumblr	54%	46%
Twitter	14%	86%
Vine	1%	99%

desktop ▪ mobile

Source: comScore, December 2013

Computers in Your Career

Many people today use social tools to market themselves to employers. They use networking sites, such as LinkedIn, to connect with other professionals. Others use social tools to post comments on blogs related to their career interests to create online credentials that potential employers may notice. Some produce podcasts or upload videos about their areas of expertise on media sharing or job-posting sites to get noticed, or post online portfolios on their own websites. Next time you're looking for work, consider using the social web to help you land a job.

Take the Next Step *Online*

Activity 7.4.1 Watch	*How are businesses using social networking?*	**CORE** CONTENT
Activity 7.4.2 Experience	*How do I create a social networking page?*	e book
Activity 7.4.3 Discuss	*How might social networks have a local impact?*	e book
Activity 7.4.4 Discuss	*Should businesses ban or make use of blogs at work?*	e book

Left: You can get recommendations of sites that you'll love based on your interests at Flipora.

Below: The web is riddled with logo links like these that allow you to connect with bookmarking and other types of social services.

7.5 Social Bookmarking

Though the social web is in flux, one thing everybody can agree on is that the web contains a huge number of websites and a wealth of content. One form of social networking that helps users organize and recommend content to each other is social bookmarking. Using sites such as Symbaloo and StumbleUpon, people can share online content with individuals and groups, and organize that content in personal libraries.

> " Social bookmarking has become a phenomenon in the last couple of years. As more individuals join these social networks, the news and what is deemed important is now driven by consumers—a fundamental shift on how information was prioritized in the past. "
>
> —Michael Fleischner, Internet marketing expert

How Social Bookmarking Works

Social bookmarking allows you to make note of online content in the form of tags called **bookmarks** and share those bookmarks with others. The technology uses **metadata**, which is essentially data about data. In other words, metadata describes the location or nature of other data, allowing software such as a browser to organize and retrieve that data easily.

Bookmarking sites save bookmarks as tags rather than saving links in folders as the Favorites features of some browsers do. A tag is a keyword assigned to information on the web that is used by social bookmarking sites to locate and organize content references. Because you can sort through and organize tags, this makes social bookmarks much easier to search and catalogue.

A Wealth of Social Bookmarking Services

Today you will find tools on many sites that allow you to bookmark them instantly. Look for logos for services such as Delicious, Reddit, StumbleUpon, and Pearltrees on your favorite website, or locate a Share icon that, when clicked, displays a variety of tools that allow you to share your recommendations.

| **Activity 7.5.1**
Watch | *How are people using social*
bookmarks? | **CORE** CONTENT |
| **Activity 7.5.2**
Experience | *How can a social bookmarking site such as Diigo*
help you research a topic? | |

PRECHECK **7.6** Wikis

The social web isn't only for swapping personal stories or photos. **Wikis** provide a way to share knowledge about every topic under the sun in the form of online visual libraries, encyclopedias, and dictionaries. Wikis enable people to post and edit content in a way that creates a living network of knowledge to which anybody can contribute.

What's a Wiki?

According to http://wiki.org, a wiki "is a piece of server software that allows users to freely create and edit web page content using any web browser." The wiki technology supports hyperlinks and enables users to create links between internal pages. Wikis allow users to not only edit the content, but change the organization of that content as well. Wiki content can then be searched by users to find the information they need.

> 66 The Internet has transformed the educational landscape, giving students more scope to access information and offering them the opportunity to collaborate in research projects online. 99
>
> —Aleks Krotoski, journalist

The wiki "open editing" model encourages anybody and everybody to contribute his or her experience and knowledge in text, audio, or video format. When you use the edit feature in a wiki, it opens the content as a document that you can modify. You can add and edit text or graphics and insert links to other documents. You then save your changes so that others can view and edit the updated document.

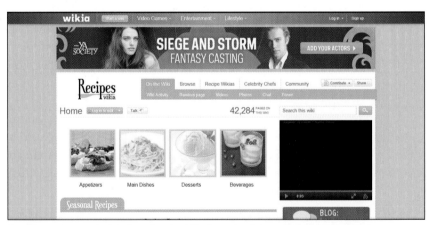

This open editing model can make the accuracy of the content less verifiable. Some sites, such as Wikipedia, have systems in place to monitor posts and edits and note where additional clarification or authentication is needed.

A wiki can be a valuable learning tool that can be integrated into courses for students of all ages.

Who's Using Wikis?

You can use wikis to coordinate projects, trips, and parties, or build online stores of shared information in the form of encyclopedias or dictionaries. Authors, artists, collectors, journalists, educators, scientists, researchers, technologists, and business people are making use of wikis to collaborate on creative works, and build business policies and procedures. People who share interests are using wikis to build content communities. In business, where companies often have to get client approval of designs or campaigns, wikis help streamline the process and keep everybody in the loop.

Here are some interesting uses of wikis you might want to check out:

- Memory-Alpha.org is a wiki where anybody can contribute and edit an encyclopedia about all things Star Trek.
- Wikitravel.org is an open content travel guide with advice and information from thousands of travellers.
- Wiktionary.org is an open, web-based dictionary that provides definitions, pronunciations, and the history (etymology) of words contributed by users.
- Teampedia.net is a collaborative encyclopedia of team-building activities, resources, and tools.

What interesting wikis can you find online?

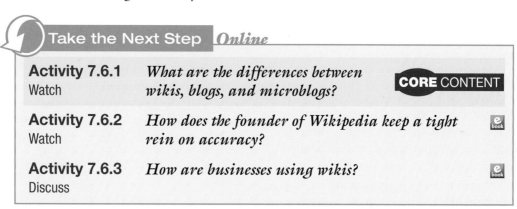

Take the Next Step *Online*		
Activity 7.6.1 Watch	*What are the differences between wikis, blogs, and microblogs?*	**CORE** CONTENT
Activity 7.6.2 Watch	*How does the founder of Wikipedia keep a tight rein on accuracy?*	
Activity 7.6.3 Discuss	*How are businesses using wikis?*	

PRECHECK

7.7 Media Sharing

Just as people want to share stories in blogs and knowledge in wikis, people have the need to share files. When you view, download, or exchange media files, such as music, videos, or photos, over the Internet, it's referred to as **media sharing**. Sites such as YouTube, Spotify, Flickr, Picasa, and Slideshare are examples of media sharing sites.

The media sharing trend began in the late 1990s with MP3 music file sharing through services such as Napster and Gnutella. MP3 sites have gone through some legal challenges because they have distributed the work of musicians and artists freely, sometimes violating copyright protections.

Sites such as YouTube tap into the grassroots version of media sharing, where individuals freely post their content in a bid for a moment of online fame. Many media sharing sites use **live media streaming**, a technology that allows them to send the content over the Internet in **live broadcasts**.

Playing It Safe

When sharing media or any content over the Internet, be aware of copyright laws and requirements. Some sites, such as Wikipedia, allow you to freely copy and share their content. Others, such as YouTube, allow you to direct people to shared content by using links to their site, but do not allow you to distribute user content yourself.

A conversation focused on shared images on VoiceThread.

How Media Sharing Works

You can easily create your own media and share it with others online. Some sites allow you to record your media right from the site; others require that you record it offline using a camera, or voice or video recorder. Media that you create in the form of a digital file can be shared as an email attachment, sent through instant messages, or posted on sites where people can then download the file.

Media is shared on many social networking sites and blogs, such as Vine and Tumblr, in web-based communities, on social bookmarking sites, and on more specialized media sharing sites, such as Flickr and YouTube.

VoiceThread is an interesting example of a site that combines media sharing with the ability to hold a conversation about the media. You can even record voice comments from your computer or any phone, including cell phones, and navigate the site through voice commands.

> " At CUNY's Graduate School of Journalism . . . we just told the students that they no longer need to commit to a media track—print, broadcast, or interactive. We believe this is the next step in convergence. All media become one. "
>
> —Jeff Jarvis, *Columbia Journalism Review*

How People Are Using Media Sharing

People are using media sharing in a variety of ways. Some artists are promoting their work by sharing it in online portfolios. People collaborating on projects, such as designing a website, may share media in environments that allow each person to comment or annotate the media file. Some media sharing sites and software allow you to build personal playlists of the media you find online.

A popular trend is to post product reviews or tutorials, for example, showing features of new cell phone models. Businesses and nonprofit organizations can use services, such as Radian6 from Salesforce.com, to troll the Internet and find content related to a theme. For example, they can find posted videos that relate to their products or brand so they can learn what their customers think of them. In response to this feedback, they can make changes or improvements.

Sites such as FriendFeed allow you to import playlists from several services and even let you share your content through Twitter and Facebook. You can also post your customized list of media content on your own website or blog.

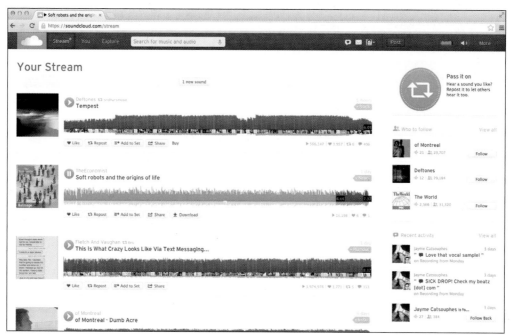

SoundCloud, launched in 2008, enables users to stream, record, share, provide feedback on, and remix music and other audio.

Ethics and Technology Blog *Online*

Posting Photos of Others to a Media Sharing Site

Do you think it's OK to take a picture or video of another person and post it online without permission?

Take the Next Step *Online*

Activity 7.7.1 Watch	*How can you safely share videos?*	CORE CONTENT
Activity 7.7.2 Research	*How do you find what you want on media sharing sites?*	e book
Activity 7.7.3 Discuss	*How did your parents or grandparents share images?*	e book

An interactive Summing Up with audio, a Study Notes document, slide presentations with audio, and Terms to Know flashcards with audio are available from the links menu on this page in your ebook.

Summing Up

The Social Web Phenomenon

Social networking sites are websites where people go to share their thoughts in text, video, or photos. Any site that allows users to interact with each other and share information or content can be considered, at some level, to be social. Services that allow you to share media are called **media sharing sites**.

A wide variety of social websites such as Facebook and Pinterest form the **social web**, a revolution in how people connect with each other, how news is delivered, and how our collective knowledge is formed. The content of most of these sites is driven almost entirely by the members, though the site owners devise and maintain the infrastructure, communication tools, and rules for behavior.

Social Technology Comes of Age

The social web is one of the most publicized and successful examples of Web 2.0. **Open content** is to the social web what open source was to software development—it means that anybody can freely share their knowledge about topics in online collections, such as Wikipedia. Although other sites already existed that allowed users to create **profiles** with information about themselves and compile lists of friends, SixDegrees was one of the first sites that combined the use of profiles and searchable **friends lists** in one service—social networking was born. Online journals called **blogs** (a term created from *web + log*) began to surface online. Blogs became one of the key tools for online social interaction. In 2003, the social phenomenon exploded with sites such as MySpace, Flickr, Facebook, and LinkedIn all launching within months of each other. Today, the social web has expanded to be accessible by a variety of devices, such as cell phones and gaming devices. These devices allow people to connect with their social sites to post text, video, and photos and interact with their friends on the go.

The social web is growing and evolving rapidly, with changes happening daily. One predicted trend is the ability to carry your **identity** (the profile you create when you join a service) with you from site to site. Another trend is the ability to gather together content from a wide variety of services. Social media has also become a real-time reporting tool. It's been suggested that in the future all websites will have social networking features.

Blogging: The Internet Gets Personal

A blog is an online journal that may be focused around a particular topic or may simply be a random collection of personal thoughts. Blogs can contain text, images, videos, and links to other online content. Many blogs focus on the written word, but there are also blogs that use other kinds of content, such as **artblogs**, **sketchblogs**, and **photoblogs**. People who read blogs can post comments. Blogs and comments are listed in reverse chronological order, with the most recent post at the top.

You may create your blog on a blog hosting site, or you may post to a blog that is part of a social networking site. Companies often host blogs on their websites, and blogs have taken on an important role in reporting news stories. Sites such as Twitter that use brief comments are called **microblogging** sites. Because of the quantity of content on social networking sites, **hashtags** (topic names preceded by the # symbol) are being used today to organize content and make it easier to search. Blogs also employ the use of **tags**, which are labels that make it easier for readers to find what they are looking for within a particular blog site.

Social Networking

Social networking sites typically include a blogging-like feature, such as Facebook's status updates and the ability to share media, but what differentiates them from other social sites is the ability to share contacts and build a network of friends. Many websites that were not traditionally considered to be social, today include social networking features, such as profiles, friends lists, and media-sharing capabilities.

Social networking trends include the increased use of social media as a business marketing tool, the emergence of **disappearing media**, higher rates of social media use by older people, and the rapid adoption of **social mobile media**. The social web is also creating a plethora of other social and business opportunities.

Social Bookmarking

Social bookmarking helps users organize and recommend content to each other. This technology uses **metadata**, which is data about data. Bookmarking sites save users' **bookmarks** as tags. Because you can sort through and organize bookmark tags, it's easy to use them to search for and catalogue information.

Wikis

Wikis are a way to share knowledge about any topic in the form of online visual libraries, encyclopedias, and dictionaries. Wikis enable people to post and edit content in a way that creates a living network of knowledge to which anybody can contribute.

Media Sharing

Viewing, downloading, or exchanging media files, such as music, videos, or photos, is referred to as **media sharing**. Many media sharing sites use **live media streaming**, a technology that allows them to send the content over the Internet in real-time broadcasts.

Media is shared on many social networking sites and blogs, in web-based communities, on social bookmarking sites, and on more specialized media sharing sites, such as Vine and Tumblr.

Terms to Know

The Social Web Phenomenon

Social Technology Comes of Age

Concepts Check

Concepts Check 7.1   Multiple Choice

Take this quiz to test your understanding of key concepts in this chapter.

Concepts Check 7.2   Matching

Test your understanding of terms and concepts presented in this chapter.

Concepts Check 7.3   Arrange It

Use the interactive tool to arrange social networking sites according to their launch dates on a timeline.

Projects

Check with your instructor for the preferred method to submit completed project work.

Project 7.1   Using Social Technologies in Business

Project 7.1.1

Identify a company that is using some form of social technology, such as blogging, microblogging, wikis, social bookmarking, social networking, or media sharing. Determine the types of social websites that the company uses, its strategies in maintaining these sites, the use of these sites to reinforce the messages on the company's website, and the ability of these sites to attract interest from diverse groups of potential customers.

Project 7.1.2   TEAM

As a team, brainstorm a start-up business that you would like to launch. Write down the name of your business and the types of products or services that your company will offer. Establish your target audience and recognize your market competition. Discuss the ways in which social technology could be an effective communications-and-marketing tool to attract potential customers. Document the various steps that you would need to take to operate a business page on Facebook. Prepare a web-based presentation that introduces your business venture and outlines your Facebook business plan, including how you will drive people to your Facebook page and what kind of content you will place there to provide the information your customers need to interact with your business.

Project 7.2 Gaining Experience with Blogging

Project 7.2.1

To understand the purposes, types, benefits/drawbacks, and popularity of blogging, research a variety of blogs on the web. Find a blog that interests you and actively engage in a dialog with other users by posting information and commentary. Prepare a memo that identifies the blog you chose and describes your experience with it. Include a transcript of your dialog exchange in the memo.

Project 7.2.2 TEAM

Go to the Chapter 7 class blog. As a group, find a news story of interest, and summarize the story on the class blog. Then have each team member respond to the summary by posting a blog entry once a day for a week. At the end of the week, prepare a transcript of the blog. Be prepared to discuss your exchange of ideas and opinions in class. Submit the transcript, as well as your source for the news article, to your instructor.

Project 7.3 How Are Social Networking Sites Being Used Today?

Project 7.3.1

Many colleges and universities today have their own social networking sites for their students. Go to your college's home page and locate the school's social networking site, if one is available. If your college does not have a social networking site, find a school that does have one. Where did you find the site? Is it current? Are there many participants? Does the site contain text, audio, photos, and/or videos? Prepare a summary of your findings.

Project 7.3.2 TEAM

As a team, investigate the impact of social networking on one aspect of our society, such as a political issue or a medical crisis. Determine the types of sites that were used, the topics that were discussed, the number of participants, and other ways social networking has influenced us today. Then, based on your research, predict the role that social networking might play in the future. Prepare a presentation of your team's findings and predictions.

Project 7.4 Sharing through Media

Project 7.4.1

Create a slideshow résumé. Post your presentation on http://ODW4.emcp.net/slideshare. Adjust your privacy settings so that your presentation can only be shared with your instructor and your class.

Project 7.4.2 TEAM

Using a video recording device, create a team video about one of the topics presented in this chapter. Upload your video to YouTube and share the link with your instructor.

Project 7.5 Wiki—Building an Online Policy

Project 7.5.1 **TEAM**

You are employed at a large publishing company that produces newspapers and magazines. Recently, several of your publications have been posted online, and your company has created blogs on these sites. You are in charge of writing the blogging policies. Write a policy on the class wiki that addresses the following user issues:

- standards for appropriate behavior or content
- reporting of inappropriate behavior or content
- privacy safeguards

Before you begin writing, review the policies of mainstream blogging sites for ideas. When you have finished your blogging guidelines, submit the document to your instructor. Be sure to include any references that you used in creating your document.

Project 7.5.2 **TEAM**

As a team, use the tools in PollDaddy or SurveyMonkey to create a survey on the use of social technology. For example, you may want to ask your survey participants how they are using personalized start pages or how blogging has benefited their businesses. Have each team member distribute the survey to 10 friends or family members. Share your survey results on the class wiki. When you post or edit content, make sure you include a notation within the page that includes your name, or the team members' names, and the date you posted or edited the content—for example, "Posted/edited by [your name or team members' names] on [date]."

Class Conversations

Topic 7.1 What privacy issues does the social web create?

The social web is used by millions of people from many cultures and backgrounds. With so many people using these technologies, one issue that users face is privacy. What privacy protections do social networking sites offer? What is meant by your social footprint? How could what you post on the web today have an impact on your future?

Topic 7.2 How could you use social technologies to make a better world?

You work for a nonprofit organization working for a cleaner environment. How could you use social technologies to raise awareness and get new members and support? Discuss ways to use wikis, blogs, media sharing, microblogging, and social bookmarking in a campaign to encourage people to take public transportation or walk rather than drive a car.

Topic 7.3 How should businesses use the social web?

People have jumped on the social web to connect with each other. Businesses are also actively using these tools to sell products and services to people by planting promotional comments in user pages. Should businesses be allowed to insert advertising into what was meant to be a way to hold a social dialog? How do you feel about businesses using your social network profile to discover how to market products and services to you?

Digital Defense
Securing Your Data and Privacy

What You'll Accomplish

When you finish this chapter, you'll be able to:

8.1 Describe the risks associated with operating a computer connected to a network and the Internet and list the tools you can use to protect your computing devices and data from those risks.

8.2 Explain the steps to secure a home network, the various types of personal computer or mobile device malware, and methods used to obtain personal information from individuals.

8.3 Recognize security risks associated with mobile devices and with storing data in the cloud and give examples of tools and services to safeguard those devices and data.

8.4 Identify hardware and software tools and strategies used by organizations to secure corporate networks and prevent loss of data.

8.5 List security defenses that both organizations and individuals should adopt to prevent cyberattacks and data loss or theft.

Why Does It Matter

Would you leave your bank card and PIN sitting on an empty table in a food court at the mall? Would you leave your home for a vacation and not bother to lock the doors or windows? Many people who are used to protecting their wallets or houses may not take steps to guard their digital information against common threats. Even if you protect your computer with antivirus software, you might overlook routine tasks that can leave you vulnerable to losing important data. Everybody should learn the basic skills of computer security because replacing a computer is easy—replacing valuable data is not.

Protecting the data on your computer and mobile device and your personal information online are important concerns in our digital age. From firewalls and antivirus software to corporate security planning and protecting your mobile devices, learn about the tools available to stay secure.

ANTIVIRUS

8.1 The Role of Security and Privacy in Your Digital World

Do a search on a news website any day of the week and you'll come up with stories like these:

- In February 2016, a hacker attack exposed 20 million accounts on Alibaba's Taobao shopping site. Chinese companies have seen a steep rise in cyber attacks in recent years.
- Bitcoin is a virtual currency that uses wallet software to make payments online. February 28, 2014, saw one of the world's largest Bitcoin exchanges, Mt. Gox, file for bankruptcy protection and become the target of a class action lawsuit after disclosing that a hacker had stolen approximately half a billion dollars of the virtual currency. Just a few days later, Flexcoin, another Bitcoin exchange, ceased operations after a security breach allowed a hacker to steal virtual currency worth approximately $600,000.
- In 2015, the second largest health insurance company experienced a breach that exposed medical IDs and social security numbers of as many as 80 million customers.
- Software giant Adobe had to contact 2.9 million customers worldwide to reset their passwords after an October 2013 attack on Adobe's systems allowed hackers to gain access to customer IDs and passwords. Encrypted credit card and debit card numbers, expiration dates, and transaction data may also have been compromised.
- Computer researchers at Britain's University of Liverpool developed a uniquely contagious Wi-Fi virus called *Chameleon* that takes control of wireless access points that have been left at factory settings. The virus then sends data across the network, looking for other vulnerable access points. Researchers warned the public that if this virus was unleashed, the virus would spread just like a common cold.

Computer security and safety are very much in the news and on the minds of both company executives and individual computer users, but just what's involved in computer security?

Computer Security: Where's the Threat?

Computer security, also referred to as information security, involves protecting the boundaries of your home or business network and individual computing devices from intruders. An important part of computer security is **data loss prevention (DLP)**, which involves minimizing the risk of loss or theft of data from within a network.

Security threats can originate from various sources. One of these sources is malware (such as computer viruses), which you will learn more about later in the chapter. In other cases, employees' own negligence can cause a company to simply lose data, in which case these companies face the hard fact that their people have been their own worst enemy.

> "I think computer viruses should count as life. I think it says something about human nature that the only form of life we have created so far is purely destructive."
>
> —Stephen Hawking, physicist

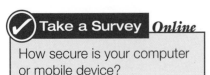
Take a Survey *Online*
How secure is your computer or mobile device?

FIGURE 8.1 **The Secure PC**
Computer security is all about keeping data, from your company's recipe for soup to your own bank account information, safe from threats and loss.

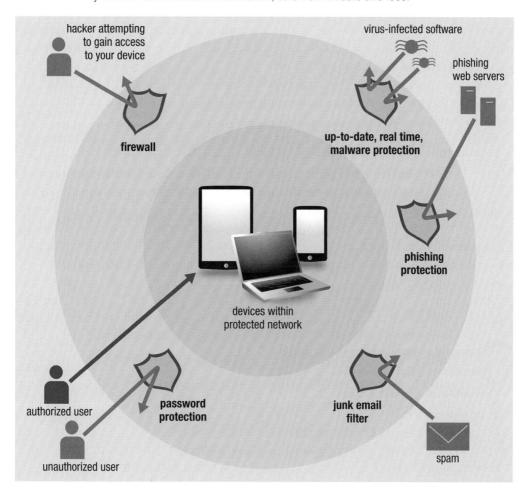

Cyberattackers may damage or steal data and can come individually or in groups. Attacks may come from a malicious **hacker** or organized crime, corporate spies, unethical employees, disgruntled colleagues, or, in the case of your home computer, from an ex-friend out to cyberbully you.

Because of the wide variety of threats out there, it's important to recognize that proper security practices are not just a matter of individual protection—they are also critical for the overall security of the Internet. If you allow your own PC to be co-opted by criminals to scam or spam others, you have become part of a bigger problem.

Figure 8.1 shows some of the measures you should put in place to keep your own digital world more secure.

What can happen if your information security is compromised? Companies can face enormous costs resulting from the theft of their customer data and intellectual property. Consider these findings from the 2015 Cost of Data Breach Study for the United States by Ponemon Institute LLC (a research center for privacy, data protection, and information security policy):

• A US organization incurs an average cost of $154 per record, with a typical incident running a total of $5.4 million, for expenses associated with a data breach.

• US businesses average $3.8 million in lost business associated with a data breach.

- Of the incidents included in the Ponemon study, 47 percent involved a malicious or criminal attack, and the average cost to clean up after such an attack is $170 per record.

The 2015 Cost of Data Breach Study also provides some positive findings, in that organizations are improving their performance to prepare for and respond to data breaches, with the average cost per record in decline for a second straight year. Still, it is worth noting that the study does not include mega data breaches, which are breaches in which more than 100,000 records are comprised. The effects of large-scale incidents such as those experienced by Adobe are not included in these statistics.

In January 2010, Google admitted that it had been the target of an **advanced persistent threat (APT)** in what has been dubbed Operation Aurora by security company McAfee. An APT is a highly targeted, sophisticated attack tailored to a specific organization, usually to gain access to sensitive information. Operation Aurora capitalized on a vulnerability in Microsoft's Internet Explorer to infiltrate Google and 30 other companies to obtain intellectual property. Security provider FireEye, Inc., in its white paper titled *Advanced Malware Exposed*, warns that targeted APTs are evading today's network defenses. In their 2015 Internet Security Threat Report, Symantec Corporation reported that one million new malware threats are released every day. Most spam emails are easily identified and quarantined when received by corporate email servers; however, a targeted attack can escape email filters. For example, an employee in the Human

 Spotlight on the Future *Online*

Growing Security Risks

As the Internet of Things grows, it's predicted that the security and privacy problems we have now will multiply as fast as the technology does.

"The experts are very worried in part because they're anticipating the internet is going to be woven even more deeply into people's lives so it becomes a much richer target in the future than it even is now," says Lee Rainie, director of the Pew Research Center Internet Project, which has produced a report predicting tech trends through 2025.

"As these systems get more complex it's almost inevitable … that the bugs and the problems that might be exploitable are going to become more evident," he says. "Since we are outsourcing lots of information about ourselves, some of our basic economic activity, health activity, some of our basic activities as citizens, it's just a real inviting target."

Talk about It

1. How are security issues expected to multiply in the future?

2. How does the connectedness of the Internet of Things contribute to security concerns?

3. What types of behaviors make us more susceptible targets for security breaches?

4. What are some of the risks or unanticipated consequences to be considered in creating a more secure system?

5. Compare the race of security vs. vulnerability to the arms race.

Resources department might receive an email with instructions to click on a link to a candidate's résumé. When the employee clicks the link, malware is unknowingly installed on his or her computer.

For individuals, the primary security risk is identity theft (ID), and the associated costs are tallied not only in dollars but in time as well. According to the Federal Trade Commission (FTC), 14 percent of complaints received in 2013 were related to identity theft, which is the topmost concern. Residents of Florida made the highest per capita rate of identity theft complaints, followed by Georgia and then California. One study reported that two-thirds of identity theft victims lost on average $1,769 each, and 10 percent spent more than one month resolving associated credit and financial problems that arose from the theft.

Basic Tools of Computer Security

High-profile hacks into companies such as Adobe and Google have companies reviewing, updating, and improving their security procedures. The tools you can use to protect your personal computer and information are similar to tools corporations use to protect their intellectual property. Both individuals and companies can implement authentication processes, security technologies, and user procedures to keep data safe.

Authentication involves the use of passwords and in some cases other identifiers such as fingerprints to make sure that the people accessing information are who they claim to be. For example, on your personal computer you can create a user name and password to ensure that others do not have access to your programs and data.

Security technologies that help keep intruders out or defend against dangerous computer code include firewalls, encryption, and antivirus software, among others.

User procedures may be as simple as teaching your kids not to follow a link online that might download a virus, or as robust as a company-wide policy identifying who can access data and establishing procedures for backing up files to avoid data loss. Operation Aurora initially started with employees clicking a link that took them to a malicious website where the Internet Explorer vulnerability was exploited to download malware onto the employees' computers. All computer users need to be suspicious of unsolicited links and follow their company's defined security practices at all times.

McAfee antivirus software is one of the products people use to protect their personal computers from damaging viruses.

The increasing number of households connected to the Internet has also resulted in an increased need for vigilance by individuals to defend against cyberattacks, identity theft, and other types of fraud. In addition, loss or damage to data resulting from inadvertently downloading damaging programs can be frustrating and costly. To date, most security threats have been targeted at Windows users, but as Mac and perhaps Linux grow their market shares, those systems are also becoming more vulnerable to cybercriminals.

The increased use of mobile devices has turned hackers' attention to mobile apps, but all platforms are not at equal risk of damage by mobile malware. According to Roel Schouwenberg, researcher for Kaspersky Labs (an anti-virus company), almost 100 percent of the mobile malware in circulation is written for Android devices.

> " Criminals want the biggest bang for their malware buck, which means the dominant operating systems, browsers, platforms, etc. are always going to be the better targets. "
>
> —Linda Criddle, privacy consultant at Intel Corporation

Tony Anscombe, a security analyst for another popular antivirus company, AVG Technologies, warns that hackers will take a popular app, such as Candy Crush Saga, insert malicious code into the program, and then publish the app on a third-party site. This allows them to avoid the malware detection mechanisms found on Google Play or the Apple store. Bluetooth users must also beware of mobile security threats. Although Bluetooth connections are short-range, they can be used to intercept data or to send harmful files or viruses.

Protecting Your Home Network

If you have set up a home network that enables your computers to connect to the Internet and you haven't thought about security, it's as if you just installed a backdoor to your house that's left wide open 24/7. An unprotected network means that anybody who is near your home can "piggyback" on your Internet connection, track your online activities, and possibly even hack into your computer.

You can take several simple steps to secure a home network. Wi-Fi home networks use an access point or router, which is a piece of equipment that comes with a preset password. The bad news is that these default passwords are pitifully predictable and simple. The good news is that you can go to the device manufacturer's website and find instructions for changing the password to something that is harder to guess.

Another important step in securing a home network is to use **encryption**, a part of cryptography, which is the study of creating algorithms and codes to protect data. Encryption scrambles a message so that it's unreadable to anybody who doesn't have the right key. Say you want your friend to send you a message that will contain data you want to protect. You use your computer to generate a **public key**,

Routers have some built-in protections for your network, if you know how to use them.

FIGURE 8.2 **Public Key Encryption**

The key for encrypted data is like your house key—it unlocks the data.

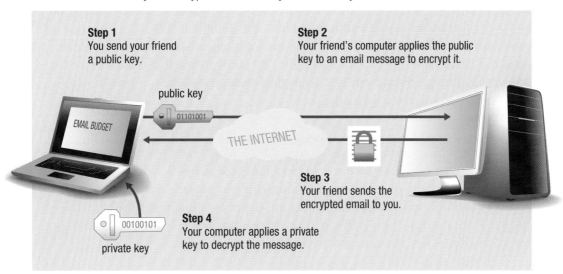

Step 1
You send your friend
a public key.

Step 2
Your friend's computer applies the public
key to an email message to encrypt it.

public key

EMAIL BUDGET

01101001

THE INTERNET

Step 3
Your friend sends the
encrypted email to you.

00100101

Step 4
Your computer applies a private
key to decrypt the message.

private key

which you send to your friend. Your friend applies the key, which encrypts the message, and sends the message to you. Your computer then applies a **private key**, known only to you, to decrypt the message. Because the message is encrypted, nobody but the intended recipient can read it. Figure 8.2 depicts this example of the **public key encryption** process. Two popular forms of encryption are **Wi-Fi Protected Access (WPA)** and **Wired Equivalent Privacy (WEP)**. **Wi-Fi Protected Access 2 (WPA2)** uses a stronger, more complex form of encryption than WPA. You should check that your router is set up with the strongest encryption available. Use WPA2 whenever possible; select WPA if WPA2 is not available, and choose WEP as a last resort.

The Menace of Malware

Collectively, nasty computer programs such as viruses and spyware are called **malware** (*mal* means bad or evil in Latin and *ware* refers to software). Malware installs itself on your computer without your knowledge or consent. Malware can do anything from pelting you with pop-up window advertisements to destroying your data to tracking your online activities with an eye toward stealing your identity or money.

In the early days of computers, individual hackers often planted viruses just to aggravate people or exploit a technological weakness. Today, most malware is created by less-than-ethical businesses, organized gangs, or criminals who aim to download dangerous code to your computer, co-opt your email contact list to send out **spam** (mass emails), or perform other illegal activities for profit-based motives. The following are descriptions of some common forms of malware.

 Ethics and Technology Blog *Online*

Taking Advantage of an Unsecured Network

My apartment is next door to a café that offers Internet access. I hardly ever go to the café, but because I can pick up its Internet connection from my apartment, I do. It saves me lots of money. Does anybody think that's a problem?

Viruses A **virus** is a type of computer program that can reproduce itself by attaching to another, seemingly innocent, file. Viruses duplicate when the user runs an infected program. A typical scenario is that a virus is part of an email attachment. This is one of the ways viruses spread from computer to computer. When the user opens the attachment, the program runs and the virus is duplicated. If the user does not open the attachment, the program does not run and the virus does not duplicate itself. Many viruses eat through your data, damaging or destroying files. Figure 8.3 illustrates the ways in which a virus attacks.

Worms A **worm** is also a self-replicating computer program, but it doesn't have to be attached to another file to do its work. A worm does not require the user to do anything. If your computer is connected to an infected network, you can put it at risk merely by powering it on. A worm has the nasty ability to use a network to send out copies of itself to every connected computer. Worms are usually designed to damage the network, in many cases by simply clogging up the bandwidth and slowing its performance. Figure 8.4 shows how a worm attacks.

Trojans Named after the infamous Trojan horse of Greek legend, a **Trojan horse** is malware that masquerades as a useful program. When you run the program, you let the Trojan into your system. Trojans open a "back door" to your system for malicious hackers, just as the Trojan horse allowed invaders to enter a city and then attack from within. Trojans are becoming more sophisticated, often disguising themselves as authentic operating system or antivirus warning messages that, when clicked, download the Trojan malware to your computer or mobile device. Figure 8.5 shows how a Trojan horse attacks.

FIGURE 8.3 **How a Virus Attacks**
When you forward an email with an attachment such as a picture, you may be spreading a damaging virus.

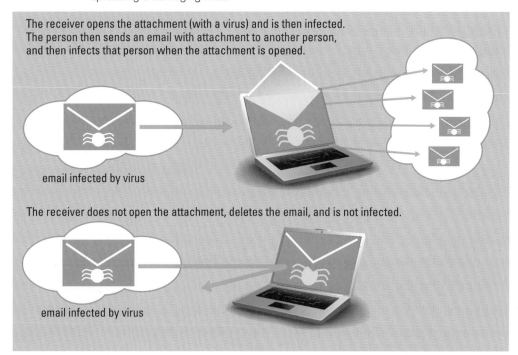

The receiver opens the attachment (with a virus) and is then infected. The person then sends an email with attachment to another person, and then infects that person when the attachment is opened.

email infected by virus

The receiver does not open the attachment, deletes the email, and is not infected.

email infected by virus

Our Digital World

FIGURE 8.4 **How a Worm Attacks**
A worm reproduces itself and attacks all the computers on a network.

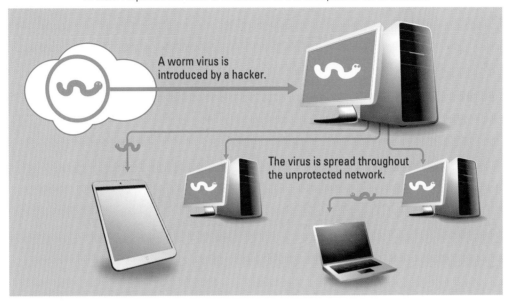

FIGURE 8.5 **How a Trojan Horse Attacks**
A Trojan horse pretends to be a useful program but ends up opening your system to hackers.

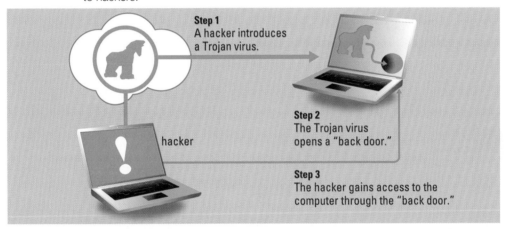

Macro Viruses and Logic Bombs Other malicious programs come in the form of small pieces of code embedded in a program. A **macro virus** is usually found in files such as word processing documents and spreadsheets and can corrupt the computer when the user opens the document and executes the macro (a recorded series of keystrokes that can be played back to perform a task). A **logic bomb virus** might be placed in a software system to set off a series of damaging events if certain conditions are met (for example, if you try to delete a set of files).

Rootkit A **rootkit** is a set of programs or utilities designed to gain access to the "root" of a computer system or the system software that controls the hardware and software. With this access, a hacker can then monitor the user's actions. This can take place on an individual system or on a network system. An important aspect of a rootkit is that it cannot be detected, at least not easily, by the user (or the administrator, in the case of a network). While rootkits can serve harmful purposes, they can also be used for legitimate purposes. For example, programs used by parents to monitor children's Internet activities can be considered rootkits.

Botnet A **botnet** is a collection of **zombie** (or robotlike) computers, which are machines that have been taken over by malware for the purpose of causing denial-of-service attacks, generating spam, or conducting other mischief. The malware sets up a stealth communication connection to a remote server controlled by the cybercriminal. Some security experts attribute most criminal activity on the Internet to botnets. Figure 8.6 shows how malware creates botnets to organize an attack.

Spyware **Spyware** is aptly named, because it spies on the activity of a computer user without his or her knowledge. Some spyware is used by legitimate websites to track your browsing habits in order to better target advertisements to you. Spyware can also be used by businesses to track employee activities online. Spyware such as a keystroke logging program can be used by criminals to learn your bank account number, passwords, social security number, and more.

Adware **Adware** is a piece of software designed to deliver ads, often in pop-up form and usually unwelcome, to users' desktops. A related type of software is ad-supported software, which shareware writers allow to be included in their programs to help pay for development effort and time.

Scareware **Scareware** is a scam in which an online warning or pop-up convinces a user that his or her computer is infected with malware or has another problem that can be fixed by purchasing and downloading software. In reality, the downloaded software may not be functional or may itself be malware. These scams are primarily used to steal the user's money and credit card information.

FIGURE 8.6 **How Malware Uses Botnets**
Your computer can be taken over by bots and used to send spam or malware to others.

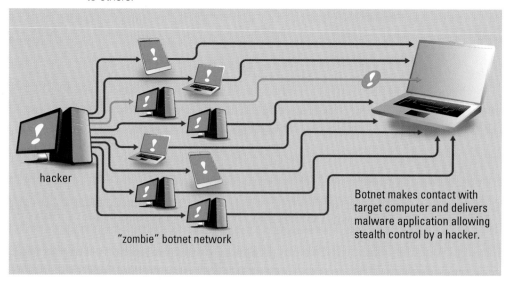

hacker

"zombie" botnet network

Botnet makes contact with target computer and delivers malware application allowing stealth control by a hacker.

Our Digital World

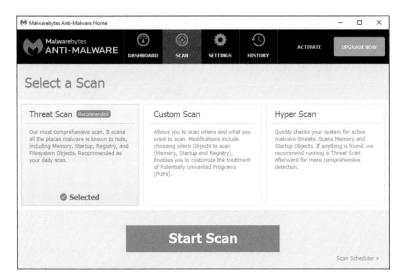

Products such as Malwarebytes' Anti-Malware scan your computer for any malware; some help prevent it from downloading in the first place.

Ransomware **Ransomware** is a scam in which access to one's computer is locked or restricted in some way. In some cases the contents of the hard drive are encrypted. A message displays to the owner of the PC or mobile device demanding payment to the malware creator to remove the restriction and/or restore the owner's data. Ransomware is a growing trend. In 2015, McAfee Labs researchers released a report that stated the company saw more than four million samples of ransomware in the second quarter of 2015, with 1.2 million that were new malware.

How Is Malware Spread?

There are several ways in which malware, depending on its nature, can be spread:

- You can infect your computer by tapping or clicking an email attachment that contains an executable file.
- Pictures you download can carry viruses stored in a single pixel of the image.
- Visiting an infected website can spread malware.
- Viruses can spread from a computer storage device such as a DVD or flash drive that you use on an infected computer and then insert into another computer drive.
- Worms can spread by simply connecting your computer to an infected network.
- Mobile devices can be infected by downloading an app, ringtone, game, or theme that carries malware.
- A mobile device with Bluetooth enabled in "discoverable mode" could be infected simply by coming within range of another Bluetooth device that has been infected and is running the same operating system.

Security threats are a reality in our digital world. What's also true is that several programs and technical tools are available to protect your computer against these potential hazards, as you'll learn later in the chapter. In addition, knowing how to recognize trustworthy websites and how to manage cookies are two proactive strategies everyone can use.

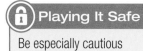

Playing It Safe

Be especially cautious when you receive a chain letter via email. These are often simply devices for delivering malware or collecting email addresses for the purpose of building spam lists.

Recognizing Secure Sites

Although even a reputable site occasionally may pass on a dangerous download to your computer, it's the sites that actively download malware that you have to be most cautious about.

Look for these symbols from various organizations that verify the secure practices of sites.

Buying only from reputable businesses that sport various accreditations such as those from TRUSTe, and ValidatedSite is one step toward safety.

Sites where you perform financial transactions should always have **Transport Layer Security (TLS)** in place. Developed from an older cryptographic protocol called **Secure Socket Layer (SSL)**, TLS is a protocol that protects data such as credit card numbers as they are being transmitted between a customer and online vendor or payment company. In more recent web browser versions, two things can signal that you are using TLS: "http" in the address line is replaced with "https," and a small closed padlock appears next to the address bar or in the status bar of the window.

Other useful tools are products such as McAfee Site Advisor or similar tools built into browsers and security programs. These display an icon next to sites in your search results indicating websites that are known to have doubtful business practices or to routinely pass on malware to visitors.

It may be safer to do business with retailers you know from the "brick-and-mortar" world. Also, you should always type a URL into your browser to go to a site rather than tapping or clicking a link in an email or advertisement.

Managing Cookies (Hold the Milk)

A **cookie** is a file stored on your computer by a web server to track information about you and your activities. Cookies can be completely harmless and even helpful. For example, if you shop at an online store often, when you next visit that site you might find that the store knows your name and has suggestions of items that might interest you. Sites can provide this personalized service by reading the information stored in the cookie.

However, some companies or individuals plant cookies on your computer for other reasons. They may be trying to track your activities to gather enough information to steal your identity, for example.

Every major browser has tools and settings for dealing with cookies. For example, in Internet Explorer, you can adjust the settings to accept all cookies, block cookies from certain sources, or block all cookies.

Cookies and site data		
Site	**Locally stored data**	Remove all Search cookies
belkin.com	4 cookies	
plug-in.bestbuy.ca	1 cookie	
bestbuy.com	24 cookies	
	UID __gads context_id mt.v s_fid s_searchTerms	
	s_vi testBucket testMonetate testVersion10-1	
	testVersion13-2 testVersion2-1 testVersion2-2	
	testVersion2-3 testVersion20-1 testVersion3-1	
	testVersion3-2 testVersion4-2 testVersion5-2	
	testVersion6-1 testVersion7-2 testVersion8-1	
	testVersion9-2 track	
www.bestbuy.com	2 cookies, Local storage	
bigstockphoto.com	13 cookies	
www.bigstockphoto.com	9 cookies, Local storage	
bing.com	4 cookies	
c.bing.com	2 cookies	

Done

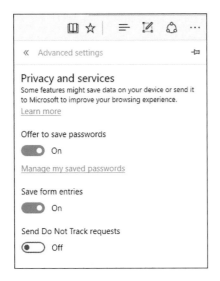

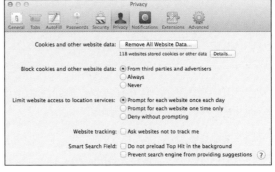

Both PC- and Mac-based browsers allow you to set privacy levels that in part control how cookies should be handled.

Foiling Phishers: No Catch Today

Phishing (pronounced *fishing*) refers to the practice of sending email that appears to be from a legitimate organization in an attempt to scam the user into revealing information. Typically, the revealed information is used for identity theft. The email directs the user to tap or click a link that then goes to a bogus website that appears valid, often containing logos and color schemes that simulate the real organization's branding. The bogus site prompts the user to update personal information such as the user name, password, credit card number, or bank account number. Once you follow these links and enter your information, you've basically handed over your sensitive information to criminals.

Delete any messages you receive that ask you to update information in a financial or retail account. Never follow a link in email messages to bank or other financial websites—always enter the URL into the browser address field yourself.

Phishing is also a problem on social media sites such as Facebook and Twitter. Popular social media sites have a high volume of users, making them frequent targets for new scams. A survey in 2013 by Harris Interactive found that 28 percent of social media users had their account hacked within the past year, and that one-third of social media users reported having received a suspicious message on their social media page. Antivirus programs do not protect users of social networking sites because the malware is operating as part of the social media application.

A warning issued by the FBI in September 2015 stated that **spear-phishing** attacks were rising and hitting individuals across all industries with the number of victims almost tripled from January to September 2015. In a spear-phishing attack, a person is targeted because of where he or she works. The hacker sends the individual a phishing email to get that the person to reveal a trade secret or other data that lets the criminal gain financially. Aryeh Goretsky, a researcher at antivirus company ESET, aptly says, "*Think before you click.*"

Activity 8.2.1 Watch	*How are botnets used on the Internet?*	**CORE** CONTENT
Activity 8.2.2 Research	*What should you know before disposing of an old computer?*	
Activity 8.2.3 **TEAM** Present	*How can you tell if your computer or mobile device has a virus?*	
Activity 8.2.4 Experience	*How prevalent are viruses where you live?*	
Activity 8.2.5 Watch	*Can you spot phishing and other tactics of identity thieves?*	

PRECHECK ⇨ **8.3** Mobile Security

Computing is no longer just a sit-at-your-desk activity—it's mobile! Mobile computing is convenient, but it also brings its own security risks. Various settings and tools can help you keep your portable device and the information stored on it safer.

Protecting Your Laptop or Tablet and Precious Data

When you bring your computer with you, you're carrying a big investment in both dollars and data, so it's important that you protect it from theft and damage. This is a concern for both personal users and corporations, who are struggling with protecting IT assets as their workforces begin to carry smaller devices that can be more prone to being lost or stolen. Consider using one or more of the following devices and procedures to help you secure your laptop or tablet computer.

Locks When you ride your bike downtown, you probably secure it with a bike lock once you reach your destination. Laptops can be secured using comparable devices that tie them to an airport chair or a desk in a field office to deter potential thieves from snatching them. As with bike locks, the determined thief with enough time can cut this cable and get away with the goods, so it's only a slight deterrent.

Remote Tracking/Wiping To protect your data in the event of a theft, consider services such as LoJack for Laptops, which allows you to remotely delete data and use GPS to track your wayward laptop or tablet. More than one Android app is available that enables you to track and lock your Android tablet remotely, and the iPad's Find My iPad feature enables you to map, lock, or wipe your Apple device clean of data from iCloud (Apple's web-based services portal). Expect remote security options to increase as tablet technology evolves. Remote tracking and wiping is not just for laptops and tablets—makers of smartphones often provide similar services to track and wipe lost or stolen phones.

Fingerprint Readers Many newer laptops include fingerprint readers. Because fingerprints are unique to each individual, being able to authenticate yourself with your own set of prints to gain access to your computer is a convenient and

Physical security is an obvious starting point in protecting data. Companies should ensure that they have locked server rooms, secured offices, and controlled access to buildings. Physical access may be controlled by using security cards that have to be swiped through or passed in front of a card reader to gain access. Closed-circuit TV monitors managed by security officers also help control physical access. When employees lose their jobs for whatever reason, corporations typically follow a specific procedure to keep company information and property secure. This policy might involve checklists to ensure that all employee access cards and keys are returned, and that passwords are changed.

Anyone who has ever lost their security card knows that getting back into the office can be a challenge—which is exactly the point!

Authentication of users is one of the most essential elements in any corporate security plan. There are several levels of authentication, ranging from the input of a simple user name and password to the use of **biometrics**, which involves devices such as a fingerprint reader or face or voice authenticator to identify individuals by a unique physical characteristic.

Criminals constantly try to find ways around authentication systems that require simple user names and passwords. For example, **spoofing** is a technique used by malicious hackers to make it appear that they are someone else so that they can convince a user to give up valuable information. Corporations have become more and more aware of such social engineering attacks. For example, a criminal might call into the company office at midnight, tell a security officer that he is an employee working on the road, providing enough personal information gained by various means to convince the officer. The story usually goes that while on a business trip he lost his access information to get into the network where vital files reside for his meeting the next morning. The officer goes to the requested office, locates secure information, and provides access to the network. The crook is in and can have a field day with company data.

Our fingerprints are unique, so a fingerprint scan is a good way to prove identity.

Denial-of-Service Attacks

A **denial-of-service (DoS) attack** targets a corporate system with continuous service requests so constant that response time on the system slows down and legitimate users are "denied service." A DoS attack typically causes an Internet site to become inefficient or to completely crash (fail). Targets of these attacks are quite often high-profile

FIGURE 8.8 | Denial-of-Service Attack

Denial-of-service attacks might target a company network or government.

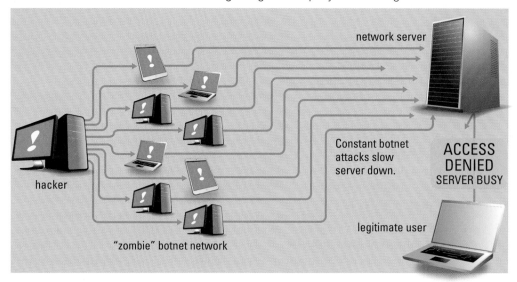

sites such as banks or Internet service providers such as AOL. Attacks may involve a set of distributed computers all pumping out requests to the target system until the system slows or fails. A DoS attack can result in slow performance of a site, unavailability of a site, or a huge number of spam emails being received. Figure 8.8 shows how a DoS might occur.

What are the motives for DoS attacks? Some are launched by spiteful individuals or groups. Others may be terrorist attacks or an assault by a competitor to damage the competing business.

Whatever the motive, companies typically use a three-pronged approach to combat DoS attacks:

- Prevent attacks.
- Detect intrusions.
- Block malicious actions.

Many software tools are available to address the three parts of this strategy, and the security industry is continually developing new programs to counteract the latest DoS threats. Network administrators often use a combination of firewalls, antivirus products, and the like to prevent attacks. Detection software looks for behavior patterns and characteristics of known attack types. Ideally, products recognize the content of network traffic quickly enough to block attacks.

Data Protection in Disastrous Times

Just as individuals have a first aid kit and some extra water and a flashlight around in case of disaster, companies typically have a data **disaster recovery plan (DRP)** in place. Damage of records, from paper to electronic files, can happen on a large scale when an earthquake or hurricane hits or when an unauthorized user gains access to the company network.

Companies typically set up their networks to back up regularly, which may be daily or more often so all information stored on their computers is kept safe. Individuals may also use automated backup features that run at regular intervals, or they may back up manually to a storage medium such as a DVD or flash drive.

To back up company servers that contain a great deal of vital company data, there are three options:

- A **cold server** is simply a spare server that can take over server functions.
- A **warm server** is activated periodically to get backup files from the main server.
- A **hot server** receives frequent updates and is available to take over if the server it is connected to fails. (The process of redirecting users to this spare server is called **failover.**)

Disasters that can destroy important company data come in all shapes and sizes, and are best prepared for by backing up data.

Many large corporations use an off-site backup. For example, a television or movie company might create copies of their programming and store them at another facility in case an original is lost or damaged or there is a natural disaster.

To avoid loss of data from a sudden surge in power such as might occur during a thunderstorm, individual computers can be plugged into a **surge protector**. In addition, an **uninterruptible power supply (UPS)** can provide a battery backup that takes over in the event of a power failure. UPS systems typically provide backup for about 15 minutes and require an auxiliary power supply to kick in during that time.

Employee Training

The final piece of corporate security is to train employees in the procedures that will keep corporate intellectual property and other data safe. Employees are more likely to comply with security policies if they understand why they are needed.

Employees should be trained in security measures such as using strong passwords and changing them frequently; using a swipe card to access the company premises; and keeping certain company information, such as network access codes, confidential. Many IT departments offer employees regular security training to educate them about the latest cyberattack methods and best practices for keeping data secure.

 Ethics and Technology Blog *Online*

Protecting Company Assets

My employer recently instituted new data security rules, stating that employees would be responsible for any sensitive data such as company secrets exposed to the public or any lost company property. I often take information home with me on a flash drive so I can work after hours or on weekends. If I make an honest mistake and lose data or property while I'm trying to do my work at a more convenient time, should I be held liable?

Cyberforensics, also known as computer forensics or digital forensic science, is a field that requires special skills and training. If you worked in this field, you would spend your day extracting information from computer storage that can be used to provide evidence in criminal investigations or identify terrorists. This might involve decrypting data or finding residual data on a hard drive that somebody has tried to wipe clean. **Mobile forensics** relates to finding data saved or sent via a mobile device. Several colleges offer majors in the field, so if you like to solve mysteries, consider cyberforensics as a career.

Take the Next Step *Online*

Activity 8.4.1 Watch	*How does encryption work?*	**CORE** CONTENT
Activity 8.4.2 **TEAM** Present	*Does the average person back up often and use encryption?*	e book
Activity 8.4.3 Discuss	*What is the role of employees in keeping data secure?*	e book

8.5 Security Defenses Everybody Can Use

Whether protecting a large business or your personal laptop, there are certain common security defenses that help to prevent attacks and avoid data loss, including firewalls, software that detects and removes malware, and strong password protection.

Building Firewalls

As you learned in Chapter 6, a firewall is a part of your computer system that blocks unauthorized access to your computer or network, even as it allows authorized access. Firewalls can be created by using software, hardware, or a combination of software and hardware. You can use a firewall feature in Windows, for example, that you turn on and off from within the Windows control panel.

Firewalls are like guards at the gate of the Internet. Messages that come into or leave a computer or network go through the firewall, where they are inspected. Any message that doesn't meet preset criteria for security is blocked. You can set up trust levels that allow some types of communications and block others, or designate specific sources of communications that should be allowed access.

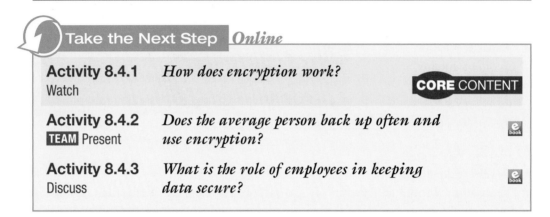

Windows Firewall blocks unwanted intruders from reaching your computer or network. This is an example of a software firewall.

Project 8.2   Mobile Device Security

Project 8.2.1

Read the article titled "10 Quick Tips to Mobile Security" at http://ODW4.emcp.net /10QuickTipstoMobileSecurity. Jump to page 7 in the PDF document and then read the section titled Top 10 Mobile Safety Tips. Prepare a one-page document in a checklist format that lists each of the ten tips. Next to each tip, provide a brief description in your own words. Then, using the checklist, interview a parent, friend, or relative who uses a smartphone for work and determine which best tips the interviewee follows. After you have completed the checklist, ask the interviewee if his or her place of employment has a mobile security policy. If so, modify the checklist to include any tips or practices that are not on the original form. Prepare a summary of the interview that details which practices were and were not followed. Submit the completed checklist and summary to your instructor.

Project 8.2.2   TEAM

A local company has hired your team to consult on a new mobile device security policy to protect its IT assets. The company employs five consultants who travel around the country conducting training presentations on individual taxation reporting requirements. Each consultant travels with a company smartphone, laptop, and in some cases a tablet and is typically away from the office for three days. To prepare you for this consultation, read the slides in the presentation titled "The Billion Dollar Lost-Laptop Study" at http:// ODW4.emcp.net/LostLaptopStudy as a starting point and then research examples of mobile security policies. Discuss with your team the main elements that should be covered in a mobile device security policy to safeguard the company from the disruption in service and large costs associated with lost mobile devices. Prepare a presentation for the company's executive board that outlines the main points that your team recommends be included in the mobile device security policy for smartphones, laptops, and tablets. Include a slide at the end of the presentation with links to the sources used for sample policies.

Project 8.2.3

With use of Bluetooth devices expected to expand in the marketplace, especially with the newer Bluetooth LE standard that uses less power, an unfortunate consequence of Bluetooth's popularity may be an increase in attacks by hackers targeted to Bluetooth devices. Yet, Bluetooth hacking is not a new phenomenon. Research the terms bluejacking, bluesnarfing, and bluebugging. Learn how to protect yourself from these types of attacks on Bluetooth devices. Prepare a brief summary with a description of each term in your own words and the best practices to use to avoid being hacked via Bluetooth. Include the URLs of the articles you read.

Project 8.3   Thwarting Social Engineers

Project 8.3.1

You have been asked by your company's human resources department to prepare a training proposal for employees on the security threats posed by social engineers. Read the article titled "Francophoned: A Sophisticated Social Engineering Attack" at http://ODW4.emcp.net/Francophoned. This article, published by Symantec, provides details about the use of emails and telephone calls by cybercriminals that led to money being stolen from accounts. Find two additional articles that describe the manipulative practices of social engineers. Next, consider the information that needs to be covered in your employee training program in order to safeguard your company's confidential information. What topics should be included in the training? What would be the best training method? How can you test employee understanding of the training and compliance with proper security protocols and procedures? Prepare a training proposal that includes a rationale for the training, an outline of the content, a description of the methodology you would use, and suggestions for testing employee knowledge and compliance. At the end of the proposal, include references to the two additional articles you read for this project.

Project 8.3.2 TEAM

Your IT manager has decided she wants to perform a test to evaluate the company's social engineering training that was recently completed. The manager has targeted two positions that she believes are the most vulnerable targets of social engineers: the help desk staff and the front desk receptionists. Develop a script for a telephone conversation in which a social engineer calls the help desk and attempts to get a staff member to reveal the user name and password of an employee. Develop another script for a face-to-face conversation in which a social engineer walks into the main reception area of the company and tries to obtain the name of the IT manager from a front desk receptionist.

Project 8.3.3 TEAM

Your team has volunteered to help senior citizens at a local community center. Recognizing that this age-group is easily victimized by social engineers, your team would like to inform individuals about the manipulative practices of social engineers and the ways in which they can protect themselves. Develop a presentation that demonstrates the tactics that a social engineer uses to trick senior citizens into sending money to cybercriminals or into revealing private information. Include tips for seniors on how to avoid being scammed.

Project 8.4   The Best Defense Is a Good Offense

Project 8.4.1

Research two to three free mobile security apps that guard against malware and hackers for your smartphone or tablet. If you don't own a smartphone or tablet, research apps for Android, the most widely used mobile operating system. Read reviews of the apps from a credible source. Create a document that summarizes in point form and in your own words what you learned about each app and the reviewers' feedback. Conclude by indicating the app you would download and install to protect your mobile device and give your reasons for your choice. Include the URLs of articles that you read for this project at the end of the document.

Project 8.4.2 TEAM

Your team has been hired to consult about security with a small-business person who is opening a new catering business. The owner has told your team she has a business manager who will provide price quotes and meet with customers to plan menus, an

clock speed The speed at which a processor can execute computer instructions, measured in gigahertz. Ch 3

cloud computing A model of software delivery in which software is hosted on an online provider's website and you access it over the Internet using your browser; you don't have to have the source application software installed on your computer in order to use the software. Also called *utility computing*. Ch 5

cloud storage Services that allow users to store documents and other files online. Ch 1

coaxial cable The cable used to transmit cable television signals over an insulated wire at a fast speed (millions of bits per second). Ch 6

cold boot Starting a computer from a no-power state. Ch 4

cold server A spare server used to take over server functions. Ch 8

command-line interface Refers to operating systems where you typed in text commands, such as DOS. Ch 4

comma-separated-values (CSV) format A format that separates each piece of data in a file with a comma. Ch 5

communications system In the context of a computer network, a system that includes sending and receiving hardware, transmission and relay systems, common sets of standards so all the equipment can "talk" to each other, and communications software. Ch 6

computer An electronic, programmable device that can assemble, process, and store data. Ch 1

computer cluster A group of computers joined together to provide higher computing power. Ch 1

computer engineering (CE) The study of computer hardware and software systems, and programming how devices interface with each other. Ch 1

computer memory Temporary storage areas on your computer, including random access memory (RAM) and cache memory. Ch 1

computer network Two or more computing devices connected by a communications medium, such as a wireless signal or a cable, that is managed via the operating system to share resources. Ch 6

computer science (CS) The study of how to design software, solve problems such as computer security threats, or come up with better ways of handling data storage. Ch 1

computer security Activities that protect the boundaries of individual computing devices and home and business networks from intruders. Ch 8

computing power Tasks accomplished by a computing system compared to the resources used. Ch 1

consumer-to-consumer (C2C) e-commerce A product, service, or payment between two online consumers. Ch 2

contact management software A type of software used to store, organize, and retrieve contact information. Ch 5

converged device A type of device that combines several technologies, such as the ability to calculate, store data, and connect to the Internet. Examples of this type of device include your cell phone, GPS navigation system, digital camera, or an appliance you can program remotely to perform tasks at a certain time. Ch 1

cookie A small file stored on your computer by a web server to track information about you and your activities. Ch 8

copyright Legal ownership of a work or symbol. Ch 2

Cortana The personal assistant/search feature introduced in Windows 10. Ch 4

crawler An intelligent agent that follows a trail of hyperlinks to locate online data. Ch 2

customer relationship management (CRM) software Generally a suite of software or online services used to store and organize client and sales prospect information, and automating and synchronizing other customer-facing business functions, such as marketing, customer service, and technical support. Ch 5

cyberforensics A field of study or a career that involves extracting information from computer storage that can be used to provide evidence in criminal investigations. This might involve decrypting encrypted data or finding residual data on a hard drive that somebody has tried to erase. Ch 8

D

data Raw facts; what you put into a computer. Ch 1

data integration Combining data from several online sources into one search result. In the context of online search, cross referencing various sources of data and including those references in the results. Ch 2

data loss prevention (DLP) Activities that involve minimizing the risk of loss or theft of data from within a network. Ch 8

database administrator (DBA) A technology professional responsible for making sure that information stored in a database is available to and usable by those who need access to the information and that the information is secure from unauthorized access. Ch 1

database software A type of software used to query, organize, sort, and create reports on sets of data such as customer lists. Also called *database management system* (DBMS). Ch 5

decryption The process of decoding an apparently random sequence of characters into meaningful text. It reverses the process of encryption and takes place as the final step in sending and receiving a secure communication. Ch 8

deep web Databases and other content on the web that aren't catalogued by most search engines. A typical search engine won't return links to these databases or documents when you enter a search keyword. Also called the *invisible web.* Ch 2

denial-of-service (DoS) attack An attack against a corporate system that slows performance or brings a website down. Ch 8

desktop The background image shown on the screen upon which graphical elements such as icons, buttons, windows, links, and dialog boxes are displayed. Ch 4

desktop computer A non-portable computer whose central processing unit (CPU) might be housed in a tower configuration or, in some cases, within the monitor, as with the Apple iMac. Ch 1

desktop publishing (DTP) software Software used to lay out pages for books, magazines, and other print materials such as product packaging or brochures. Ch 5

dial-up modem A piece of hardware that works with telephone transmissions and changes or manipulates an analog signal so that it can be understood by a computer or fax machine (which only understand digital signals). Ch 6

digital certificate An electronic document used to encrypt data sent over a network or the Internet. Ch 8

digital computer A computer that represents data using binary code. Ch 1

digital rights management (DRM) A set of technologies used by owners of digital content to control access to, and reproduction of, their material. It is used primarily to enforce copyright protection for digital content. Ch 8

digital pen A device used to write or draw on a touchscreen. Ch 3

digital signal A discrete electronic signal that is either high or low. In computer terms, high represents the digital bit 1; low represents the digital bit 0. Ch 6

digital signature A mathematical way to demonstrate the authenticity of a digital certificate. Ch 8

disaster recovery plan (DRP) A formal set of policies and procedures that guides the preparation for a possible disaster and subsequent recovery of computer resources and information thereafter. Ch 8

Disk Cleanup A utility included with Windows that gets rid of unused files on your hard disk. Ch 4

disappearing media Social media posts that can be viewed for only a short amount of time before they disappear and are deleted from the site's servers; a trend driven by social apps such as Snapchat. Ch 7

distributed application architecture A network architecture that distributes tasks between client computers and server computers. Ch 6

document camera An output device that is often used in educational settings to display text from a book, slides, a 3-D object, or any other printed material. Ch 3

domain name An identifier for a group of servers (the domain) hosting a particular website. Ch 2

DOS (disk operating system) An early operating system for personal computers which used a command-line interface. Ch 4

download To transmit data, such as a digitized text file, sound, or picture from a remote site to one's own computer via a network, such as the Internet. If you are receiving content from the Internet, you are downloading. Ch 2

DRAM (dynamic random access memory) The type of memory most commonly found in computers, and works quickly, is compact, and affordable. Requires electricity and is fragile, meaning that the data held in RAM must constantly be refreshed. Ch 1

drive A device that stores data on media. Can be integrated into the computer, or be external or removable. Ch 3

driver Software that allows an operating system to interface with specific hardware, such as a printer or keyboard. Ch 4

DSL modem A piece of hardware that allows you to connect to your existing telephone system, but separates voice from data traffic so you don't lose the use of your telephone while your computer is transmitting or receiving data. DSL stands for *digital subscriber line.* Ch 6

DVD (digital video disc) A storage device from which you can read data, write data, or both. This type of media can store larger quantities of data than a CD. Ch 3

E

e-commerce The transaction of business over the Internet. Ch 2

edutainment Software and/or media that contain both entertainment and educational value. Ch 5

email (electronic mail) A message that is shared over the Internet. Ch 2

email address A unique identifier for an email sender or recipient, comprised of user name, domain name of the email service, and domain suffix. Ch 2

email client A program stored on your local computer that is used to manage multiple email accounts and contacts when you connect to your email service. Ch 2

email server A computer dedicated to managing the sending, receiving, and storing of email messages. Ch 6

embedded object An object that has been inserted into a software file using object linking and embedding (OLE) technology, where the object is not connected to the object in the source file and therefore will not be altered when the source file is changed. Ch 5

embedded technology Placing computing power in your environment as with, for example, a system in your house that senses and adjusts lighting or temperature. Also called *ubiquitous computing*. Ch 1

encryption The process of using a key to convert readable information into unreadable information to prevent unauthorized access or usage. Ch 8

entertainment software A category of software that includes computer games you play on a computer or game console. Ch 5

entry A value entered into one field of a table. Ch 5

Ethernet A standard that specifies that there is no central device controlling the timing of data transmission. With this standard, each device tries to send data when it senses that the network is available. Ch 6

exabyte A unit of computer data storage equal to 1 billion gigabytes. According to SearchTarget.com, this amount is roughly equivalent to storing 50,000 years' worth of DVD-quality video. Ch 6

expansion card A device inserted on the computer motherboard that adds capabilities such as sound, graphics handling, or network communications. Ch 3

export To send data to another document. Ch 5

external hard drive A disk drive that connects to your computer via a cable connected to a port where you can store data and retrieve it from another computer. Ch 3

extranet An extension of an intranet that allows interaction with those outside the company, such as suppliers and customers. Ch 6

F

failover The process of redirecting users to a hot server. Ch 8

fax machine A device used to transmit a facsimile (copy) of a document to another location using a phone line. Ch 3

fiber-optic cable A transmission medium that uses a protected string of glass that transmits beams of light. Fiber-optic transmission is very fast, sending billions of bits per second. Ch 6

field A column of data in a table, which contains similar information. Ch 5

file A computer's basic storage unit, which might contain a report, spreadsheet, or picture, for example. Ch 1

file allocation table (FAT) A table maintained by the OS to keep track of the physical location of the hard disk's contents. Ch 4

file extension The part of a file name that identifies the program that is to launch when the file is double-clicked. It is commonly a set of 3 or 4 characters following a period at the end of the file name. For example, for the file index.htm, "index" identifies the file and "htm" is the extension, indicating in this case that a browser such as Internet Explorer would launch to view the HTML (web page) file. Ch 5

FireWire Based on the same serial bus architecture as a USB port, this type of port provides a high-speed serial interface and is generally used for devices that require high performance, for example, for digital cameras, camcorders, or external hard disk drives. Ch 3

firewall Software and hardware systems that stop those outside a network from sending information into the network or taking information out of it. Ch 6

firmware Code built into electronic devices that controls those devices and may include instructions to start the system. Ch 4

flash drive A small, convenient device that lets you store data and take it with you. Also known as a *USB stick* or *thumb drive*. Ch 3

flash memory A type of computer memory used to record and erase stored data and transfer data to and from your computer; used in mobile phones and digital cameras because it is much less expensive than other types of memory. Ch 3

flop A measurement of computing power representing one floating-point operation per second. Ch 1

freeware Software that is made available to use free of charge. Ch 5

frequency The speed at which a signal can change from high to low; a signal sent at a faster frequency provides faster transmission. Ch 6

friends list The people you have allowed to access your profile on a social network. Ch 7

G

gaming device A piece of equipment such as an Xbox that allows a user to play a computer game using software or an online connection. Ch 3

gateway A device that helps separate, dissimilar networks to communicate with each other. Ch 6

generic top-level domain (gTLD) Common top-level domains with three or more characters, in contrast to two-character country code TLDs. Common gTLDs include .com, .org, and .net. Ch 2

gigabit per second (Gbps) A transmission at a rate of 1 billion bits per second. Ch 6

gigabytes (GB) The average computer's hard drive capacity for data storage is measured in gigabytes; one gigabyte is approximately 1 billion bytes. Ch 3

gigahertz (GHz) A measurement of processor speed; one gigahertz is approximately 1 billion cycles per second. Ch 3

GNU General Public License A policy that specifies polices about creating open source software, including that source code has to be made available to all users and developers. Ch 5

graphical user interface (GUI) The visual appearance of an operating system that uses graphical icons, buttons, and windows to display system settings or open documents. Ch 4

graphics software Software that allows you to create, edit, or manipulate images. Ch 5

H

hacker A person who has knowledge of computer technology and security settings, which can be used for benign or malicious purposes. Ch 8

handwriting recognition software A type of software that enables a computer to recognize handwritten notes and convert them into text. Ch 5

hard disk The disk that is built into your computer and is the primary method of data storage. The disk rotates under a read/write head that reads and writes data. Ch 3

hashtag The pound symbol (#); placed in front of topic names on social media sites as a way to help organize content and make it searchable. Ch 7

home page The main page of a website or the page a browser first lands on when you specify a universal resource locator (URL). Ch 2

honeypot As part of a corporate security strategy, a computer set up to be easily hacked into to help identify weaknesses in the system. Ch 8

hot server A spare server that receives frequent updates and is available to take over if the server it mirrors fails. Ch 8

hotspot A location where Wi-Fi access is available. Ch 6

hub Used on older LAN networks to coordinate the message traffic among nodes connected to a network. Ch 6

hybrid cloud An information technology system in which some computing resources and data are managed internally in conjunction with other computing resources and data that are managed externally by cloud service providers. Ch 6

hyperlink Describes a destination within a web document and can be added to text or a graphical object such as a company logo. Used for navigation. Generally, clicking on a hyperlink sends the user to the specified web document. Ch 2

hypertext Text that represents a hyperlink. Used for navigation. Generally, clicking on hypertext sends the user to the specified web document. Ch 2

I

identity The profile you create when you join a social networking service. Ch 7

import To bring content into a document. Ch 5

information Raw facts that are processed, organized, structured, or presented in a meaningful way; what you get out of a computer. Ch 1

information processing cycle A cycle of handling raw data and information that has four parts: input of data, processing of data, output of information, and storage of data and information. Ch 1

information systems (IS) A computer profession that bridges the needs of an organization and the way their information is handled to solve business problems. An IS professional considers who needs what data to get work done and how it can be delivered most efficiently. Ch 1

information technology (IT) The study, design, development, or management of computer systems, software applications, and computer hardware. Ch 1

Infrared Data Association (IrDA) port Ports that allow you to transfer data from one device to another using infrared light waves. Ch 3

infrared (IR) technology A technology that enables transfer of data over short distances using light waves in the infrared spectrum. Ch 3

input Data that is entered into a computer or other device, or the act of reading in such data. Ch 1

input device A device that allows a user to put data into a computing device. Translates into electronic (digital) form. Ch 3

Institute of Electrical and Electronics Engineers (IEEE) One of the organizations that establishes network communications standards. Ch 6

instant message (IM) A message transferred over a network and requiring that the sender and receiver have the same messaging software. Ch 2

instruction register A holding area on your computer where instructions are placed after the fetch portion of the machine cycle is completed. Ch 1

intellectual property Creations of the mind; inventions, literary and artistic works; and symbols, names, images, and designs. Ch 2

interactive whiteboard (IWB) A display device that receives input from the computer keyboard, a stylus, a finger, a tablet, or other device. Ch 3

Internet The physical infrastructure that provides us with the ability to share resources and communicate with others across a network of computers. The Internet is made up of hardware such as servers, routers, switches, transmission lines, and towers, that store and transmit vast amounts of data. Ch 2

Internet law A legal specialty that includes writing the legal terms and policies for websites. Ch 1

Internet Message Access Protocol (IMAP) A communications protocol that receives email from a mail server and delivers it to the proper mailbox. Has replaced POP on some email servers. Messages will not be deleted from the server until requested by the recipient. Ch 2

Internet of Things (IoT) Any physical object (excluding personal computers, tablets, and smartphones) that contains embedded technology and communicates or senses and interacts with other devices via the Internet. Ch 1

Internet peer-to-peer (P2P) network A modification of the peer-to-peer network architecture, used on the Internet to share files. Ch 6

Internet Protocol (IP) address A series of numbers that uniquely identifies a location on the Internet. An IP address consists of four or eight groups of numbers separated by a period, for example: 225.73.110.102. Ch 2

Internet service provider (ISP) A company that lets you use its technology to connect to the Internet for a fee, typically charged monthly. Ch 2

intranet A private network within a company's corporate "walls." Ch 6

Intrusion Prevention System (IPS) A robust form of anti-malware program that offers network administrators a set of tools for controlling access to the system and stopping attacks in progress. Ch 8

invisible web Databases and other content on the web that aren't catalogued by most search engines. A typical search engine won't return links to these databases or documents when you enter a search keyword. Also called the deep web. Ch 2

iOS The Apple operating system for the iPhone, iPad, iPod Touch, and Apple TV devices. Ch 4

K

keyboard An input device that consists of keys a user types on to input data. Ch 3

keystroke logging software A kind of malware that is used to track the keystrokes typed by a computer user. Ch 3

keyword Word or phrase that you include in search text to look for content using a search engine. Ch 2

kilobit per second (Kbps) A transmission at a rate of 1 thousand bits per second. Ch 6

L

laptop A portable computer with a built-in monitor, keyboard, and pointing device, along with the central processing unit (CPU) and a battery. Also known as a *notebook computer*. Ch 1

least possible privileges A principle applied by network operating systems that means that each user is only given access to what he or she needs in order to get his or her work done. Ch 4

LED display A type of monitor that uses light-emitting diodes, saving power and delivering a high-quality image. Ch 3

linked object An object that has been inserted into a software file using object linking and embedding (OLE) technology, where the object is connected to the object in the source file and therefore is altered when the source file is changed. Ch 5

Linux First developed by Linus Torvalds in 1991, Linux is an open source operating system, meaning that the source code for it is freely available for use and modification. Ch 4

liquid crystal display (LCD) projector A device that projects light through panels made of silicone colored red, green, and blue. The light passing through these panels displays an image on a surface such as a screen or wall. Ch 3

live broadcast Live, or real-time, delivery of media over the Internet. Also called *live media streaming*. Ch 7

live media streaming Live, or real-time, delivery of media over the Internet. Also called *live broadcast*. Ch 7

local area network (LAN) A type of network where connected devices are located within the same room or building, or in a few nearby buildings. Ch 6

logic bomb virus A piece of code that is placed in a software system to set off a series of potentially damaging events if certain conditions are met. Ch 8

Long Term Evolution (LTE) A set of 4G wireless standards that involves changes to the wireless infrastructure to increase speed and bandwidth by installing transmitters that operate on different frequency bands to avoid interference. Ch 6

M

machine cycle A cycle a CPU goes through when handling an instruction; a process in which four basic operations are performed: (1) fetching an instruction, (2) decoding the instruction, (3) executing the instruction, and (4) storing the results. Ch 1

Mac OS X The operating system produced by Apple Inc. Ch 4

macro virus A form of virus that infects the data files of commonly used applications such as word processors and spreadsheets. Ch 8

malware Collectively, damaging computer programs such as viruses and spyware, which can do anything from displaying pop-up window advertisements to destroying your data or tracking your online activities. Ch 8

media sharing Sharing video, photos, music, or presentations with individuals or groups using the Internet. Ch 7

media sharing site A service that allows you to share media, such as music and video, on the web. Ch 7

megabit per second (Mbps) A transmission at a rate of 1 million bits per second. Ch 6

megahertz (MHz) A measurement of RAM access speed; 1 megahertz is approximately 1 million cycles per second. Ch 3

memory capacity The amount of memory (RAM) on your computer, which it uses to run programs and store data. Ch 3

metadata Data about other data, which describes that data and how to process it. Ch 7

metasearch engine A type of search engine that can search for keywords using several search engines at the same time. Ch 2

metropolitan area network (MAN) A type of network that connects networks within a city or other populous area to a larger high-speed network; typically made up of several LANs that are managed by a network provider. Ch 6

microblogging A form of blogging where brief comments rather than personal blogs are the main form of interaction, as on Twitter. Also called *social journaling*. Ch 7

microphone An input device for sound. Ch 3

microprocessor A computer chip that can accept programming instructions that tell a computer what to do with the data it receives. Ch 1

Microsoft Edge The browser introduced with Windows 10. Ch 2

Microsoft Windows The operating system produced by Microsoft Corporation, first released in 1985. Ch 4

microwave A high-frequency radio signal that is sent from one microwave tower to another. Because the signal cannot bend around obstacles, the towers have to be positioned in line of sight of each other. Ch 6

MID (mobile Internet device) A category of devices that fall between netbooks and phones, putting the Internet in a pocket-sized form. Ch 3

MIDI (musical instrument digital interface) A protocol that allows computers and devices, such as musical synthesizers and sound cards, to control each other. Ch 3

mobile broadband stick A USB device that acts as a modem to give your computer access to the Internet and that can easily be moved between computers. Ch 6

mobile forensics The field of study or career that involves finding data saved or sent via a mobile device to use as evidence in criminal prosecutions. Ch 8

mobile instant messaging (MIM) A message that is transferred by a mobile device over a Wi-Fi network and requires that the sender and receiver have the same messaging software. Ch 2

mobile operating system Operating system used on mobile phones and tablets. Often called *mobile OS* or *mobile platform*. Ch 4

modem A piece of hardware that sends and receives data from a transmission source such as your telephone line or cable television connection. The word *modem* comes from a combination of the words *modulate* and *demodulate*. Ch 6

monitor A visual output device that displays data and information as well as provides the ability to view the computer's interface. Ch 3

MOOC (massive open online course) A free, online course typically with open registration and publically shared curriculum that is objective driven and includes required assessments and some student-student and student-instructor interaction. Ch 5

Moore's Law A theory proposed by Gordon Moore, one of the founders of Intel, which states that over time the number of transistors that can be placed on a chip will increase exponentially, with a corresponding increase in processing speed and memory capacity. Ch 3

motherboard The primary circuit board on your computer that holds the central processing unit (CPU), BIOS, memory, and expansion cards. Ch 3

mouse An input device, referred to as a *pointing device*, that is able to detect motion in relation to the surface you rest it on and provides an onscreen pointer representing that motion. Ch 3

MP3 blog A blog where people post audio or music files. Ch 7

multicore processor A CPU chip that contains more than one processing unit (core), for example dual core (two cores) or quad core (four cores). Ch 3

multihomed device A device capable of connecting to a network in multiple ways. For example, your smartphone may be able to connect using either cell service or Wi-Fi. Ch 2

multimedia software Software that enables you to work with media, such as animation, audio, or video. Ch 5

Multipurpose Internet Mail Extensions (MIME) format A format for messages that are sent over the Internet. MIME permits text, graphics, audio, and video. Ch 2

multitasking The ability to have two or more tasks running at the same time. Also refers to the CPU's ability to execute several processes simultaneously. Ch 4

N

netbook A style of laptop computer with screen sizes ranging from 8 to 10 inches, and weighing only 2 to 3 pounds. Popular in the early 2000s, it was a precursor to tablets used for browsing the Internet or using email. Ch 1

network adapter A device that provides the ability for a computer to connect to a network. Ch 6

network architecture The design and layout of the communications system; how computers in a network share resources. Ch 6

network attached storage (NAS) A networked hard drive. Ch 3

network interface card (NIC) One kind of network adapter card. In most current computers, NICs take the form of a circuit board built into the motherboard of a computer that enables a client computer on a LAN to connect to a network by managing the transmission of data and instructions received from the server. Ch 6

network operating system (NOS) Programs that control the flow of data among clients, restrict access to resources, and manage individual user accounts. Ch 6

network protocol A rule for how data is handled as it travels along a communications channel. Ch 6

node A device connected to a network. Ch 6

nonvolatile memory A type of computer storage specifically designed to retain information, even when the power is switched off. Ch 3

notebook A portable computer with a built-in monitor, keyboard, and pointing device, along with the central processing unit (CPU) and a battery. Also known as a *laptop*. Ch 1

O

object linking and embedding (OLE) A technology that allows content to be treated as objects that can be inserted into different software documents, even if they were not created using that software. Ch 5

open content A creative work or other content that anybody can copy or edit online. Ch 7

open source Operating system software built with contributions by users whose source code is free to anybody to modify and use. Ch 4

open source software A type of software whose source code can be used, edited, and distributed by anybody. Ch 5

operating system (OS) A type of software that provides an interface for the user to interact with computer devices and software applications. Ch 4

operating system package Packaged software, such as Windows or Linux, which includes an operating system and utilities (collectively known as *system software*). Ch 4

optical drive A drive that allows your computer to read and write data using optical technology, such as a DVD or CD drive. Ch 3

optoelectronic sensor Technology used in devices, such as optical drives, which detects changes in light caused by irregularities on a surface. Ch 3

organic light emitting diode (OLED) A display technology that projects light through an electroluminescent (a blue/red/green–emitting), thin film layer made of up of organic materials. Ch 3

output The information that results from computer processing or the act of writing or displaying such data. Ch 1

output device A device that allows a computer user to obtain data from a computer. Translates from electronic (digital) form to some other format. Ch 3

P

packaged software Software saved to a physical medium such as a DVD and sold in a box or other package. Ch 5

packet A small unit of data that is passed along a packet-switched network, such as the Internet. Ch 6

packet switching The process of breaking data into packets, sending, and then reassembling the original data. Ch 6

parallelized Software design that allows tasks to run pieces of a task on two or more processors. Ch 3

path The hierarchy of folders that leads to a stored file. Ch 4

PC Card An add-on card that slots into a built-in card reader to provide other kinds of functionality, such as adding memory or networking capabilities. Ch 3

peer-to-peer (P2P) file sharing program A program that allows people to share music, video, and other types of files by downloading them from each other's hard drives, rather than from a central location on the Internet. Ch 2

peer-to-peer (P2P) network A network architecture in which each computer in the network can act as both server and client. Ch 6

performance The speed with which your computer functions. Ch 4

peripheral device A device that physically or wirelessly connects to and is controlled by a computer, but is external to the computer. Ch 3

petabit per second (Pbps) A transmission at a rate of 1 quadrillion bits per second. Ch 6

petaflop A measurement of supercomputing power representing a thousand trillion floating-point operations per second. Ch 1

phishing The practice of sending email that appears to be from a legitimate organization in an attempt to convince the reader to reveal personal information. Ch 8

photo editing software Software designed to enhance photo quality or apply special effects such as blurring elements or feathering the edges of a photo. Ch 5

photo printer An output device that allows you to print high-quality photos directly from a camera's flash memory to the printer without having to upload the photos to a computer first. Ch 3

photoblog A blog used to share amateur or professional photography. Ch 7

physical port A type of port that uses a physical cable to connect a computer to another device. Ch 3

pixel A single point in an image; short for picture element. Ch 1

plasma display A flat panel display, mainly used for televisions. This type of monitor uses a great deal of power, but has a very true level of color reproduction compared to an LCD monitor. Ch 3

platform The hardware architecture of a computer and the operating system that runs on it. Ch 4

platform dependency Applications and hardware that are only designed to work with a particular operating system. Ch 4

player A typically freely downloadable program that enables you to view or hear various types of online multimedia content. Ch 2

plotter An output device used to print large blueprints and other design or engineering documents. Ch 3

Plug and Play A feature that recognizes and makes available for use devices you plug into your computer, for example into a USB port. The OS installs the correct driver in order for the device to operate if the driver is available. Ch 4

plug-in A freely downloadable program that adds functionality to your browser. Ch 2

podcast A short audio presentation that can be posted online. Ch 5

port A slot in your computer used to connect it to other devices or a network. Ch 3

Post Office Protocol, Version 3 (POP3) A communications protocol that receives email from a mail server and delivers it to the proper mailbox. By default, messages are deleted from the server when the recipient retrieves his/her mail unless the user changes the settings. Ch 2

power supply Switches alternating current (AC) provided from a wall outlet to lower voltages in the form of direct current (DC). Ch 3

preferences Settings on your social networking page, including privacy settings. Ch 7

presentation software Software that enables you to create slideshows that include text, graphics, and multimedia. Ch 5

primary key A field that is used to ensure each row of data in a table is unique and to help the database software locate the correct row(s) in response to a query. Ch 5

printer A peripheral device used to produce printed output, sometimes called *hardcopy*. Ch 3

private key A code key used in encryption that is known to only one or both parties when exchanging secure communications. Ch 8

processing The manipulation of data by the computer to create information. Ch 1

processor speed The speed at which the CPU interprets and carries out instructions that operate the computer and its devices. Ch 3

productivity software Software applications that people typically use to get work done such as word processing, spreadsheet, database, or presentation software. This type of software is often compiled into suites of applications. Ch 5

profile A blogger or social networking user's information, such as name, location, and interests. Ch 7

protocol A standard that specifies how two devices will communicate by providing rules such as how data should be formatted and coded for transmission. The Internet transmission protocol is indicated in the first part of a website's universal resource locator (URL). Ch 6

public key A code key used in encryption. Creates an encrypted message that is decrypted by a private key. Ch 8

public key encryption A system of encrypting and decrypting data using a public key and private key combination. Ch 8

Q

query A question that can be used by database software to return information. Ch 5

quick response (QR) code A 2-D bar code that provides a shortcut to a website. Rather than entering the web address, you use your smartphone (with a reader application installed) to scan the code and let your phone's browser use the code to connect to the site. Ch 2

R

Radio Frequency Identification (RFID) A wireless technology primarily used to track and identify items using radio signals. An RFID tag placed in an item contains a transponder which is read by a transceiver or RFID reader. Ch 6

random access memory (RAM) A holding area for data while your computer processes information. When you turn your computer off, the data temporarily stored in this holding area disappears; RAM is therefore also referred to as *volatile memory*. Ch 1

ransomware A scam in which a user's computer is locked or data encrypted with a message from the malware creator demanding payment to restore access or data. Ch 8

read-only memory (ROM) Memory that holds information such as the BIOS and instructions the computer uses to start up the operating system. Also called *nonvolatile memory*. Ch 3

record A row of data in a table. Ch 5

relational database A database in which data is arranged into tables that are related on a common field. Ch 5

release to manufacturing (RTM) version A final version of the software with all identified bugs reconciled so that the software can be duplicated and sold to the public or deployed to internal users. Ch 5

render farm A custom-designed connection between groups of computers joined in a computer cluster. Ch 1

repeater An electronic device that takes a signal and retransmits it at a higher power level to boost the transmission strength. A repeater can also transmit a signal to move past an obstruction, so that the signal can be sent further without degradation. Ch 6

resolution A measurement of the number of pixels on a screen. Ch 1

RFID reader An input device often used in retail or manufacturing settings to scan an embedded tag using radio frequency. Ch 3

rich text format (RTF) A text format that includes only basic formatting information that most software products are likely to be able to open or import. Ch 5

ring topology An arrangement that has computers and other devices connected, one after the other, in a closed loop. Data transmitted on a ring network travels from one computer to the other until it reaches its destination. Ch 6

rootkit A set of programs or utilities designed to allow a hacker to control a victim computer's hardware and software and permit a hacker to monitor the user's actions. Ch 8

router A hardware device that connects two or more networks in a business setting. At home, a router allows you to connect multiple devices to one high-speed connection. Ch 6

S

satellite communication Space-based equipment that receives microwave signals from an earth-based station and then broadcasts the signals back to another earth-based station. Ch 6

scanner A peripheral input device used to create an electronic file from a hard copy document. Ch 3

scareware A scam where an online warning or pop-up convinces a user that his or her computer or mobile device is infected with malware or has another problem that can be fixed by purchasing and downloading software, which may do nothing or install malware. Ch 8

screen capture software Software that enables you to capture an entire computer screen or only a portion of it. Ch 5

SDRAM (synchronous dynamic random access memory) An updated version of DRAM that provides significant improvements in access speed. Most modern computer memory is some variation of SDRAM, including DDR-SDRAM, DDR2-SDRAM, and DDR3-SDRAM. Ch 1

search directory A site that allows you to locate web content within categories. Ch 2

search engine A website that permits you to search for information by entering keywords. Ch 2

Secure Socket Layer (SSL) A cryptographic protocol that is required for creating Transport Layer Security (TLS). Ch 8

Semantic Web The next (third) phase in online usage, also called *Web 3.0*, which will make it possible for websites to "understand" the relationships between elements of web content. Ch 2

serial port A port, built into the computer, used to connect a peripheral device to the serial bus, typically, by means of a plug with 9 pins. Network routers use serial ports for administration, although they are being replaced by web-based administration interfaces. Ch 3

server Any combination of hardware and software that provides a service, such as storing data, to a client, such as your computer. Ch 6

shared feature A small application that cannot run on its own, but that allows suites of software products to share functionality, such as diagramming or drawing. Ch 5

shareware Software for which you pay a small fee. Ch 5

Short Message Service (SMS) A service that carries text messages and is used by cell phone providers. Ch 2

Simple Mail Transfer Protocol (SMTP) A communications protocol installed on the ISP's or online service's mail server that determines how each message is to be routed through the Internet and then sends the message. Ch 2

sketchblog A blog consisting of drawings and sketches. Ch 7

smartphone Mobile phone devices with a mobile OS and rich feature set that essentially makes them into very small computers. Ch 4

social bookmarking A method of sharing bookmarks with others using tags. Ch 7

social engineer A con artist who employs tactics to trick computer users into giving up valuable information. Ch 8

social journaling A form of blogging where brief comments rather than personal blogs are the main form of interaction, as on Twitter. Also called *microblogging*. Ch 7

social mobile media Social services accessed from mobile phones. Ch 7

social networking site A site that offers the ability to share contacts and build a network of "friends" along with tools that allow individuals and groups to connect and communicate. Ch 7

social web The collective description of websites that offer the ability to communicate, interact, and network with others. Ch 7

software as a service (SaaS) A software delivery model where a provider licenses an application to customers to use as a service on demand. Ch 5

software development life cycle (SDLC) The general flow of creating a new software product; includes performing market research and business analysis, creating a plan and budget for implementing the software, programming the software, testing the software, releasing the software to the public, and debugging the software. Ch 5

software engineering (SE) A field involving writing software programs, which might be developed for a software manufacturer to sell to the public, or involve a custom program written for a large organization to use in-house. Ch 1

software on demand A software delivery model where a provider licenses an application to customers to use as a service on demand. Also called *software as a service (SaaS)*. Ch 5

software suite A collection of productivity software applications sold as one package that use tools common to all the products in the suite. Ch 5

solid-state drive (SSD) A flash-based replacement for an internal hard disk that is lighter and more durable than a traditional hard disk, and which should pave the way for smaller, portable computers with longer battery life. Ch 3

source code The programming code used to build a software product. Ch 5

spam Mass emails sent to those who haven't requested them, usually for the purpose of advertising or fraud. Ch 8

speaker A device that provides audio output. Ch 3

spear-phishing A targeted phishing attack sent to individuals employed by certain companies for the purpose of obtaining trade secrets or other confidential information, leading to financial gain for the hacker. Ch 8

speech recognition software A type of software that enables a computer to recognize human speech and convert it into text. Ch 5

spoofing Attempting to gain valuable information via electronic communications by misleading a user as to your identity. Ch 8

spreadsheet software An application with which you can perform calculations on numbers and display other data. In addition, most spreadsheet products offer sophisticated charting and graphing capabilities. Ch 5

spyware Software that tracks activities of a computer user without the user's knowledge. Ch 8

SRAM (static random access memory) A type of memory that is about five times faster than DRAM. Though dependent upon electricity, this type of memory does not require constant refreshing and is more expensive than DRAM. It is therefore often used only in cache memory applications. Ch 1

standards Allow different devices to talk to one another. Standards ensure compatibility among devices, specifying how computers access transmission media, the speeds used on networks, the design of networking hardware such as cables, and so on. Ch 6

star topology An arrangement where all the devices on the network, called nodes, connect to a central device that is a hub or a switch. Ch 6

Start menu A menu that appears when you click the Start button on the taskbar that displays commands, apps menus, and rectangular tiles used to launch apps, the web, documents, or programs. Ch 4

storage A permanent recording of information, data, and programs on a computer's storage medium, such as a magnetic disk or optical disc, so that they can be retrieved as needed. Ch 1

streaming video Video that is delivered to your computer as a constant stream of content, usually requiring a media player. Ch 2

strong password A password that is difficult to break. Strong passwords should contain uppercase and lowercase letters, numbers, and punctuation symbols, but not contain dictionary words nor repeating characters. Ch 8

Structured Query Language (SQL) The standard language used to query a database. Pronounced "sequel." Ch 5

stylus A special device, usually with a rubber tip, used to tap on a touchscreen. Ch 3

supercomputer A computer with the ability to perform trillions of calculations per second, usually custom-made for a particular use or used as a large server. Ch 1

surface-conduction electron-emitter display (SED) A display technology that uses nanoscopic electron emitters (extremely tiny wires smaller than human hairs) to send electrons that illuminate a thin screen. Ch 3

surge protector Protects an individual device from loss of data caused by a spike in power, such as might occur during a thunderstorm. Ch 8

swap file A file created when data is stored or "swapped" into virtual memory. Ch 4

switch A hardware device that joins several computers together to coordinate message traffic in one LAN network. Although a switch performs a role similar to a hub, a switch checks the data in a packet it receives and sends the packet to the correct destination using the fastest route. Ch 6

symmetric encryption A system of encrypting and decrypting data where in the sending and receiving computers each have a matching private key. Ch 8

sync The process of updating data on one device based on changes made to the data on another device. Short for synchronize. Ch 2

system configuration The entire computing system, including the identity of the computer, the devices connected to it, and some essential processes that the computer runs. Ch 4

system files Files that provide instructions needed to run the operating system on your computer. Ch 4

system software Software that includes the operating system and utilities for maintaining a computer and its performance. Ch 4

T

table A row-by-column layout of data. Ch 5

tablet A portable computer that enables you to give commands via a touchscreen using easy controls. Tablets also enable you to add functionality via downloadable apps and are often used as e-readers and media-consumption devices. Ch 1

tags Labels assigned to blog posts that describe the various topics covered in each post so that users can easily search a blog by topic. Ch 7

TCP/IP Short for Transmission Control Protocol/Internet Protocol. A protocol that breaks transmissions into small packets of data that are sent on the network. Each packet specifies the order in which the data is to be reassembled. This is the protocol for the Internet. Ch 6

technological convergence When a device begins to use technologies traditionally thought to belong to another device, as when a cell phone performs tasks traditionally performed by a computer. Ch 1

terabit per second (Tbps) A transmission at a rate of 1 trillion bits per second. Ch 6

tethering The ability to share the Internet connection of a mobile device with another device via a cable, Bluetooth, or Wi-Fi. Ch 6

text message A brief, written message of 160 characters or less sent between mobile phones or other portable devices using the short message service (SMS). Ch 2

texting The process of sending a text message. Ch 2

TFT active matrix liquid crystal display (LCD) The most prevalent type of monitor technology used today. It uses a thin film transistor (TFT) to display your computer's contents. Ch 3

thermal printer A type of printer that heats coated paper to produce output. Ch 3

thumb drive A small, convenient device that lets you store data and take it with you. Also known as a *USB stick* or *flash drive*. Ch 3

Thunderbolt port A port connection technology introduced by Apple that provides a high-speed serial interface using multiple channels to transmit data; used on devices such as cameras, camcorders, and audio and video equipment. Ch 3

top-level domain (TLD) The suffix (the period and the letters that follow) of a domain name. Ch 2

topology How devices in a network are physically arranged and connected to each other. Ch 6

touchpad A type of flat mouse or pointing device often used in laptop computers, which senses finger movement. Ch 3

touchscreen A visual display that permits the user to interact with a digital device by touching various areas of the screen to provide input, and view information onscreen as output.

Transport Layer Security (TLS) A protocol that protects data, such as credit card numbers as they are being transmitted between a customer and online vendor or payment company. Ch 8

Trojan horse Malware that masquerades as a useful program. When you run the seemingly useful program, you let this type of malware into your system. It opens a "back door" through which hackers can access your computer. Ch 8

twisted-pair cable A type of cable consisting of two independently insulated wires twisted around one another. This type of cable is used to transmit signals over short distances. Twisted-pair cables are used to connect a home's hardware telephone system or an Ethernet network, for example. Ch 6

U

ubiquitous computing Placing computing power in your environment as with, for example, a system in your house that senses and adjusts lighting or temperature. Also called *embedded technology*. Ch 1

UEFI (Unified Extensible Firmware Interface) A new specification for booting your computer that will eventually replace the aging BIOS firmware and could make booting computers a much faster process. Ch 4

ultrabook A type of lightweight laptop. Ch 1

Unicode An encoding standard used to represent different languages and scripts by assigning each letter, digit, or symbol a unique numeric value. This value is applied across different platforms and programs and is recognized internationally. Ch 1

uniform resource locator (URL) A naming system used to designate unique website addresses that you enter into a browser to navigate to a particular site. Also called *web address*. Ch 2

uninterruptible power supply (UPS) A battery backup that provides a temporary power supply in case of a power failure. Ch 8

universal serial bus (USB) port A port in the form of a small rectangular slot that can be used to attach everything from wireless mouse and keyboard toggles (the small device that transmits a wireless signal to a wireless device) to USB flash drives for storing data. Ch 3

UNIX A server operating system written with the C programming language. Ch 4

upload To transmit data, such as a digitized text file, sound, or picture from one's own computer to a remote site via a network, such as the Internet. If you are sending content to the Internet, you are uploading. Ch 2

USB stick A small, convenient device that lets you store data and take it with you. Also known as a *flash drive* or *thumb drive*. Ch 3

user interface The visual appearance that software presents to a user. Ch 4

utility computing A model of software delivery in which software is hosted on an online provider's website and you access it over the Internet using your browser; you don't have to have the source application software actually installed on your computer in order to use the software. Also called *cloud computing*. Ch 5

utility software A category of system software that you use to optimize and maintain your system performance and provides information about system resources. Ch 4

V

video blog A blog where people post video content. Also called *vlog*. Ch 7

video conferencing Technology that transfers video and audio signals over the Internet so users can see as well as hear one another. Ch 2

video editing software Software used to create and edit video files. Ch 5

virtual memory A capability of the computer's operating system that handles data that cannot fit into RAM when running several programs at once. When RAM is used up, data is stored or "swapped" into virtual memory. Ch 4

virtual reality system A system that connects you to a simulated world. It creates a connection between user and computer that allows both input and output in various forms and can be used to create sophisticated training programs such as those used by pilots, doctors, and astronauts. Ch 3

virus A type of computer program that is placed on your computer without your knowledge. The key characteristic of a virus is that it can reproduce itself and spread from computer to computer by attaching itself to another, seemingly innocent, file. Ch 8

virus definitions Information about viruses used to update antivirus software to recognize the latest threats. Ch 8

vlog Short for *video blog*. A blog where people post video content. Ch 7

Voice over Internet Protocol (VoIP) A transmission technology that allows you to make voice calls over the Internet using a service such as Skype. Ch 2

volatile memory A type of computer memory whereby stored instructions and data are lost if the power is switched off. Ch 1

W

warm boot Restarting a computer without turning the power off. Ch 4

warm server A server activated periodically to get backup files from the main server. Ch 8

wearable computer An electronic device that is worn and provides computing functionality in the form of everything from clothing to objects such as glasses or watches. Ch 1

Our Digital World

text-based data, Activity 1.4.3
texting, 52
text messages, 52
TFT active matrix liquid crystal displays (LCDs), 76
thermal printers, 77
3-D polarized lenses, 76
3-D printing, 12, 77, Activity 3.4.2
3G, Activity 4.4.1
thumb drives, 16, 71
Thunderbolt ports, 68-70
top-level domains (TLDs), 40, **40**
topology, 179
Torvalds, Linus, 104
touchpads, 73
touchscreens, 73, 100, Activity 3.3.1
Tracking and Data Relay Satellite (TDRS) system, 170
transmission speed, **166**, 166-167, **167**
transmission systems, 168-169, **169, 170**, 171, **171**
Transport Layer Security (TLS), 236
Trojan horses, 232, **233**
Trojan viruses, 103
twisted-pair cables, 168, **169**
Twitter
    launch date, **202**
    media sharing, 216
    microblogging and, 29, 207
    time spent on, **212**

U

ubiquitous computing, 10
Ubuntu, **102**
ultrabooks, 6
Unicode, Activity 1.4.3
Unified Extensible Firmware Interface (UEFI), 97, **98**
uniform resource locators (URLs), 40, **40**, 41, **41**, 50, Activity 2.4.1
uninterruptible power supply (UPS), 245
UNIVAC I, 99
universal serial bus (USB), 69
UNIX, 99, 104
upload, Activity 2.3.1
USB (flash) drives, 16, 71
user authentication, 243
user interfaces, 106-107, **107**
utility software, 96, 114, **115,** 240

V

video blogs, Activity 7.3.1
video conferencing, 53, **53**
video editing software, 138
video sharing, Activity 7.7.1
virtual memory, 109, **109**
virtual reality systems, 78
virus definitions, 247
viruses, 226, 232, **232,** 247
Voice over Internet Protocol (VoIP), 51, 53, **53,** 184-185
VoiceThread, 216
volatile memory, 14

W

WANs (wide area networks), 176, **177**
warm boots, 97
warm servers, 245
WBAN (wireless body area network), 74
wearable computers, 4
wearable devices, 74
web, Activity 2.2.1. *See also* Internet
    browsing/searching, **41**, 41-44, **42, 43, 44, 45,** 48
    described, 31
    evaluating content, 46, **46-47**
    invisible, 48, Activity 2.5.2
    navigating, 39-40, **40, 41**
    regulating, 33
Web 2.0, 32-33, Activity 2.2.2. *See also* social web
Web 3.0, 33
web addresses, 39-40, **40, 41**
web authoring software, 138-139
web-based email, 51
web-based software, 146. *See also* cloud-based software
web-based training, Activity 5.2.2
webcams, 73-74
web conferencing, 53
web development, 10
webmail, Activity 6.4.1
web pages, 31, **41**, 41-42
websites. *See also* specific sites
    components, **32**
    described, 31
    recognizing secure, 235-236
    specialized, 44, **44**
WEP (Wired Equivalent Privacy), 231
wide area networks (WANs), 176, **177**
Wi-Fi
    Chameleon virus, 226
    networks, 36, **37,** 171, **173,** 173-175, 184-185
    using safely, 239
Wi-Fi Protected Access (WPA), 231
Wi-Fi Protected Access 2 (WPA2), 231
WiGig, **174**
Wii U, 74
Wikipedia, 201, 214
wikis, 214-215
Wikitravel, 215
Wiktionary, 215
WiMAX (Worldwide Interoperability for Microwave Access, 802.16 standard), 173, 174
WiMAX towers, 36
Windows
    about, 103
    Defender, 139, 247
    Disk Cleanup, 96
    drives, 70
    8.1, 33, **100,** 101, **109,** 121, 247
    10, Windows, **102,** 103, 106, 109, 110, 113, 115, 117, 119, 121, 125, 137, 139, 247
    manufacturers of, 4
    Media Player, 44, **45**
    operating system, 81, 100, Activity 4.1.1

Photo Credits

Chapter 1

Page 3, Apple watch image courtesy of Apple Inc; *Page 4*, (clockwise from top) courtesy of Nikon Inc., courtesy of Samsung Electronics Co., Ltd., courtesy of Microsoft, courtesy of Apple Inc.; *page 5*, courtesy of Apple Inc.; *page 6*, courtesy of Sony Mobile Communications; *page 9*, Google autonomous car image courtesy of Google Inc.; *page 11*, © iStock.com/baranozdemir; *page 12*, © iStock.com/bunhill; *page 13*, courtesy of Xerox Corporation; *page 14*, courtesy of Intel Corporation; *page 15*, Adobe product screenshot reprinted with permission from Adobe Systems Incorporated, computer image courtesy of Dell, Inc. *Page 16*, (left) courtesy of SanDisk Corporation, (right) courtesy of Seagate Technology, LLC.

Chapter 2

page 28, (top) © iStock.com/STEEX, (bottom) © Jordan Tan/Shutterstock.com; *page 29*, © Simon Jarratt/Corbis; *page 37*, © zeljkodan/Shutterstock.com; *page 38*, screen courtesy of Mozilla Firefox; Google search engine and the Google logo are used courtesy of Google Inc.; *page 39*, screen courtesy of Opera Software ASA, phone image courtesy of Samsung Electronics Co., Ltd.; *page 41*, courtesy of Copyright.gov; *page 43*, (top) Google search engine and the Google logo are used courtesy of Google Inc.; (bottom) reproduced with permission of Yahoo. ©2014 Yahoo. YAHOO! and the YAHOO! logo are registered trademarks of Yahoo; *page 44*, BizRate screen courtesy of Connexity Inc.; *page 45*, courtesy of Microsoft; *page 46*, the Wikipedia unified mark is a trademark of the Wikimedia Foundation and is used with the permission of the Wikimedia Foundation. We are not endorsed by or affiliated with the Wikimedia Foundation; *page 47*, courtesy of Nasa.gov; *page 50*, these materials have been reproduced with the permission of eBay Inc. © 2014 EBAY INC. ALL RIGHTS RESERVED; *page 51*, © Daniel L. Murphy; *page 53*, Skype screen courtesy of Microsoft.

Chapter 3

Page 66, (clockwise from top left) courtesy of Sony Mobile Communications, courtesy of Sony Corporation of America, courtesy of Apple Inc., courtesy of Hewlett-Packard Company, courtesy of Dell Inc., screen image courtesy of Microsoft; *page 67*, courtesy of ASUSTeK Computer Inc.; *page 68*, courtesy of Energizer; *page 69*, © iStock.com/Chelnok; *page 71*, © iStock.com/calvio; *page 72*, courtesy of V-MODA; *page 73*, (top) courtesy of Hewlett-Packard Company, (bottom left) courtesy of Microsoft, (bottom right) © LDprod/Shutterstock.com; *page 74*, (top) courtesy of Microsoft, (bottom) courtesy of National Science Foundation; *page 76*, (top, left and right) courtesy of iStock, (bottom) courtesy of Panasonic; *page 77*, © Brian A Jackson/Shutterstock.com; *page 78*, (top) courtesy SMART Technologies, (bottom) © Barone Firenze/Shutterstock.com; *page 80*, © Adam Ziaja/Shutterstock.com; *page 81*, courtesy of Apple; *page 83*, courtesy of Dell Inc.

Chapter 4

Page 97, courtesy of Apple Inc.; *page 98*, courtesy of Microsoft; *page 99*, courtesy of Hagley Museum and Library; *page 100*, courtesy of Apple Computers; *page 101*, courtesy of Microsoft; *page 102*, (top to bottom) courtesy of Microsoft, courtesy of Apple Inc., courtesy of Canonical Ltd.; *page 104*, (top) courtesy of Microsoft, (bottom) courtesy of Apple Inc.; *page 105*, (top) courtesy of Linux Online, Inc., (bottom) courtesy of Acer Inc.; *page 107*, (top) courtesy of Microsoft, (bottom) courtesy of Hewlett-Packard Company; *Page 108*, courtesy of Microsoft; *page 110*, (top) courtesy of Microsoft, (bottom) courtesy of Apple Inc.; *page 112*, courtesy of Microsoft; *page 113*, (top) courtesy of Apple Inc., (bottom) courtesy of Microsoft; *page 116*, (left to right) courtesy of Apple Inc., courtesy of Google Inc., courtesy of Microsoft Mobile.

Chapter 5

Page 132, courtesy of Microsoft; *page 133*, courtesy of Microsoft; *page 134*, all courtesy of Microsoft; *page 135*, (top and bottom) courtesy of Microsoft; *page 136*, (top and bottom) courtesy of Microsoft; *page 137*, (left to right) TechSmith Snagit logo reprinted with permission from TechSmith Incorporated, box shot reprinted with permission from Corel Corporation, courtesy of Quark Software Inc., Adobe Creative Cloud Logo reprinted with permission from Adobe Systems Incorporated; *page 139*, (top) courtesy of Intuit Inc., (bottom) courtesy of World Food Programme; *page 140*, (top) courtesy of Intuit Inc., (bottom) courtesy of Microsoft; *page 141*, © iStock.com/Adivin; *page 142*, © 2014 SAP SE. All rights reserved; *page 146*, courtesy of Google Inc.; *page 147*, courtesy of Tucows Inc.; *page 151*, courtesy of Microsoft.

Chapter 6

Page 165, © Alexlukin/Shutterstock.com; *page 170*, © iStock.com/cpku; *page 174*, © iStock.com/PIKSEL; *page 179*, © iStock.com/Alec051, *page 180*, © iStock.com/baloon111; *page 181*, (clockwise from top left) courtesy of Cisco, courtesy of TRENDnet, courtesy of TRENDnet, courtesy of Amped Wireless.

Chapter 7

Page 201, (top to bottom) © iStock.com/Imagesbybarbara, © iStock.com/bo1982, © wavebreakmedia/Shutterstock.com; *page 203*, © iStock.com/atakan; *page 204*, courtesy of Khan Academy. NOTE: All Khan Academy content is available for free at www.khanacademy.org; *page 205*, courtesy of HootSuite Media Inc.; *page 206*, courtesy of The White House; *page 207*, courtesy of Tumblr, Inc.; *page 210*, courtesy of Facebook; *page 211*, © Sean Locke Photography/Shutterstock.com; *page 213*, (left) courtesy of Flipora; *page 214*, courtesy of Wikia.com; *page 216*, courtesy of VoiceThread.com; *page 217*, courtesy of SoundCloud.

Chapter 8

Page 229, courtesy of McAfee; *page 230*, courtesy of Cisco Systems, Inc. Unauthorized use not permitted; *page 236*, (clockwise from top left) courtesy of TRUSTe Inc., courtesy of Validatedsite.com, copyright © 2014 Symantec Corporation. All rights reserved. Reprinted with permission from Symantec Corporation, (bottom) courtesy of Google Inc.; *page 237*, (left) courtesy of Microsoft, (right) courtesy of Apple Inc., (bottom) © iStock.com/mbolina; *page 239*, (left to right) courtesy of Kensington Computer Products Group, a division of ACCO Brands; U.are.U® 4500 Fingerprint Reader by DigitalPersona, Inc.; © ptnphoto/Shutterstock.com, (bottom) © Kzenon/Shutterstock.com; *page 240*, © iStock.com/sturti; *page 243*, (top) © gifted/Shutterstock.com, (bottom) © iStock.com/chaowalit407; *page 245*, © iStock.com/JoeBiafore; *page 246*, courtesy of Microsoft; *page 247*, courtesy of Microsoft; *page 248*, © AVG Netherlands B.V. and the AVG group of companies.

Concepts Check

1-3, courtesy of Apple Inc., courtesy of Opera Software ASA, courtesy of Dell Inc., courtesy of Sony Mobile Communications, courtesy of International Business Machines Corporation; *1-4*, © Creativa/Shutterstock.com, courtesy of International Business Machines Corporation, courtesy of Epson America, Inc., courtesy of SanDisk Corporation; *3-4*, © Julio Embun/Shutterstock.com, © Paradigm Education Solutions, © Paradigm Education Solutions, © iStock.com/greg801, courtesy of Logitech, courtesy of Logitech.